AF566831

Ethics Among Academic Professionals

Ethics Among Academic Professionals

Manmohanjit Singh Hundal

Bookwell
Delhi

ISBN: 978-93-80574-58-5

First Published in 2014 by:

Bookwell

3/79, Nirankari Colony,
Delhi 110009, India
Ph: 91-11-27601283
E-mail: bkwell@nde.vsnl.net.in
bookwelldelhi@gmail.com
Website: www.bookwellindia.com

Typeset by:
Unique Typeset Processing, Delhi

Printed at:
D.K. Fine Art Press (P) Ltd., Delhi

Acknowledgement

It gives me a deep sense of pride and satisfaction that I have been able to complete this socially significant extensive research work. The present thesis is the outcome of the continuous effort for the past few years and during this sociological study a number of people have been kind enough to guide me and lend me their invaluable help to make it inclusive. It is indeed very difficult for me to prioritise all these personalities but still I would name a few who have made all the difference.

The success of my work largely depends on the person under whose inspiration and guidance, it is accomplished. I must first of all express my heartiest gratitude to my supervisor Prof. R. S. Sandhu, whose patience, experience and scholarly advice has been invaluable. His access, kind suggestions and consistent encouragement in laying down the format of the study were extensively helpful in improving the quality of work.

I also extend my great thanks to Prof. Paramjit Singh Judge, Chairperson, Department of Sociology, for his cooperation at every stage. I am also thankful to Prof. Gurpreet Bal, formerly Chairperson, Department of Sociology, for helping me in completing other official requirements. I am also indebted to Prof. Jasmeet Sandhu for her statistical guidance in the tabulation of data. I am thankful to all other faculty members, fellow research scholars, librarians and all the staff members of the department for helping me in my research work.

I also extend my great thanks to Prof. S. L. Sharma, formerly Chairman, Department of Sociology, Punjab University, Chandigarh, for his able guidance in the reformation of my research proposal. I am also thankful to various officials of I.C.S.S.R. at Chandigarh and New Delhi for helping me in access to their database and libraries. Further I am thankful to various respondents for their patience, cooperation and confidence they have reposed in me.

I am also indebted to my cousin sister Mrs. Khushwinder Kaur, Senior Lecturer in English, Government Training College, Jalandhar, for sparing her precious time in editing my thesis.

I would like to thank all those who in one way or another might have helped me in the project but whose names might have slipped out of my mind.

Manmohanjit Singh Hundal

Content

Acknowledgement *v*
List of Tables *ix*

1. Introduction 1

2. Socio-economic Profile of the Teachers 35

3. Prevalence of Unprofessional Practices Among Teachers 77

4. Correlates of Unprofessional Practices 93

5. Reasons and Remedies for Unprofessional Practices 117

6. Summary and Conclusions 179

Appendices
1. Study of Professions According to Country, Professions and Themes/Content Areas 193
2. Interview Schedule 198

References 209

Index 221

List of Tables

2.1 Distribution of Respondents According to Type of School and Age 37

2.2 Distribution of Respondents According to Sex and Age 37

2.3 Distribution of Respondents According to Place of Employment and Age 38

2.4 Distribution of Respondents According to Type of School and Marital Status 39

2.5 Distribution of Respondents According to Sex and Marital Status 40

2.6 Distribution of Respondents According to Place of Employment and Marital Status 41

2.7 Distribution of Respondents According to Type of School and Religion 41

2.8 Distribution of Respondents According to Sex and Religion 42

2.9 Distribution of Respondents According to Place of Employment and Religion 42

2.10 Distribution of Respondents According to Type of school and Caste 44

2.11 Distribution of Respondents According to Sex and Caste 45

2.12 Distribution of Respondents According to Place of Employment and Caste 46

2.13 Distribution of Respondents According to Type of School and Their Educational Qualifications 47

2.14 Distribution of Respondents According to Sex and Their Educational Qualifications 48

2.15 Distribution of Respondents According to Place of Employment and Their Educational Qualifications 48

2.16 Distribution of Respondents According to Type of School and Their Schooling in Childhood 50

2.17 Distribution of Respondents According to Sex and Their Schooling in Childhood 50

2.18 Distribution of Respondents According to Place of Employment and Their Schooling in Childhood 51

2.19 Distribution of Respondents According to Type of School and Their Father's Educational Level 52

2.20 Distribution of Respondents According to Sex and Their Father's Educational Level 53
2.21 Distribution of Respondents According Place of Employment and Their Father's Educational Level 53
2.22 Distribution of Respondents According to Type of School And Their Father's Occupation 54
2.23 Distribution of Respondents According to Sex and Their Father's Occupation 55
2.24 Distribution of Respondents According to Place of Employment and Their Father's Occupation 56
2.25 Distribution of Respondents According to Type of School And Their Family Income While Joining Teaching Profession 57
2.26 Distribution of Respondents According to Sex and Their the Family Income While Joining Teaching Profession 57
2.27 Distribution of Respondents According to Place of Employment and Their Family Income While Joining Teaching Profession 59
2.28 Distribution of Respondents According to the Type of School and Type of Family 60
2.29 Distribution of Respondents According to Sex and Type of Family 60
2.30 Distribution of Respondents According to Place of Employment and Type of Family 60
2.31 Distribution of Respondents According to Type of School and Family Size 61
2.32 Distribution of Respondents According to Sex and Family Size 62
2.33 Distribution of Respondents According to Place of Employment and Family Size 62
2.34 Distribution of Respondents According to Type of School and Their Family Income 63
2.35 Distribution of Respondents According to Sex and Their Family Income 64
2.36 Distribution of Respondents According to Place of Employment and Their Family Income 65
2.37 Distribution of Respondents According to Type of School and Aim in Life 66
2.38 Distribution of Respondents According to Sex and Aim in Life 67
2.39 Distribution of Respondents According to Place of Employment and Aim in Life 67

2.40 Distribution of Respondents According to Type of School and Age at Which First Thought of Becoming a School Teacher Came in Mind 69
2.41 Distribution of Respondents According to Sex and Age at Which First Thought of Becoming a School Teacher Came in Mind 70
2.42 Distribution of Respondents According to Place of Employment and Age at Which First Thought of Becoming a School Teacher Came in Mind 70
2.43 Distribution of Respondents According to Type of School and Role of Career Decision Makers 72
2.44 Distribution of Respondents According to Sex and Role of Career Decision Makers 72
2.45 Distribution of Respondents According to Place of Employment and Role of Career Decision Makers 73
2.46 Distribution of Respondents According to Type of school and Length of Service 74
2.47 Distribution of Respondents According to Sex and Length of Service 74
2.48 Distribution of Respondents According to Place of Employment and Length of Service 75
3.1 Prevalence of Unprofessional Practices Among Public and Private School Teachers 87
3.2 Relative Prevalence of Unprofessional Practices Among Public and Private School Teachers on a Five Point Scale 87
3.3 Prevalence of Unprofessional Practices Among Male and Female Teachers 88
3.4 Relative Prevalence of Unprofessional Practices Among Male and Female Teachers on a Five Point Scale 89
3.5 Prevalence of Unprofessional Practices Among Rural and Urban School Teachers 89
3.6 Relative Prevalence of Unprofessional Practices Among Rural and Urban School Teachers on a Five Point Scale 90
4.1 Distribution of Respondents According to Age and UPPs 95
4.2 Distribution of Respondents According to Marital Status and UPPs 95
4.3 Distribution of Respondents According to Religion and UPPs 97
4.4 Distribution of Respondents According to Castes and UPPs 97
4.5 Distribution of Respondents According to the Designation and UPPs 100

4.6 Distribution of Respondents According to Childhood Schooling and UPPs 100
4.7 Distribution of Respondents According to Education Level of Father and UPPs 103
4.8 Distribution of Respondents According to Occupation of the Father and UPPs 104
4.9 Distribution of Respondents According to the Income of the Family While Joining Teaching Profession and UPPs 105
4.10 Distribution of Respondents According to the Income of the Family and UPPs 106
4.11 Distribution of Respondents According to Aim in Life and UPPs 110
4.12 Distribution of Respondents According to the Age at Which First Thought of Becoming a School Teacher Came in Mind and UPPs 111
4.13 Distribution of Respondents According to the Career Decision Makers and UPPs 112
4.14 Distribution of Responses for UPP According to the Length of Service and UPPs 113
5.1 Distribution of Respondents According to Reasons for Absenteeism and Type of School 120
5.2 Distribution of Respondents According to Reasons for Absenteeism and Sex 121
5.3 Distribution of Respondents According to Reasons for Absenteeism and Place of Employment 123
5.4 Distribution of Respondents According to Remedies for Absenteeism and Type of School 124
5.5 Distribution of Respondents According to Remedies for Absenteeism and Sex 125
5.6 Distribution of Respondents According to Remedies for Absenteeism and Place of Employment 128
5.7 Distribution of Respondents According to Reasons for Dereliction of Duty and Type of School 129
5.8 Distribution of Respondents According to Reasons for Dereliction of Duty and Sex 130
5.9 Distribution of Respondents According to Reasons for Dereliction of Duty and Place of Employment 133
5.10 Distribution of Respondents According to Remedies for Dereliction of Duty and Type of School 134
5.11 Distribution of Respondents According to Remedies for Dereliction of Duty and Sex 136

5.12 Distribution of Respondents According to Remedies for Dereliction of Duty and Place of Employment 137
5.13 Distribution of Respondents According to Reasons for Lack of Responsibility and Type of School 139
5.14 Distribution of Respondents According to Reasons for Lack of Responsibility and Sex 140
5.15 Distribution of Respondents According to Reasons for Lack of Responsibility and Place of Employment 143
5.16 Distribution of Respondents According to Remedies for Lack of Responsibility and Type of School 144
5.17 Distribution of Respondents According to Remedies for Lack of Responsibility and Sex 145
5.18 Distribution of Respondents According to Remedies for Lack of Responsibility and Place of Employment 146
5.19 Distribution of Respondents According to Reasons for Discrimination Against Students and Type of School 148
5.20 Distribution of Respondents According to Reasons for Discrimination Against Students and Sex 149
5.21 Distribution of Respondents According to Reasons for Discrimination Against Students and Place of Employment 151
5.22 Distribution of Respondents According to Remedies for Discrimination Against Students and Type of School 152
5.23 Distribution of Respondents According to Remedies for Discrimination Against Students and Sex 154
5.24 Distribution of Respondents According to Remedies for Discrimination Against Students and Place of Employment 155
5.25 Distribution of Respondents According to Reasons for Authoritarianism and Type of School 157
5.26 Distribution of Respondents According to Reasons for Authoritarianism and Sex 158
5.27 Distribution of Respondents According to Reasons for Authoritarianism and Place of Employment 160
5.28 Distribution of Respondents According to Remedies for Authoritarianism and Type of School 161
5.29 Distribution of Respondents According to Remedies for Authoritarianism and Sex 163
5.30 Distribution of Respondents According to Remedies for Authoritarianism and Place of Employment 165
5.31 Distribution of Respondents According to Reasons for Commercial Venality and Type of School 166
5.32 Distribution of Respondents According to Reasons for Commercial Venality and Sex 170

5.33 Distribution of Respondents According to Reasons for Commercial Venality and Place of Employment 171
5.34 Distribution of Respondents According to Remedies for Commercial Venality and Type of School 172
5.35 Distribution of Respondents According to Remedies for Commercial Venality and Sex 173
5.36 Distribution of Respondents According to Remedies for Commercial Venality and Place of Employment 175

1

Introduction

1.1 Overview

Education as envisaged besides an agency of socialisation of individuals at different organisational levels (school, college, university etc.) also puts its impact on various social institutions like family, economy, polity, stratification and religion through its individual and societal functions and in return is impacted by them in modern society. No social institution is immune to each other in any society. The functions of education in totality, while complementing and supplementing each other, influence various social institutions in society. If education enables the individual to internalise ideologies, values, norms, attitudes and behaviour patterns institutionalised in the society, then it also contributes to the formation of social personality, an individual function of education. Formation of social personality of individuals helps them assume the roles of responsible citizens in society and then it leads to social stability, a societal function of education. Acquisition of knowledge and skills through education at different organisational levels enables the individual to earn a livelihood thus putting him/her in a social position in society. Education also provides the individual requisite knowledge, skills and behaviour patterns for placing him/her in higher occupational position called social mobility. Differential forms of education enable individuals to assume different tasks in society, thus resulting in division of labour, the societal function of education. When new values, ideologies, attitudes and behaviour patterns, which are consonant with the social order that the society aspires for as more desirable, are successfully inculcated, the educational system performs its function towards social change (Aikara 2004).

In this way, the qualitative educational system holds the key to maintain social order in the society. But erosion and decline in the quality of basic education in developing countries has assumed the proportions of global emergency (Chattergee and Khan 2003). In the whole educational system, besides the infrastructural part (buildings, materials, tools etc.) the other component is various role-performers (teachers, students, administrators and parents) whose role performance has a direct bearing on the outcome of the education system. One pivotal role-performer is the teacher, whose status-role performance has a direct bearing on the entire educational system because he is a professional status-role performer. The status-role definition, performance and evaluation of a teacher fall in the jurisdiction of sociology of professions. The emphasis of sociology of professions, a sub-discipline of sociology, is to study the professional organisations, background of professionals and their values and roles. According to Hall (1948) sociological approach to profession is to look at the profession as an organised group that is constantly interacting with the society that forms its matrix, which performs its social functions through a network of formal and informal relationships, and which creates its own sub-culture requiring adjustments to it as a pre-requisite for career success.

The discrepancy between the ideal-typical conception of profession and the way in which many professions are actually found to function in India is so alarmingly wide as to render their title as profession of exceedingly doubtful value. While this is to some extent understandable in the case of relatively new professions, it can hardly be justified in the case of the oldest professions of medicine, law and teaching. These are not merely the oldest, but at the same time also the true classic model of professions and often described as the learned professions.

1.2 Profession as Defined

According to Webster (1969) it is believed that profession comes from the word 'profess' which means to receive formally into a religious community following a novitiate by acceptance of required vows. It might have something to do with the word 'priest' who is authorised to perform the sacred rites of a religion especially as a mediatory agent between man and God. According to Shaffer (1968) may be that priesthood was the oldest profession with special knowledge. A priest was capable of doing such things, which an ordinary person could not do. Seen in this context, profession is originally meant to be a calling requiring specialised knowledge and often long and intense academic preparation. *Oxford English Dictionary* defines a profession as "a vocation in which professed knowledge of some department of learning or science is used in its application to affairs of others or in the practice of an art founded on it". *Cambridge International Dictionary of English* defines a profession as "any type of work which needs a special training or a particular skill, often which is respected because it involves a high level of education". Both definitions lay emphasis on intellectual and skill aspects of the profession.

1.3 Sociological Orientation of a Profession

A brief review of literature into the work done by Hall (1948); Shaffer (1968); Webster (1969); Chattergee and Khan (2003) and Aikara (2004) on the study of professions clearly indicates that the sociologists have held a special fascination for this area of investigation for the last part of nineteenth century but the work done is not as much as compared to other sub-disciplines of sociology.

There are two major approaches pertaining to the study of professions:-

1.3.1 Structural-functional Approach

Discarding the definitional approach and cynicism towards professions, structural-functionalists talked of emphasising on evolving attributed or 'ideal type' of professions. Max Weber while describing the concept of 'process of rationalising' used some variant of 'rational' as synonymous with systematic, profitable, intellectualised, efficient, logical, accumulative, cognitively encompassing, disenchanted, and/or as any change from status quo (Gerth and Mills 1948). The approach found its best exposition in Durkheim's (1933) 'division of labour' and its function in maintaining 'social order' and 'cohesion'. To avoid 'anomic' form of division of labour, Durkheim emphasised on the increasing roles of occupational professional groups and syndicates. They were to his mind a midpoint between state and the family. Professions did not represent only the unrestricted economic interest but they were rooted in the moral codes and ethics.

Parsons (1968) saw in the growth of professions, the emergence of a new 'social force', which he was inclined to regard as a universal trait of all modern societies, including the socialistic ones. The massive emergence of the 'professional complex' had displaced first the 'state' in the relatively early modern sense of that term, and then, 'the capitalist or socialistic' organisation of economy. He tried to substantiate this by stating that "professional men were neither 'capitalists' nor 'workers', nor were they typically government administrators or 'bureaucrats'. They certainly were not independent peasant proprietors or members of small urban proprietary groups". Parsons (1939) gave an ideal-typical view of a profession that involved such attributes as prolonged socialisation, collective identity, control and regulation of the behavior of the professional by the professional body, professional fraternity etc.

According to Carr-Saunders (1928), "a profession may be defined as an occupation based upon specialised intellectual study and training, the purpose of which were to supply skilled service or advice to others for a definite fee or salary". He was of the opinion that while certain occupational groups were unambiguously professions, in case of others it was a matter of degree. These groups of specialists sooner or later formed associations to protect their interests, firstly to secure monopoly for members of the association to practice that profession; secondly to prescribe and enforce a proper standard of professional and honourable conduct; and thirdly, to improve the status of the profession, which among other things, was a function of the monetary rewards offered by it.

Greenwood (1957), who also shared the view that the difference between professions and non-professions was a matter of degree and not quality, and attempted to construct an ideal type of professions in terms of five attributes namely (i) systematic theory, (ii) authority, (iii) community sanction, (iv) ethical codes, (v) culture.

There were many other scholars like Webb and Beatrice (1917); Tawney (1920); Marshall (1939); Cogan (1953); Millerson (1963); Goode (1957); Sciulli (2005) and Torstendahl (2005) who listed the characteristics of the profession.

1.3.2 *Conflict Approach*

The key concepts of this approach are conflict, change and coercion. Marxists viewed professions as a part of stratification and class structure. In their view, knowledge and professional skills is a commodity having its market value. It can be exchanged for money. They defined the 'profession' as positions defined with in the technical relations of production and 'class' on the other hand, the social relations of production (Marx 1967). Followers of Marxian approach defined the profession as those occupations which are based on practice and ideology of people who call their occupation a profession and claim certain prerogatives, and, in exchange, they offer or claim to offer certain services due to expertise they possess by way of specialised training which, in turn, results in creation and control of a protected, or institutional market (Oppenheimer and Dale 1982).

The Bowles (1972) was of the view that the rise of public education in capitalist economies occurred along with, and as a consequence of advancing capitalism. Capitalism, he argues, first requires a skilled and disciplined labour force, one which cannot be adequately socialised by the traditional institutions of family and church. Secondly, it could supply workers who had already learned the values and behaviour conducive to productive labour. Children could be taught punctuality, discipline, deference to authority, and acceptance of responsibility for their work. The social relations of the school (the relationship between teacher and students for example) could replicate the social relations of the workplace and ease the transition from the family to the world of work. Third, the schools could teach loyalty to the state and obedience to law. This loyalty could be achieved by convincing children that the system was benevolent and just. The schools, then, could provide the capitalist economy with a ready, willing, and able supply of workers, while at same time assimilating foreign and potently disruptive groups with in the population. Bowles argues that it was for these reasons that a system of mass education was finally established in capitalist economies.

Waller (1961) sees the school as a coercive institution. At the top are teachers, given their authority by the community outside the school. At the bottom are the children, relatively (but not totally) helpless under their yoke. Here, the interests of teachers are in unavoidable and universal conflict with the interests of the children. The teacher is the task-master, attempting to make the students learn the formal curriculum. The students are subordinate to them, but are much less interested in schoolbooks than in their classmates and informal activities. The teacher then must coerce the students into obedience and learning.

1.3.3 *Attributional Analysis of Professions*

Because of the difficulties inherent in accepting any one definition; scholars chose a different path; they defined professions by *criteria*. And various attempts were made to itemise the traits of profession which emerged in response to new market opportunities, created by industrialisation and the decline of communal warrants of professional probity (Goode 1960; Carr-Saunders and Wilson 1933).

1.3.3.1 A Body of Abstract Knowledge

"It is this characteristic, the possession of an intellectual technique acquired by special training, which can be applied to some spheres of everyday life that forms the distinguishing mark of a profession" (Carr-Saunders 1962). Continued employment of the scientific method is nurtured by, and, in turn, reinforces the element of what Parsons, following Weber, calls rationality (Parsons 1939; Weber 1947). The source of abstract knowledge could be a university or a training institution, which culminates in the production of knowledge with the standardised production of professional producers. Higher education is thus, a key variable in professionalisation.

1.3.3.2 Service-orientation

It is assumed that the abstract body of knowledge and skill, acquired through extensive training by the members of the professional group, would be utilised for the other members of the society. The professionals are assumed to be altruistic; for them, their own interest is secondary and the interest of the other members of the society is primary.

1.3.3.3 *Professional Authority*

The prolonged specialised training in the body of abstract knowledge imparts the professional a type of knowledge, which is lacking in the common man. This creates a sense of uniqueness, of having claim to a special territory, forbidden to the outsiders. The concept of professional authority can be simplified by drawing a distinction between a 'customer' and a 'client'. A client is related to a professional occupation while a customer to a non-professional occupation. A customer can safeguard his interests through his own judgement in non-professional occupations whereas in professional occupations, the professional has to decide what is good and bad for the client because the client lacks the requisite theoretical knowledge. This monopoly of judgement is limited to the professional field only. Parsons calls it 'functional specificity' (Parsons 1939).

1.3.3.4 *Community Sanction*

The community gives power and authority to the professions in a formal and an informal manner to have control over the training centers run by the professions. The formal authority of the professions is enforced by the community's state power. This is done through accrediting process. This helps profession in maintaining monopoly over the clients.

1.3.3.5 *Professional-client Relationship*

Another quality of a profession is professional-client relationship. There are three types of professional-client relationship. The first type of relationship is based on the belief that the client is in the need of the expertise of the professional. The second type of relationship is governed by the norms that require that the interaction be initiated by the client and the termination of interaction be initiated by the professional when the clients' problem has been solved, or the professional has reached the limits of his capability in aiding the client. The third type of relationship is the interaction itself which is based on privileged communication, competency of the professional, duration and type of the client and un-accountability of the professional (Wilensky 1984).

1.3.3.6 Professional Ethics

The monopolies acquired by a profession get abused if its members do not adhere to its ethical code. Rousseau wrote "The strong is never strong enough", "To be always the master, unless one transforms strength into right and obedience into duty" (Rousseau 1950). No doubt, the ethical codes vary among professions, nevertheless the essentials are uniform. The client-professional ethics comprise cosmopolitanism, emotion neutrality, universalism and disinterestedness (Parsons 1939). The colleague-colleague relations, governing ethics demand behaviour that is co-operative, equalitarian and supportive.

1.3.3.7 Professional Culture

Another characteristic of the profession is that there emerges a professional culture consisting of values, norms and symbols (Bledstein 1976). One of the central concepts of the professional culture is the career concept. A career is essentially a 'calling', a life devoted to 'good work'.

1.3.3.8 Professional Associations and Code of Conduct

Professionals form associations that would nurture the growth of the profession, defend the rights of the members, achieve satisfactory working conditions, and engage in action research and other developmental activities to add to the corpus of prevailing knowledge, maintain standards, enjoy autonomy, be accountable and strive to raise the social status of the practitioners. Members of the association should also be bound by certain ethics and a code of conduct.

1.4 Professionalisation and Professionalism

These organisational strategies transform non-professional occupation into a professional occupation and structuralists put this process as professionalisation. These attributes are not the exclusive monopoly of the professions; non-professional occupations also possess them, but to lesser degree. In the Marxist approach professionalisation is a process by which producers of special services seek to constitute and control a market for their expertise. Professionalisation is, thus, an attempt to translate one order of scarce resource, special energy and skills into other social and economic rewards (Larson 1977). Professionalisation is a process by which persons in an occupational category struggle to gain the advantage of being professional (Oppenheimer 1982).

The professionalism is used to denote the ideology and value system of professions. The professional ideology is related with culture and value system of a society. Social values and the culture settings, to a great extent, decide attitudes towards work, and provide norms and standards of work, performance and techniques for the application of knowledge. Structural-functionalists view professionalism as observance of codes and ethics, service, community orientation, effectual-neutrality, rationality and objectivity. According to Marxists professionalism may be characterised by the extension of exchange relations and use value. Thus, the professions are labor market (Larson 1977). Many scholar's studied the work and non-work activities of professional groups and how they and allied parties use the discourse of professionalism to realise their goals (Aldridge and Evetts 2003; Cohen et al. 2005; Hanlon 1998). Evetts (2006) viewed how and in what ways the discourse of professionalism is being used (by states, by employers and managers, and by some relatively powerful occupational groups themselves) as an instrument of occupational change (and resistance to change) and social control.

1.5 A Review of Literature

The preoccupation of sociologists in India was with the study of tribes, castes, families and rural/urban India. There are certain studies on occupations such as Mukerji (1958) and Ghurye (1961) but they studied occupations in the framework of caste only. It was in seventies only; the need for the study of professions was felt after Nehru's efforts to modernize India and United Nations Organisation declaration of sixties as the decade of development. All these studies of professions emerged as a part of the study of class structure. The review of study of professions published between 1960 and 2005 according to frequency of country, frequency of professions and frequency of themes/content areas are presented in Appendix-(i).

Notable contributions have been made by Madan (1972, 1980); Chandani (1985); Oommen (1978); Rika and Wegar (1993); Johnson et al. (1995); Benoit and Heitlinger (1998) and De Vries et al. (2001) on the medical profession, by Galanter (1972); Morrison (1972); Gandhi (1982) and Orzack (1998) on legal profession, by Aurora and Rao (1977) and Evetts (1999) on scientific and technological profession, by Mishra (1961); Swanson (1971); Dubey (1975); Tilly (1975); Skocpol (1979); Wallerstein (1984); Abbott (1988); Torstendahl and Burrage (1990); Burrage and Torstendahl (1990); Brint (1994); Esping-Andersen (1996); Hanlon (1998); Hellberg et al. (1999); Swank (2002); Abbott (2002); Torstendahl (2005); Sciulli (2005) and Evetts (2006) on professions in general and Damale (1970); Ruhela (1970c); Dutt (1970); Malavika (1970); Shah (1970); Gore et al. (1970a); Singh (1969); Chitnis (1973); Goyal (1973); Gupta (1974); Khanna (1979); Derebello (1979); Singh (1979); Altbach (1979): Sharma (1979); Jayaram and Sriramakrishnan (1979); Chitnis and Altbach (1979); Heredia (1979); Wadhawan (1980); Sharma (1980); Sinha (1982); Gupta (1982); Nahar (1984); Malaviya (1984); Rao and Venkataramana (1984); Gupta and Rani (1988); Srivastava (1988); Ramana (1986); Rao (1986); Britto (1987); Bhoite (1987); Singhal (1988); Chubb and Moe (1990); Tapodhan (1991); Garg (1992); Raju (1992); Gauba (1993); Kaur (1994); John (1994); Chauhan (1995); Saroha (1995); Davis and Guppy (1997); Kapoor (2000); Singh (2001); Harinder (2002); Atal (2003) and Davis and Quirke (2007) on academic profession.

1.5.1 Teaching Profession

Teaching profession falls under a special category among other professions. For instance, the job of a doctor as a professional is finished when the cure is attained and that of a lawyer when the case is decided in the court of law. But the influence of a teacher as a professional does not cease merely after passing of an examination by a student. The professional role of a teacher is not analogous to that of a lawyer or a doctor, because the former's influence endures and is reflected in the minds sharpened (or not sharpened), personalities shaped (or not shaped) and characters moulded (or not moulded). Moreover, the teacher as a professional is the maker of other professionals.

In the light of these observations, it seems pertinent to investigate to what extent teachers as professionals have fulfilled their social obligations.

Ruhela's work (1970c) on schools is based on the collection of articles contributed by educationalists, psychologists and sociologists. It covers the rich variety of issues relating to the social backgrounds, professional equipment and professional behaviour of teachers. It also covers an equally impressive range of issues relating to the structure of the school system, teacher's role, status and problems of the teachers. In a systematic study of professional role of secondary school teachers, Shah (1970) notices considerable evidence of role consensus among various role definers in that they almost unanimously rejected the old authoritarian concept of the teacher's role and, instead, conceived of it in more diffused terms. Comparing school teachers with other white-collar professionals, Dutt (1970) finds the former lacking in professional attributes such as extended training, code of professional ethics, strong professional associations, work autonomy, etc. Examining the attitudes and values of teachers, Gore et al. (1970a) discerns college teachers to be secular and activist. Majority of them seemed to regard the simplification of ideas as their major pedagogic function and one-third to two-third had never published anything.

Chitnis (1973) in her study opines that, college teachers do not seem to measure up as professionals. From among the seven indicators in terms of which their occupational standing has been examined, they seem to qualify satisfactorily only in one; their idealism and commitment to their work. On the other six indicators– their foundation upon advanced learning, the importance of function the occupation fulfils in society, their organisation and solidarity, their autonomy and the status accorded to their occupation– they fail to fit in the concept of professionals. Khanna's (1979) study of the teachers of Jodhpur University examines the level of aspiration and commitment of teachers, and comes to the conclusion that majority of the university teachers have neither high aspirations nor high commitment. The work of Derebello (1979) is on the impact of schooling on students. It presents a research project to be tried in Hyderabad and Secunderabad as a replication of a study done in California on the relationship between schooling and personal efficacy. The findings of the California study is that the more formal schooling a child received, the higher would be its rating on the personal efficacy scale.

Singh (1979) has tried to measure the extent of modernisation in the attitudes and values of university teachers. He has found that teachers of social sciences seemed to have better understood the values of objectivity and rationality, while the science teachers appeared to have imbibed the mechanistic aspects of science without having grasped its basic stance of skepticism and inquiry. He finds teachers role structures as more transitional than either purely traditional or purely modern. Those who were pure modern in their outlook– that is committed, having high aspirations and demanding autonomy in the pursuit of their profession– were a small majority and so were pure traditional– that is, those low in aspirations, low in commitment and prone to acquiesce in the decisions made by those in authority.

Sharma's (1979) study of 770 students of Punjab University is based on to see the effect of education on modernity. He discovers that the quality and content of education and the type of early schooling, rather than education *per se*, have a role to play in inculcating modern attitudes and values. Analysing the role preference of university teachers, he finds that the majority of them rated the teaching role (conserver and conveyer of knowledge) as the most important, the research role (creator of knowledge) as of considerable importance, the character-building role as relatively less important, and the perspective-shaping role (socio-political outlook molding) as the least important. At any rate, the fact remains that teachers perceive their professional self-image more as 'subject specialist' than as 'student welfarist'. In his study of college teachers of Bombay University, Altbach (1979) observes that the college teaching role is marked by a sense of 'ambivalence' - a conflict between the broader ideology of the academics, which does stress research and writing, and his or her own reality, which does not. The basic structure of the college in India is autocratic with little pretence of the collegial decision-making and for this as well as several other reasons college teaching according to him, has failed to develop fully into a profession.

In a study of Bangalore University Teachers Association, Jayaram and Sivaramakrishna (1979) notices that teachers viewed their union as some sort of insurance agency, expecting the office-bearers to 'cover their risks'. They were reluctant to accept responsibilities or participate in deliberations. In effect, even as the union was complete in terms of enrolment of members, it was weak in terms of the involvement of members. Thus, unlike trade unions, teachers unions evoke neither feeling of solidarity nor of professional pride, despite the often-high calibre of leadership. Most important of all, the authors point out that teacher organisations function more as economically oriented unions than as learned societies, with teacher's interest in them being one of economism rather than professionalism. Analysing the internal organisational environment of college academics in Bombay, Heredia (1979) has advanced significant evidence of centralisation of authority and of heavy reliance on bureaucratic criteria for decision-making. This means that there is little scope for professional autonomy among college teachers. Making a distinction between unionisation and professionalisation, he has drawn attention to such consequences of the former as the increased magnitude of bureaucratisation and politicisation, which, in turn, undermine the professionalisation potential of teacher organisation.

Wadhawan's work (1980) on schoolteachers of Delhi has found that they generally belong to low socio-economic background. Social background of women teachers is slightly better than their men counterparts but men are more professional than women teachers. The latter hardly tried to enhance their subject knowledge and expressed no utility of in-service training programmes. The overall assessment in the light of the variables like evaluation of principals, evaluation of colleagues, colleague-group orientation and teacher autonomy, general ability of teachers, evaluation of students, evaluation of parents attitude, teaching assignment, professional aspirations and job satisfaction, the teachers included in the sample turned out to be less professional and less satisfied with teaching as their career. Sinha's study (1982) of the professional and social problems faced by the university teachers in Bihar finds widespread dissatisfaction among the teachers with respect to their family, professional and social life. Rao (1986) examines work adjustment and job satisfaction of teachers with rural and urban background.

Ramana (1986) focuses her study on women schoolteachers and their role performance and does not specifically discuss the issue of gerder inequality. She finds that the role performance of teachers is affected by their socio-economic background, modernity and professional aspirations and commitment. Britto (1987) analyses the issue of education and equality from a different perspective. Her study of three schools in Bombay– elite, middle-class and municipal– shows, how the schools with unequal infrastructure and inputs, function as a source of creating and maintaining inequality. The studies conducted by Bhoite (1987) and Malaviya (1984) on the whole; deal with the socio-economic background of teachers. While Bhoite studied teachers of arts and science colleges situated in the Mofussil areas of Marthwada region in Maharashtra, Malaviya studied the background of home science teachers. Singhal's study (1988) of teacher-pupil ratio, touches upon another aspect of teacher role in the schools in India. The study has shown that the existing norm of teacher-pupil ratio is different in the different states in India. Srivastava (1988) in his observation on university teaching, which is considered as the sacred 'mother' of professions, happen to be suffering from the combined effects of both, alienation and anomie. The noble, peace loving, truth-seeking, teaching-preaching-researching, intellectual-service-oriented life of the university teacher is not free from role ambivalence and conflicting ideologies. The first role conflict of the salaried university teacher is between his university authorities and his colleagues, both junior and senior; the second, closely linked, is the conflict between loyalty to the employer (Chancellor, Vice-chancellor, Syndicate, Senate etc.) and to clients (students who are not the pay masters) where the two parties are not one and the same.

The study conducted by Gupta and Rani (1988) is based on 183 teachers of three higher secondary schools of a small town Samana in Punjab and six high schools from the nearby villages. The study reveals that higher is the age more is the commitment towards the profession. Teachers in urban areas are more committed as compared to their rural counterparts. The male teachers from rural and urban areas are more committed than female teachers. Among the females, urban teachers are more committed.

The study of Tapodhan (1991) is based on 480 Gujarati speaking secondary school teachers of 19 districts of the state of Gujarat. The study is intended to measure the attitude of teachers towards the profession in relation to various variables as sex, area, caste, qualification, type of the school, marital status, and various faculties of education, age and experience. The findings of the study are that female teachers have more favourable professional attitudes than male teachers, urban teachers have more favourable professional attitudes than rural teachers, B.C. teachers have more favorable professional attitudes than non B.C. teachers, qualification has no effect on professional attitudes, non government teachers have more favourable professional attitudes than government teachers, marital status has no effect on professional attitudes, arts teachers have more favourable professional attitudes than science and commerce teachers, age and experience have no effect on professional attitudes of the teachers.

Raju's work (1992) is carried out with a sample of 454 teachers of senior secondary schools drawn from 28 schools of Delhi, to study the factors contributing to the commitment to teaching profession using 18 psychosocial variables. The five predictor-factors identified from 18 psychosocial variables that contribute more to less significantly towards the professional commitment of the teachers are perceived characteristics of the profession, work-related personality, professional satisfaction and importance, desire for skill improvement and professional choice satisfaction.

John's study (1992) is based on 390 teachers of 27 colleges affiliated to Gorakhpur University. His findings infer that gender difference, teaching experience and rural/urban background have no bearing on teacher's professional values, but minority community managed college teachers; have higher professional values than their counterparts of non-minority community managed colleges. Same trend is found in terms of professional growth of the college teachers. In terms of principal's decision making style, those who followed heuristic type of decision making style have direct bearing on teacher's professional growth and values, than those, who followed supportive, compromise and routine type of decision making style. Chauhan's work (1995) is based on 700 teachers working in 52 government and privately managed high schools in the state of Haryana. The study is based mainly on three professional aspects of teachers, namely, professional responsibility, teaching attitude and organisational climate. One of the significant findings of the study is that gender difference and type of the school have no bearing on the professional responsibility of the teachers. In terms of attitude towards teaching, government schoolteachers have higher degree as compared to their private school counterparts but gender difference has no bearing towards teaching attitude. He found that there is hardly any difference in the organisational climate of both type of schools. Teaching attitude and organisational climate jointly contribute for the variance of teacher's professional responsibility.

The study of Saroha (1995) is based on 104 male and 96 female teachers working in 16 government high schools of Faridabad district of the state of Haryana. The three variables used in the study are self-concept, socio-economic status and social adjustment. The findings of the study are that gender has no role to play in achieved or ascribed socio-economic status, self-concept and social adjustment. An association has been found between socio-economic status and self-concept in terms of male and female as well as ascribed and achieved. An association has also been found between socio-economic status and social adjustment in terms of male and female as well as ascribed and achieved. A close association is found between self-concept and social adjustment in terms of male and female teachers.

Kapoor's study (2000) is based on the students and teachers of an Arunachal Pradesh school. He tried to investigate the affect of socio-economic background of students and teachers towards the acquisition of environmental education and attitude towards the environment awareness. The study of Singh (2001) is based on the teachers of a physical education college. In his study, he has tried to investigate socio-personal background, achievements, adjustment and job satisfaction of the teachers. Harinder's work (2002) is based upon the students of Punjab studying in urban primary schools. An attempt is made to study the television viewing behaviour of the students.

1.5.2 School Teaching: A Critical Review

From the brief review of the literature on teaching profession in general, it is found that college and university teaching has had been the preferred area of investigation for sociologists as compared to school teaching. Ruhela's work (1970c) on schools is a collection of articles based upon the theoretical principles of psychology, sociology and education. Shah's work (1970) on schoolteachers covers only a single professional aspect of role transition from authoritarian to liberal. Dutt in her study (1970) compared schoolteachers with other white-collar professionals in terms of degree of professionalisation. The work of Derebello (1979) is on the impact of formal schooling on the personal efficacy of the students. He compared his sample of California with that of Hyderabad and Secunderabad.

Wadhawan's work (1980) is a notable study on 375 schoolteachers of Delhi. The set of criteria adopted to judge the degree of professionalisation of teachers is drawn from the sociology of professions. The overall assessment of data reveal that the teachers included in the sample turned out to be less professional and less satisfied with school teaching as their career. The type of schools whether government or private is not mentioned in the study. The findings based on the teachers of a metropolitan city can hardly represent the state of affairs of the teachers coming from the major rural India. Raman's study (1986) is limited only to the women school teachers of Vishakhapatnam municipal schools and does not specifically discuss the issue of gender inequality. In his study Singhal (1988) touches upon only a single aspect of teacher-pupil ratio of a teacher's role. The study of Gupta and Rani (1988) is based on 183 schoolteachers of a small town Samana in Punjab. The professional commitment of the teachers is measured in terms of their professional training, earlier occupation, future plans, and responsibility they feel towards students and membership of teacher organisations. Certain significant attributes of professionalisation like attitude towards work, observance of professional ethics, professional authority and autonomy, prevalence of professional culture etc., are missing in the measurement of professional commitment of the teachers. The type of the schools covered for the study is not clear. Moreover the small size of the sample put it in the doubtful value in terms its statistical significance.

The study of Tapodhan (1991) of 480 Gujarati speaking secondary school teachers restricted to individualistic characteristics of the schoolteachers based on the discipline of psychology of education. The whole state of affairs cannot be described on the base of individualistic characteristics. Raju's work (1992) is carried out with a sample of 454 teachers of 28 senior secondary schools of Delhi, and covers the behavioural aspect of the teachers. It is not mentioned whether the schools selected are government or private schools. This study may have relevance while selecting the schoolteachers that only right people join the profession. The work of Saroha (1994) based on 104 male and 96 female teachers working in 16 government high schools of Faridabad district of the state of Haryana, is again limited to behavioural attributes of the teachers based on the principles of psychology of education.

Chauhan's work (1995) is based on 700 teachers working in 52 government and privately managed high schools. The study is based on to find the inter-relationship between three behavioural aspects namely professional responsibility, teaching attitude and organisational climate, drawn from the theoretical principles of educational psychology. It is not mentioned whether the schools included in the sample are rural or urban. Kapoor's (2000) research project is based on the students and teachers selected from a single school of Arunachal Pradesh. The sample is too small to generalise the findings of the study. Harinder's work (2002) is based on primary school students and is restricted to the urban schools. Sharma (1979) in his study of 770 students of Punjab University finds that the quality and content of education and the type of early schooling, rather than education *per se*, has a role to play in inculcating modern attitudes and values. Atal (2003) in his review of education profession has discovered some priority areas of study in school system as: teachers as role models, monitoring teaching-learning process in formal educational institutions, work culture in educational institutions etc.

There is no dearth of studies like Gore et al. (1970a); Chitnis (1973); Altbach (1979); Heredia (1979); Bhoite (1987) and Malaviya (1984); John (1992); Singh (2001) on college teachers and Khanna (1979); Singh (1979); Sharma (1979); Jayaram and Sivaramakrishna (1979); Sinha (1982); Srivastava (1988) on university teachers, which are based on the theory and principles drawn from sociology of professions. Except the studies conducted by Wadhawan (1980); Gupta and Rani (1988); Chubb and Moe (1990); Davis and Guppy (1997) and Davis and Quirke (2007), all other studies on school teachers are either based on to study the behavioural aspects of the teachers or investigated one or two attributes of professionalisation of teachers.

Education being a social institution has individual level functions (formation of social personality, social placement and social mobility) as well as societal level functions (social stability, division of labour and social change) to perform (Aikara 2004). In the process of acquisition of formal education the desirable status-roles, contents and context of learning are predefined and determined. For the education to be functional is dependent to a large extent upon the roles performed by various status-role performers at different organisational levels (school, college and university). Various status-role performers in education can be broadly classified into two categories as ultimate beneficiaries and supportive role performers. Students and parents constitute the first category whereas teachers and administrators (members of management in privately run educational institutions and officials in the upper hierarchy in state run educational institutions) fall in the second category of status-role performers. In any context the status roles (student, teacher and administrator) generate six types of social relationships. These are student-teacher, student-administrator, teacher-administrator, student-student, teacher-teacher, and administrator-administrator.

Another status-role of parent adds four more social relationships viz. student-parent, teacher-parent, administrator-parent and parent-parent. The various social relationships generated by these status-roles are characterised either by cooperation and healthy competition or by conflict. In any context if a social relationship is based on cooperation and healthy competition then it is functional to education and if it is based on conflict then it is dysfunctional to education. In case of education the hub of the structure of social relationships is that of teacher-student and all other social relationships are supportive of it. The status-role of a teacher is characterised by the possession of knowledge and the required skill to communicate it to the student effectively and the status-role of the student is defined to acquire the knowledge. If the teacher does not have competence (knowledge and skill to impart it) and his/her commitment to role performance and the student does not accept it as a value then the outcome of this social relationship will not materialise. Other additional status-roles of administrator and parent form the part of the social structure in education in order to facilitate the teacher-student interaction.

The World Bank report authored by Chand and Mishra (2004) reveals gloomy dimension of the schools of the state of Punjab. The report says "On any one day 36.0 per cent of Punjab's primary school teachers are absent from school. The rate is third highest across Indian states, following Bihar and Jharkhand".

An IIM-A study (2006) of 400 districts of 13 states, have found that Sarva Shiksha Abhiyan, the Centre's flagship scheme to improve primary education, is a success in numbers. The study explains that more than 50.0 per cent of Indian children are dependent on private schools, among the highest in the world, due to the failure of state-run schools to provide quality education. Study suggests that quality can be assured if besides infrastructure, teaching staff, support staff and monitoring system, are in place. Field reports reveal that state-run schools in both rural and urban India now cater only to the most deprived sections of the population. In many parts of rural India, it is now rare to find children of the professional class or the village elite attending a local school. Such segregation of children along caste and class lines, even if not by design, is unwelcome and needs to be addressed immediately. Involvement of communities, in the running of state schools, say parent-teacher associations, has had significant impact in Kerala and Nagaland. The study explored the significance of another status-role of that of community (parent-teacher association and village educational development committee) in ensuring the quality education, in the form of four more social relationships viz. community-teacher, community-student, community-parent and community-administrator.

The UNESCO's International Institute of Educational Planning study (2007) on corruption in education says that 25.0 per cent teacher absenteeism in India is among the highest in the world and second only after Uganda that has a higher rate. It also says teacher absenteeism not only affects quality of education but also a huge drain on resources, resulting in the wastage of 22.5 per cent educational funds in India. Teachers also believe strongly in private tutoring, a practice identified by UNESCO as unethical. "It (private tuition) does not complement learning at school and leads to corruption", the report said. The practice of ghost teachers and involvement of teachers in mismanagement of schools were other grey areas identified in Indian education system. The recruitment of school teachers, which has been a rare thing in the state of Punjab, if it happens, is full of corrupt practices. A recent enquiry report has found that many teachers made to the selection list by acquiring fake experience certificates countersigned by higher officials.

An analytical report of education indicators by National University of Educational Planning and Administration (NUEPA 2005-06) reveals the fact that only teachers are not to be blamed for this, sometime they are working as paramedic, enumerator and election staff at the cost of children and teaching. The Punjab Education Development (amendment) Bill, (2007) which makes provision for private-public partnership for Adarsh schools to be set up at the cost of 500 crore to take care of 75,000 children neglecting 34 lakh students studying in public schools, is another measure of the state to segregate the children in terms of equality in access to quality education. The situation is so grim that community has come forward through Public Interest Litigations (PIL), (2007) in the court of law quoting the alarming drop-out rate in public schools due to the shortage of teachers. The majority of sufferers were the rural poor residing in far flung areas and the state has not devised any plan to ensure their return.

A survey conducted by People Forum (2008), on education and social reforms in 15 public schools of Faridkot district in the state of Punjab, have revealed that the number of general category students in public schools is continuously falling. The percentage of general category students in 2000-01 was 42.5 per cent and continuously decreased to 22.8 per cent in 2008-09. Since most of the educated persons and middle class families prefer private schools for their children, this has led to poor quality of education in public schools. As most of the students in public schools are the children of labourers and daily wagers, so there is no one to question the teachers to make them responsible. The survey puts forward a very distinct trend which is hitting the concept of social equality and harmony hard.

Sen (2008) while talking about a just society in reality in the era of globalisation, emphasised the indispensable role of qualitative and quantitative public school education system for the marginalised. Blaming the broken down inspection system of Indian public schools, for teacher absenteeism, delayed arrival in the school and private tutoring, that has a profound effect on the schooling of poor and underprivileged children - sometimes first-generation school goers - unsure of their rights and unable to raise their voice. He advocated the role of parents and teacher associations instead of teacher unions, in inculcating the work culture among the school teachers, in the delivery of school education.

The rural school education is more in a state of neglect as compared to urban school education in the state of Punjab. The phenomenon had begun more than a decade back and state may have to pay a heavy price in the form of lack of availability of skilled workers for lower category jobs and rural unemployment thus leading to unrest and chaos in the countryside. A study conducted by Ghuman (2006) of Punjabi University, Patiala, depict this fact that only 4.07 per cent students are from rural areas in the universities and professional colleges of the state of Punjab against 66.0 per cent of rural population. Another, similar study (2006) conducted by PRATHAM, an NGO in its ASER (rural) report, reveal the extent of poor quality of education being delivered in the rural schools of India. The data collected from 10726 households of 522 villages, from 18 districts of the state of Punjab, depict that 5.0 per cent children were out of school, 60.0 per cent of the 4th standard and 36.5 per cent of the 5th standard students could not read a 2nd standard text book in the state of Punjab. The condition of rural school education is more shocking in educationally backward and border districts of the state of Punjab.

A survey report (2008) brought out by a daily about Tarn Taran, a border district; reveal that 40 primary and middle schools have been closed due to non-availability of teachers and in others, 50.0 per cent of posts of teachers have been lying vacant since last five years. In the district, 51 out of total 52 public secondary schools sans principals while 74 posts of headmasters are lying vacant. The inspection system is totally shattered due to the non-availability of vehicles and financial resources to maintain and ply them. In the Public Interest Litigation (2007), submitted before the court of law, it is mentioned that the shortage of 25000 posts of teachers and 2200 posts of heads, are taking the toll of public school education in the state of Punjab besides other factors.

Due to lack of effective governance and monitoring of the system, school teachers have started practicing unprofessional practices. The prevalence of unprofessional practices among schoolteachers like absenteeism, dereliction of duty etc., have further added to the plight of trailing and frailing school system of Punjab what to talk of professionalisation or professionalism. It seems that the effect of liberalisation, privatisation and globalisation have changed the role of the 'Guru' of the traditional Indian educational system of 'Gurukul' from 'social good' to 'self good'. The dependency of more than 50.0

per cent of Indian children on private schools is a shift in paradigm of state from a 'welfare state' to 'lais-sez-faire' in the era of privatisation and liberalisation.

At the core of Michel Foucault's picture of modern 'disciplinary' society are three primary techniques of control: hierarchal observation, normalising judgment, and the examination. From hierarchal observation, he was of the view that, there is a need for 'relays' of observers, hierarchically ordered, through whom observed data passes from lower to higher levels. From normalising judgment, Foucault meant the discipline through imposing precise norms that are pervasive in society, though different for different social institutions. The examination is a method of control that combines hierarchal observation with normalising judgment. It is a prime example of what Foucault calls power/knowledge, since it combines into a unified whole "the deployment of force and the establishment of truth" (Foucault 1975). It is obvious from the account of Foucault that a well-oiled hierarchal monitoring system in social institutions is indispensable for the thought of a 'Good Society'.

According to Giddens, "the driving force of the new globalisation is the communication revolution", and beyond its effects on the individual, this revolution is fundamentally altering the way public institutions interact (Giddens 2000). Giddens talk of the nation, the family, work, tradition, nature, as if they were all the same as in the past. They are not. They are institutions that have become inadequate to the tasks they are called upon to perform. The pessimistic view of globalisation would see it as destroying local culture, widening world inequalities and worsening the lot of impoverished, in the developing societies. Globalisation, creates a world of winners and losers, a few on the fast track to prosperity, the majority condemned to a life misery and despair (Giddens 1999). Neo-liberal political philosophy of the world nations have too much dominance by the marketplace over the effective modes of active governments and a more effective global civil society, thus leading to all troubles (Giddens 2000). Education, a public institution, is not an exception in the globalised world. The beneficiaries of the globalised world are those who have access to or are a part of the knowledge-based society. That is to say, those who have access to globalised educational institutions, not those who are devoid of these institutions. The role of the welfare-state is either intentional or ineffective, in creating inequalities in this public institution.

In the era of globalised knowledge-based society, Pierre Bordieu's concern for those who benefited least from it, deserve to be mentioned here. Pierre Bordieu's work emphasized how social classes, especially the ruling and intellectual classes preserve their social privileges across generations despite the myth that contemporary post-industrial society boasts equality of opportunity and high social mobility, achieved through education. According to Bourdieu, social capital that is the accumulated form of economic and cultural capital could be used to produce or reproduce social inequality (Lane 2008). It is obvious from the account of Bordieu that differential forms of educational institutions could be the potential source of propagation and preservation of social inequalities in the society.

Durkheim was of the opinion that excessive individualism in education can lead to personal defeat and social chaos. For him, education is above all a social means to a social end - the means by which a society guarantees its own survival. The teacher is society's agent, the critical link in cultural transmission. It is his task to create a social, a moral, being. Through, him society creates man in its image. 'That,' says Durkheim, 'is the task and glory of education'. The family is out since the indulgent warmth of kinship ties is incompatible with the sterner demands of morality. If the family, small and intimate as it has become, can provide emotional support and tension release, it is not setting for cultivating the abstract idea of duty. On the other hand, moral education cannot be deferred until adulthood, nor it can be entrusted to adult agencies whose demands are excessive for a young child. So the task of moral education devolves upon the school (Durkheim 1973).

These observations attract some concern to the state of affairs of the schoolteachers, sometimes called as the descendents of the clergymen and learned professionals and seek the answer to the following queries:

1. Whether the education a social institution is functional in the age of liberalisation, privatisation and globalisation in achieving its objectives in the larger society?

2. Whether various status-role performers in the school education have deviated from their role performance desired by the society.

Keeping these major questions in mind the present study is planned and it has the following aims and objectives.

1.6 Aims and Objectives of the Study

1. To investigate the role of socio-economic and demographic profile of schoolteachers in the prevalence of unprofessional practices.
2. To examine the role of the type of the institution in the prevalence of unprofessional practices in schoolteachers.
3. To learn the status-role of the administrators (officials in the upper hierarchy or management) in the prevalence of unprofessional practices among schoolteachers.
4. To understand the status-role of students in the prevalence of unprofessional practices among the schoolteachers.
5. To investigate the status-role of the parents in the prevalence of unprofessional practices among schoolteachers.
6. To explore the importance of the role of the community (members of parent-teacher association and village educational development committee) in the school system in containing the prevalence of unprofessional practices in school teachers.

The primary objective of this study is to examine the prevalence of unprofessional practices among the school teachers. Six unprofessional practices to be investigated are:

Absenteeism: People are not going to work or school when they should be going. Teachers are away from school during their duty hours. Those who have equation with the principal are adjusted with non-teaching duties out of the school. Others take the advantage of higher bureaucratic and political connections in abstaining from school. Kin of the members of the management in private schools, working as teachers in the school, misuse their connections in abstaining from school.

Dereliction of Duty: Dereliction of duty is the failure on the part of the people to do something that they have to do because it is the part of their job. While in the school, teachers do not teach during their teaching hours. Other leisure activities like gossiping, sitting idle in the classroom or in school canteen etc. take priority over teaching.

Lack of Responsibility: People do not have a sense of being accountable for the work or job that is necessary or wanted. School teachers are supposed to possess the knowledge and desired skill to impart that knowledge to the students. Besides transmission of knowledge, they are expected to reconstitute personalities and create productive, moral and responsible social beings. On the contrary, they lack the required zeal and commitment to do this.

Discrimination: To treat a person or a group of people differently on the basis of their skin colour, caste, class, race, religion, sex etc. A sense of universality is lacking in the teachers. Personal whims do play a role while doing one's duties. Students are not treated without the distinction of caste, class and creed.

Authoritarianism: A manner in which total acquiescence is demanded and there is no freedom for the people to act as they wish. Total obedience is expected from the students and there is no space for empathetic understanding of their feelings.

Commercial Venality: Commercial venality is a corrupt practice that is connected with, profit, and not quality or morality. Public funding funds the professional knowledge and skill acquired by the teachers. This knowledge should be used for the welfare of the society and students, but on the contrary, it is used for individual welfare and self-development of the teachers through private tutoring.

1.7 Method of Research

The universe of present study is Roopnagar district in the state of Punjab. The district of Roopnagar is named after its district headquarters, the town of Roopnagar. Formerly known as Ropar, is said to have been founded by a Raja called Rokeshar, who ruled during the 11th century and named it after his son Roop Sen. Roopnagar district, falls in Patiala Division of Punjab, between north latitude 30^{0}-32^{1} and 31^{0}-24^{1} and east longitude 76^{0}-18^{1} and 76^{0}-55^{1}. It is 42 Km from Chandigarh, the state capital. The district adjoins Una district (Himachal Pradesh) in the north, Hoshiarpur district in the northwest, Ludhiana and Patiala districts in the southwest and Chandigarh in the southeast. The district comprised of 4 Tehsils, 894 villages and 9 towns. The population of the district was 1110000, with 593638 males and 516362 females (Census 2001). With the formation of Mohali as a new district in the state of Punjab some towns of Roopnagar district have become a part of Mohali. There were total 708 schools in the Roopnagar district. Of which, 257 were government schools and 451 were private schools. There were total 4763 teachers in the upper primary public schools. Of that 3336 were posted in rural schools and 1427 in urban schools. The number of female teachers was 3119 and that of male was 1644 (SAIES 2002). Data was not available regarding the private school teachers.

To achieve the set objectives of the study, four types of respondents namely teachers, inspectors, students and parents were included in the sample. The reason behind selecting four types of respondents in the sample was that their status-roles form the part of the structure of various social relationships in education, a social institution, and has a cause and effect role to play, in the prevalence of unprofessional practices in schoolteachers. Nevertheless, the teacher respondents were the real core of the sample because they are professional role performers in student-teacher social relationship which has a direct bearing on the outcome of education. To achieve the second objective of the study, the respondents were chosen from government as well as private schools of Roopnagar district. To observe the preferred area of prevalence of unprofessional practices in schoolteachers, rural and urban schools were included in the sample. To examine the role of gender in the prevalence of unprofessional practices among schoolteachers, male and female teachers formed part of the sample. The administrator category of respondents included principals, other officers in the upper hierarchy and members of the management. The student category of the respondents included high and secondary standard students of both rural and urban schools. Parents of the students who were frequent visitors to the school formed parent category of the respondents.

Interview schedule that has been attached at Appendix-(ii) was used as the technique for data collection in terms of teachers as respondents. Case study method was used for all other categories of respondents to supplement the empirical findings of the study. The core for the choice of various unprofessional practices to be studied and questions for the interview schedule was based on the inputs collected from the students and parents. Students were asked to name the most liked and most disliked teacher of their school. They were then asked which qualities made that teacher the most liked teacher. Soft spoken, regular and empathetic towards students coming from low socio-economic background were some qualities stated by them for the most favoured teacher of their school. Those who guided them regarding medical health and nutrition, personal hygiene, cleanliness; guided them in solving psychological/personal problems and maintained discipline in the classroom were in the list of favourite teachers. Those who involved themselves with students through co-curricular activities in the school, maintained good communication with the students and took pains to develop the personalities of the students were the most liked teachers by the students. On the contrary, who were arrogant, did not take interest in school affairs, did not maintain good relations with fellow teachers, always looked for opportunities to run away from school, indulged in factionalism to spoil the atmosphere of the school, behaved badly with the students and humiliated students in the presence of peer group and other teachers were the most disliked teachers. Those who were always burdened by fatigue and personal problems in the classroom, did not attend the Morning Assembly rather chose to have breakfast in the staffroom, indulged in gossiping/reading newspapers or sitting in the principal's office, took overtime to cover up the absence from scheduled classes, were in the list of disliked teachers among the student community.

Some of the parents, who were aware of the future prospects of their wards, were also critical about such teachers who boycotted or punished students over frivolous reasons. Parents play an active role in pinpointing such type of teachers in private schools due to direct access to the members of management who happen to be locals. On the other hand, the parents most of them labourers and petty shopkeepers whose children study in urban government schools have no courage to raise voice against such type of teachers. If some one has the courage to raise voice against such teachers he/she has no access to higher authorities or to the Parent Teacher Association (PTA) of the school whose members happen to be politically ambitious locals having no wards in the school. At the most if a parent approaches the principal of the school against the teacher he is persuaded to settle down the matter by the principal and the school staff using lip service and the concerned teacher is left unscathed and morally boosted to keep up the conduct. The 73rd and 74th amendment in Act (1992) of the Constitution have delegated powers to members of the community to have a say in the running of day to day affairs of the educational institutions of their area in the form of self government.

The formation of Village Education Development Committees in rural areas and PTAs in urban areas are the result of this empowerment through 73rd and 74th amendment in the Constitution respectively. Their effectiveness seems doubtful after getting the inputs from the parents. Members of PTAs are either politically ambitious people or members of political parties and are selected by the principal of the school to maintain links with the political masters to settle down problems arising out of administrative lapses on his/her part. They are hardly approachable to the humble parents of the students. Even if they are approachable they are hardly enthusiastic to raise a voice against the teacher of the school in order to maintain his/her legacy of being member of PTA without being a parent of a ward in the school. On the other hand, VEDC members are found proactive as compared to members of PTA in taking interest in school affairs due to the small size of village community and better inter personal communication. Members of VEDC have greater participation in school development programmes and thus greater interaction with the teachers. There have been many instances of locking of schools by the members of VEDC due to teacher absenteeism, unacceptable behaviour of the teachers, poor results etc. But such instances are hardly found in the urban schools.

Inputs from the members of school teaching community were highly useful in the construction of interview schedule. Having cordial and supportive relations between the teachers of the same subject was a rare thing in urban schools with few exceptions in rural schools. Desire to maintain supremacy over the other led them to adopt all possible means to degrade the other. Factionalism on the basis of caste, class, classes being taught, designation, religion, rural/urban background, subject being taught, sincerity towards duty, relationship with the principal etc. was a common thing in schools with few exceptions of rural schools. Private schools were virtually immune to it due to two tier governing system. Teachers of private schools hardly find time to indulge in such type of practices. Female teachers do have some exceptions in doing such things but they indulge in other type of practices like indulging in group gossiping at the cost of teaching, taking their children to the school, usual refusal to do an extra work, sleeping in the classroom, always looking for excuses to run away from the school, coming late etc.

The inputs got from administrative staff to monitor the public schools reveal that it is indeed very cumbersome to back on rails highly deteriorated school system which suffers from many flaws. In a highly bureaucratic and politicised system the administrative staff has little autonomy and powers to act against the erratic teachers. Due to the shortage of clerical staff and regular summoning from the upper hierarchy there is hardly any time left to monitor the schools. Even if the administrators are determined to take action against the teachers the clerical staff at district and state level connive with the erratic teachers in tampering the charge sheets and they walk scot-free. In highly a politicised system of school education it is very cumbersome to bring to book the erratic teachers. The interview schedule contained both open-ended and closed questions. It was pre-tested. The questions that seemed difficult to answer were either dropped or changed. This process made the interview schedule precise and specific.

It was very difficult to find adequate number of respondent teachers for the study to represent rural/urban, male/female and government/private categories. Most of the private as well as government schools were dominated by female teachers. Moreover, the percentage of female teachers was quite high even in the rural schools of Roopnagar district due to its easy approach from state capital of Chandigarh and its satellite towns of Mohali and Panchkulla. A great number of female teachers who were supposed to be either spouses, daughters or daughters-in-law of the high rank officials in the state capitals of Punjab and Haryana who had the arrangement to get posting near Chandigarh, ply by chartered vehicles to attend schools in the Roopnagar district. In the absence of new appointment of teachers in government schools for several years it was very difficult to find young respondents for the sample in government schools. To overcome this problem male and young teacher from government schools were interviewed when they were in the district headquarters to attend in service training seminars at In-service Training Centre, District Institute of Education and Training and Senior Secondary Schools at district headquarter. Most of the teachers in this group were either Computer Teachers or Art and Craft Teachers who were recently appointed in government schools. Private schools also had a high representation of female teachers in rural as well as urban schools. Female teachers of private schools and experienced male teachers were interviewed in their respective schools.

A total of 385 respondent teachers were interviewed to make the sample statistically significant. To achieve the set objective of the role of the type of school in the prevalence of various unprofessional practices (UPPs) among the teachers, 195 teachers were interviewed from public schools and 190 from private schools. In the category of private schools both philanthropic and individual run schools affiliated to state school education board, made to the sample. Previously the salaries of the teachers run by philanthropic organisations were shared by the state and the management in the form of paid posts of teachers but now most of the teachers are recruited and paid by the school management. Among the interviewed teachers of private schools, 177 were male and 208 female. The number of teachers interviewed from rural schools was 200 and that from urban schools was 185. The criteria adopted to differentiate urban and rural schools was that the schools falling in towns having Municipal Committees were considered urban schools and those having Gram Panchayats were considered as rural schools.

Keeping in mind the obvious reluctance of the teacher respondents to admit to the prevalence of a particular unprofessional practice among them, they were asked, whether it is present among the teachers of their school or teachers of other schools. Even if they responded in 'No', they were asked to give the suggestions to contain that particular unprofessional practice. Many of them responded to suggestions listed in the interview schedule to contain that practice although they did not admit to it. While listing the reasons and suggestions for a particular UPP in the interview schedule 'others' item was placed in the end of each table to entertain the reasons and suggestions not covered in the list to supplement the findings. At the end of the interview schedule respondents were asked to rate the prevalence of each of the UPP to be studied on a five point scale to avail another chance to admit to various UPPs under investigation. All respondents attempted even though did not admit to that UPP earlier. The objective behind this was to reassess the obviously deniable practice among the respondent teachers.

The data thus collected were posted to the coding forms for each respondent before posting to computer to minimise the posting errors, on a spread sheet in MS-Excel. All the columns on the spread sheet were checked for correctness against the response code. Data were then sorted out after copying on temporary spread sheet according to the different variables and responses summated to form frequency tables manually. Percentages for making comparisons were calculated manually but Standard Deviations and Means were computed using mathematical functions in Ms-Excel.

This study consists of six chapters. In the first chapter the significance of the study is highlighted in the light of sociological orientation of the school teaching profession and the plight of the profession as depicted in numerous survey reports. The second chapter is dedicated to know the socio-economic profile of the school teachers. In the third chapter prevalence of six unprofessional practices among teachers are presented against type of the institution, sex and place of posting. The fourth chapter depicts the, correlation between socio-economic variables and the prevalence of various UPP. Reasons and remedies for the prevalence of various UPP in the light of type of the institution, sex and place of posting are presented in chapter five. The sixth chapter contains a brief discourse on major findings of the study.

1.8 Theoretical Importance and Practical Significance of the Study

In the process of acquisition of formal education the desirable status-roles, contents and context of learning are predefined and determined. Desirable status-role is the action or behaviour expected of the individual holding a particular status in a particular situation of interaction. Sometimes personal belief system, priorities of life, context of activity cast such an effect that a particular status-role holder deviates from the desired role. If the deviance is to such an extent that it starts affecting the outcome of a particular activity, then the role of the particular status-role holder becomes undesirable.

If the status-role holder is a professional then his/her role becomes unprofessional.

In case of education if various status-role holders deviate from the desired roles then the structure of social relationships change, which ultimately affect the functions of education in society. To study the change in the social structure of education as a social institution is the concern of sociology. To study the change in the behavioural pattern of a professional (school teacher in this case) is the concern of sociology of professions.

The present study is an endeavour to assess the prevalence of unprofessional practices, reasons behind the prevalence of a particular unprofessional practice and remedial measures in containing that unprofessional practice among school teachers. Findings of the study may help the policy makers for the prevention and remedy of the prevalence of unprofessional practices among school teachers in general. Inferences drawn from the study may also help the researchers for doing the comparative studies and formulating hypothesis for the future studies.

2

Socio-economic Profile of the Teachers

2.1 Introduction

Socio-economic status or social class of a person, in one way or another, influences the formation of attitudes and aspirations towards life and in the development of value system. Socio-economic status can be measured in a number of different ways. According to Parelious (1978) socio-economic status is measured by an index constructed from father's education, mother's education, parent's income and their characteristics, father's occupation and household possessions. Innumerable studies have documented the relationship between socio-economic status, education and occupational accomplishment. When we talk of characteristic possession of individuals and their families, they are already the complex products of their genetic endowments and social experiences by the time they enter school after several years of their life. They enter school with a variety of talents and handicaps that already predispose them towards school success or failure and as they move through school they continue to be influenced by these factors and by others that are beyond the control of educational institutions. For example, some predispose acquisition of wealth, power and prestige as the ultimate aim of life, while other's inclination is towards excellence, commitment and studiousness in life. Bowles and Gintis (1976) have found that middle-class families are more likely than working-class and poor families to encourage independence, self-discipline, creativity and self-actualisation. Working-class families are more concerned with obedience, respect and, cleanliness. Learning this pattern of behaviour prepares children to enter and accomplish occupations similar to their parents. Kahl (1953) in his study discovered that the working-class families with sons, who were successful in school were more likely than others to stress the importance of getting ahead. These families tended to be dissatisfied with their own situation in life and parents were anxious that their sons do better than they had done importantly; these parents also believed that the key to success was education.

In this chapter an attempt is made to have a look into the socio-economic profile of the teachers in the light of the variables like age, marital status, religion, caste, educational attainment, place of origin and rearing, educational level of the previous generation, occupational mobility, family income at the time of joining teaching profession, type and size of the family, family income, occupational preference, age at which first thought of becoming a school teacher came in mind, career decision makers, and length of service.

2.2 Age

Distribution of the age of the respondents is given in Table 2.1. The range of age variation was from a low of twenty-one years to a high of fifty-eight years. The table shows that, a close to 44.0 per cent respondents belonged to the age group of 21-30 years. Another 26.8 per cent of the total sample fell in the age group of 31-40 years. A vast majority (71.2 per cent) of the respondents were below the age of 40 years. Only 28.8 per cent accounted on the elderly side of the age group. The percentage of private school respondents was almost double (57.9 per cent) than public school respondents (31.3 per cent) in the age group of less than thirty-one years whereas; the percentage of public school respondents was substantially high (68.7 per cent) than private school (42.1 per cent) respondents in the same age group. This indicates that teachers in private schools were younger than their public school counterparts. Average age of private school respondents was lower (32.4 ± 9.5years) than public school respondents (37.6 ± 10.3 years). The vast difference in the average age of the respondents is due to fact that there have been no appointments in public schools for last ten years and high reshuffling rate among private school teachers due to poor pay and lack of job security. In private schools, teachers are asked to leave the school whenever there is a demand for pay hike, thus keeping the youngsters on move. Meager salary and job insecurity is keeping the private school teachers on tenterhooks.

Table 2.1: Distribution of Respondents According to the type of School and Age

Age in Years	Type of School				Total	
	Public		Private			
	No.	Percentage	No.	Percentage	No.	Percentage
21 - 30	61	31.3	110	57.9	171	44.4
31 - 40	60	30.8	43	22.6	103	26.8
41 - 50	47	24.1	25	13.2	72	18.7
51 - 60	27	13.8	12	6.3	39	10.1
Total	195	100.0	190	100.0	385	100.0
Mean Age	37.6	-	32.4	-	35.0	-
S.D.*	10.3	-	9.5	-	10.2	-

* Standard Deviation

Distribution of the respondents in various age groups according to the gender is shown in Table 2.2. The table reveals that the percentage of male respondents was more (50.3 per cent) than female respondents (39.4 per cent) in the age group of 21-30 years whereas percentage of female respondents was more (35.6 per cent) than their male counterparts (16.4 per cent) in the age group of 31-40 years. Percentage of male respondents was more (33.3 per cent) as compared to female respondents in the age group of above fourty years. A large number of male teachers in the younger age group is due to the fact that many computer teachers who were appointed three years

Table 2.2: Distribution of Respondents According to Sex and Age

Age in Years	Sex				Total	
	Male		Female			
	No.	Percentage	No.	Percentage	No.	Percentage
21 - 30	89	50.3	82	39.4	171	44.4
31 - 40	29	16.4	74	35.6	103	26.8
41 - 50	35	19.8	37	17.8	72	18.7
51 - 60	24	13.5	15	7.2	39	10.1
Total	177	100.0	208	100.0	385	100.0
Mean Age	35.4	-	34.7	-	35.0	-
S.D.*	11.2	-	9.3	-	10.2	-

* Standard Deviation

back made to the sample despite the fact that female teachers were in a majority. However, there was not much difference in the average age of male (35.4 ± 11.2 years) and female (34.7 ± 9.3 years) respondents.

Distribution of respondents in various age groups, teaching in rural and urban schools is presented in Table 2.3. The table depicts that percentage of respondents teaching in rural schools was more (56.5 per cent) than urban school respondents (31.3 per cent) in the age group of 21-30 years where as percentage of urban respondents was more (68.7 per cent) than their rural (43.5 per cent) counterparts in the age group of 30 years and above. On the average rural school respondents were quite young (32.4 ± 9.2 years) than their urban school colleagues (37.9 ± 10.5 years). This large difference in the average age of the teachers was due to the reason that a majority of the computer teachers who joined the service a few years back and made to the sample, were posted in rural schools. The average age of the sample was 35.0 ± 10.2 years.

Table 2.3: Distribution of Respondents According to the Place of Employment and Age

Age in Years	Place of Employment				Total	
	Rural		Urban			
	No.	Percentage	No.	Percentage	No.	Percentage
21 - 30	113	56.5	58	31.3	171	44.4
31 - 40	47	23.5	56	30.3	103	26.8
41 - 50	28	14.0	44	23.8	72	18.7
51 - 60	12	6.0	27	14.6	39	10.1
Total	200	100.0	185	100.0	385	100.0
Mean Age	32.4	-	37.9	-	35.0	-
S.D.*	9.2	-	10.5	-	10.2	-

* Standard Deviation

The average age of the respondents in the study of Gupta and Rani was 33.1 years and that of urban and rural schoolteachers were 35.5 years and 30.6 years respectively (Gupta and Rani 1988). The average age of the respondents teaching in urban schools was also more than those teaching in rural schools in the sample same as in the sample of Gupta and Rani, though the average age of teachers in the sample of Gupta and Rani was less than that of respondents in our sample.

2.3 Marital Status

Distribution of respondents teaching in public and private schools and their marital status is presented in Table 2.4. The table reveals that more than two third of the respondents were married; only one was widowed and other two separated or divorced. The percentage of married respondents was more in public schools (79.0 per cent) than in private schools (58.4 per cent) and that of unmarried respondents was more in private schools (40.0 per cent) than in public (21.0 per cent) schools. Table 2.1 also revealed that the percentage of teachers in lower age group was more in private schools as compared to teachers of public schools which had higher percentage in upper age groups. It is evident from the analysis that public school teachers were generally married and older than their private school counterparts who were unmarried youngsters. Some of the reasons for this are that posts of teachers are lying vacant and experienced teaches are serving in public schools. In private schools due to poor pay and job insecurity teachers kept on changing jobs for better avenues thus leading to unmarried youngsters joining and leaving the job frequently.

Table 2.4: Distribution of Respondents According to the type of School and Marital Status

Marital Status	Type of School				Total	
	Public		Private			
	No.	Percentage	No.	Percentage	No.	Percentage
Married	154	79.0	111	58.4	265	68.8
Unmarried	41	21.0	76	40.0	117	30.4
Widowed	-	-	1	0.5	1	0.3
Separated/ Divorced	-	-	2	1.1	2	0.5
Total	195	100.0	190	100.0	385	100.0

Male and female respondents are distributed according to their marital status in Table 2.5. The table portrays that percentage of married female respondents was more (73.0 per cent) than married male respondents (63.8 per cent) and that of unmarried male respondents was more (35.6 per cent) than unmarried female respondents (26.0 per cent). One female teacher was widowed and another was separated or divorced besides one male counterpart. Table 2.2 also revealed that the percentage of male respondents was more in the younger age group and that of female respondents was more in the age group of 31 - 40 years. This is due to the fact that computer teachers who joined service recently, are unmarried males.

Table 2.5: Distribution of Respondents According to Sex and Marital Status

Marital Status	Sex				Total	
	Male		Female			
	No.	Percentage	No.	Percentage	No.	Percentage
Married	113	63.8	152	73.0	265	68.8
Unmarried	63	35.6	54	26.0	117	30.4
Widowed	-	-	1	0.5	1	0.3
Separated/Divorced	1	0.6	1	0.5	2	0.5
Total	177	100.0	208	100.0	385	100.0

Distribution of respondents teaching in rural and urban schools according to their marital status is exhibited in Table 2.6. The table shows that percentage of married respondents, teaching in urban schools was more (77.3 per cent) than those teaching in rural schools (63.8 per cent) and that of unmarried respondents, teaching in rural was more (38.0 per cent) than those teaching in urban schools (22.2 per cent). The only widowed respondent was teaching in urban school and another two separated or divorced respondents were teaching in rural schools. Table 2.3 also indicated that percentage of younger respondents teaching in rural schools was more than those teaching in urban schools. The higher percentage of unmarried teachers in rural schools was due to the reason that newly appointed computer teachers in public schools and young teachers of private schools that made to the sample were located in rural area. Urban schools are dominated by married female teachers. This shows that domain of private schools is no more limited to urban area but also spreading towards the rural area.

Table 2.6: Distribution of Respondents According to Place of Employment and Marital Status

Marital Status	Place of Employment				Total	
	Rural		Urban			
	No.	Percentage	No.	Percentage	No.	Percentage
Married	122	61.0	143	77.3	265	68.8
Unmarried	76	38.0	41	22.2	117	30.4
Widowed	-	-	1	0.5	1	0.3
Separated/Divorced	2	1.0	-	-	2	0.5
Total	200	100.0	185	100.0	385	100.0

2.4 Religion

The whole population of Punjab is divided into many religions but Sikh and Hindu religions are in dominance. The Sikhs constitute 59.0 per cent, where as the Hindus constitute 39.4 per cent of the total population of Punjab. The percentage of Christians is 1.2 per cent and that of Jains is 0.16 per cent (Census 2001). The religious composition of the respondents teaching in public and private schools is presented in Table 2.7. The percentage of Sikh respondents was 52.5 per cent and that of Hindu respondents was 46.8 per cent in the sample. One respondent each from Jain and Christian religion also represented the sample. One respondent declined to disclose his religion. The percentage of Hindu respondents was slightly more (49.0 per cent) in private schools than in public (44.6 per cent) schools where as the percentage of Sikh respondents was more in public schools (54.9 per cent) as compared to private (50.0 per cent) schools.

Table 2.7: Distribution of Respondents According to the Type of School and Religion

Religion	Type of School				Total	
	Public		Private			
	No.	Percentage	No.	Percentage	No.	Percentage
Sikh	107	54.9	95	50.0	202	52.5
Hindu	87	44.6	93	49.0	180	46.8
Christian	-	-	1	0.5	1	0.3
Jain	1	0.5	-	-	1	0.3
Others	-	-	1	0.5	1	0.3
Total	195	100.0	190	100.0	385	100.0

The only respondent that belonged to Jain religion was a public school teacher and the only Christian respondent was teaching in a private school. The other one who refused to disclose the religion was a private school teacher.

The religious composition of the respondents according to the gender is shown in Table 2.8. The table reveals that among the Hindu respondents the percentage of male was more (51.4 per cent) than female (42.8 per cent). The Sikh religion was represented more (57.2 per cent) by female respondents than male (46.8 per cent) respondents. All three respondents that belonged to other religions were male respondents.

Table 2.8: Distribution of Respondents According to Sex and Religion

Religion	Sex				Total	
	Male		Female			
	No.	Percentage	No.	Percentage	No.	Percentage
Sikh	83	46.8	119	57.2	202	52.5
Hindu	91	51.4	89	42.8	180	46.8
Christian	1	0.6	-	-	1	0.3
Jain.	1	0.6	-	-	1	0.3
Others	1	0.6	-	-	1	0.3
Total	177	100.0	208	100.0	385	100.0

Table 2.9 shows that percentage of Hindu respondents was slightly more (48.1 per cent) in urban schools than in rural schools (45.5 per cent) where as percentage of Sikh respondents was more (53.5 per cent) in rural schools than in urban (51.4 per cent) schools.

Table 2.9: Distribution of Respondents According to Place of Employment and Religion

Religion	Place of Employment				Total	
	Rural		Urban			
	No.	Percentage	No.	Percentage	No.	Percentage
Sikh	107	53.5	95	51.4	202	52.5
Hindu	91	45.5	89	48.1	180	46.8
Christian	1	0.5	-	-	1	0.3
Jain	-	-	1	0.5	1	0.3
Others	1	0.5	-	-	1	0.3
Total	200	100.0	185	100.0	385	100.0

The ratio of respondents belonging to Sikh and Hindu religion was little less (1.1 to 1.0) in the sample than that of the ratio of Sikhs to Hindus (1.5 to 1.0) in Punjab. A similar trend was noticed in the ratio of Sikh to Hindu respondents except male respondents, according to the type of the institution, gender and location of the institution though meagre in magnitude.

2.5 Caste

Indian society is rigidly divided into relatively closed groups known as castes. Membership of a caste is determined by birth and there is little, rather no opportunity for an individual to change the caste. Caste plays a vital role in the social life of the people in Indian society. The major classification of Indian society can be done on the basis of three groups namely Scheduled Castes, Other Backward Castes and General Castes, though there are thousands of castes. According to Indian Census (2001) Scheduled Castes constitute 16.2 per cent of Indian population. Punjab state constitutes the highest Scheduled Caste population of 28.9 per cent among the other states. There are problems to assess the exact composition of Other Backward Castes and so is the case of General Castes. For the sake of enjoying the benefits of reservation of Other Backward Castes, various social and political movements have been taking place from time to time for inclusion in the group. National Sample Survey (2000) put the composition of Other Backward Castes as thirty two per cent where as Mandal Commission (1980) put it fifty two per cent consisting of total 3000 castes of Indian population. According to DISE (2005) in the department of school education of Punjab the composition of teachers belonging to Scheduled Castes was 18.9 per cent and that of Other Backward Castes was 10.4 per cent. Teachers belonging to General Castes constituted 66.4 per cent in the whole teaching community.

In the Roopnagar district Scheduled Caste teachers constituted 19.7 per cent and Other Backward Caste teachers were 7.5 per cent of the whole fraternity. Teachers belonging to General Castes in Roopnagar district were 69.8 per cent. Composition of teachers according to caste composition in our sample is depicted in Table 2.10. The table shows that, a vast majority (80.3 per cent) of the respondents that could make to the sample belonged to General Castes. The percentages of Other Backward Castes and Scheduled

Castes were 7.5 per cent and 12.2 per cent respectively. Among the General Caste respondents, 74.9 per cent were teaching in public and 85.8 per cent were teaching in private schools. In the category of Other Backward Castes, public school respondents outnumbered (11.8 per cent) their private school (3.2 per cent) counterparts. The percentage of respondents belonging to Scheduled Castes was slightly more (13.3 per cent) in public schools as compared to private (11.0 per cent) schools.

Table 2.10: Distribution of Respondents According to the Type of school and Caste

Caste	Type of School				Total	
	Public		Private			
	No.	Percentage	No.	Percentage	No.	Percentage
General	146	74.9	163	85.8	309	80.3
S C	26	13.3	21	11.0	47	12.2
O B C	23	11.8	6	3.2	29	7.5
Total	195	100.0	190	190	385	100.0

Analysis of data reveals a considerable imbalance in the existing composition of three major caste based groupings in the society, in the department of school education, and even in the sample. Teachers belonging to General Castes are in dominance even though there are recruitment and promotion benefits for Scheduled Castes and Other Backward Castes. According to Indian Census (2001) the percentage of male population in the state of Punjab was 53.3 per cent and females were 46.7 per cent. Among the Scheduled Castes 52.8 per cent were male and 47.2 per cent were female. According to DISE (2005) in the department of school education the percentage of female teachers was 40.1 per cent and that male was 26.3 per cent belonging to General Castes in the state of Punjab. Among the Scheduled Caste teachers 10.0 per cent were male and 8.9 per cent were female. Male teachers constituted 5.3 per cent and females were 5.1 per cent belonging to Other Backward Castes in the state of Punjab. In Roopnagar district male teachers were 24.2 per cent as compared to 45.6 per cent of females belonging to General Castes. In the Scheduled Castes percentage of male teachers was 8.9 per cent and that of females were 10.8 per cent. In the district teachers belonging to Other Backward Castes 3.8 per cent were male and 3.7 per cent were females.

Composition of male and female teachers belonging to various castes is presented in Table 2.11. The table depicts that percentage of male respondents was 11.8 per cent and that of female respondents was 12.5 per cent in the category of Scheduled Castes and in the category of Other Backward Castes the percentage of male respondents was 8.8 per cent and that female respondents was 7.2 per cent. The representation of male was (80.2 per cent) and that of female was (80.3 per cent) in the category of General Castes. This shows an equal representation of male and female respondents belonging to different castes in the sample. But in the case of General Castes, the gap in the percentages of male and female teachers is quite noticeable in Roopnagar district as well as in the state of Punjab different from that of present sample. In other castes male and female teachers were almost equally represented.

Table 2.11: Distribution of Respondents According to Sex and Caste

Caste	Sex				Total	
	Male		Female			
	No.	Percentage	No.	Percentage	No.	Percentage
General	142	80.2	167	80.3	309	80.3
S C	21	11.8	26	12.5	47	12.2
O B C	14	8.0	15	7.2	29	7.5
Total	177	100.0	208	100.0	385	100.0

The rural population of the state of Punjab was 66.1 per cent as compared to urban population which was 33.9 per cent. The rural population of Scheduled Castes was 75.7 per cent and that of urban was 24.3 per cent. In Roopnagar Scheduled Castes constituted 82.1 per cent in rural areas and only 17.9 per cent Scheduled Castes were living in urban area. The distribution of respondents teaching in rural and urban schools belonging to different caste groups is presented in Table 2.12. The table shows that percentage of respondents belonging to General Castes, teaching in urban schools was more (84.3 per cent) than those teaching in rural schools (76.5 per cent). Among Scheduled Castes, 14.5 per cent were teaching in rural schools and 9.7 per cent in urban schools. Other Backward Caste respondents were more (9.0 per cent) in rural schools than their urban school (6.0 per cent) counterparts.

Table 2.12: Distribution of Respondents According to Place of Employment and Caste

Caste	Place of Employment				Total	
	Rural		Urban			
	No.	Percentage	No.	Percentage	No.	Percentage
General	153	76.5	156	84.3	309	80.3
S C	29	14.5	18	9.7	47	12.2
O B C	18	9.0	11	6.0	29	7.5
Total	200	100.0	185	100.0	385	100.0

More than two third of the population is putting up in rural area of the state of Punjab and the composition of Scheduled Caste population in rural area is more than three fourth. In case of Roopnagar district it is more than four fifth of the total population. This shows the imbalance in the distribution of Scheduled Castes population which is heavily concentrated in the rural area. A similar trend is noticed in our sample.

2.6 Educational Attainment of the Teachers

As a social process, education is concerned with the transmission of various kinds of knowledge. This knowledge is reproduced, transmitted, and mediated through the relationships between the respondents and learners, within the institutional context and frameworks. For this purpose the teacher must be in the possession of esoteric knowledge and the skill to transmit it to the students.

This sample included the teachers who were teaching Secondary and Senior Secondary classes. The essential qualification for Vernacular/ Art and Craft/ Physical Education teachers was Higher Secondary/ Senior Secondary followed by one year professional Diploma in relevant field. For Masters/Mistresses the basic qualification is Graduation in relevant subject followed by Bachelor of Education in concerned teaching subjects. For Lecturers the essential qualification is Post Graduation in the relevant subject and Bachelor of Education. The others category included the Computer Teachers and Vocational Masters/Lecturers. There are two hierarchies among Computer Teachers namely Faculty and Computer Teacher. For Faculty the essential qualification is M.Sc. (Information Technology or Computer Science) or Master in Computer Applications. For Computer Teachers the basic qualification is Graduation followed by one year Diploma in Computer Applications. For Vocational Lecturers the basic qualification is Post Graduation followed by one year Post Graduate Diploma in relevant technical field or Degree in Engineering. For Vocational Masters the basic qualification is Polytechnic Diploma in technical field followed by three year experience in relevant field.

The distribution of respondents according to their qualifications is presented in Table 2.13. The table shows that a vast majority (64.4 per cent) of the respondents included in the sample was Post Graduates, 29.1 per cent were Graduates, and 2.6 per cent were Under Graduates with some technical qualification. Only one was Doctorate and another 3.6 per cent were in the possession of some other Vocational or Technical qualifications. The percentage of Post Graduate respondents was more (66.7 per cent) in public schools than in private (62.1 per cent) schools whereas the percentage of Graduate respondents was more (31.6 per cent) in private schools than in public (26.7 per cent) schools. The only Doctorate teacher included in the sample was teaching in a private school and the majority of (6.1 per cent) Technical/ Vocational teachers were from public schools.

Data shows that there is no dearth of highly qualified teachers in the schools of state of Punjab. Public schools are better equipped with highly qualified teachers as compared to private schools. Public schools are also having an array of teachers with qualifications in the multiplicity of technical fields other than private schools.

Table 2.13: Distribution of Respondents According to the Type of School and their Educational Qualifications

Educational Level	Type of the School				Total	
	Public		Private			
	No.	Percentage	No.	Percentage	No.	Percentage
High/Sr. Sec.	1	0.5	9	4.7	10	2.6
Graduation	42	26.7	60	31.6	112	29.1
Post Graduation	130	66.7	118	62.1	248	64.4
Doctorate	-	-	1	0.5	1	0.3
Others	12	6.1	2	1.1	14	3.6
Total	195	100.0	190	100.0	385	100.0

Distribution of male and female respondents according to their qualifications is presented in Table 2.14. The table shows that percentage of male Post Graduate respondents was more (66.7 per cent) than their female (62.5 per cent) counterparts whereas percentage of female Graduate respondents was slightly (30.8 per cent) more than their male (27.1 per cent) counterparts. The only Doctorate respondent was a male teacher. The percentage of female Art and Craft teachers was more (3.8 per cent) than their male (1.1 per cent) counterparts.

Table 2.14: Distribution of Respondents According to Sex and their Educational Qualifications

Educational Level	Sex				Total	
	Male		Female			
	No.	Percentage	No.	Percentage	No.	Percentage
High/Sr. Sec.	2	1.1	8	3.8	10	2.6
Graduation	48	27.1	64	30.8	112	29.1
Post Graduation	118	66.7	130	62.5	248	64.4
Doctorate	1	0.6	-	-	1	0.3
Others	8	4.5	6	2.9	14	3.6
Total	177	100.0	208	100.0	385	100.0

Distribution of respondents teaching in rural and urban schools on the basis of their academic qualifications is depicted in Table 2.15. The table displays that percentage of Post Graduate respondents was more in urban schools (67.6 per cent) than those teaching in rural

Table 2.15: Distribution of Respondents According to Place of Employment and their Educational Qualifications

Educational Level	Place of Employment				Total	
	Rural		Urban			
	No.	Percentage	No.	Percentage	No.	Percentage
High/Sr. Sec.	4	2.0	6	3.2	10	2.6
Graduation	70	35.0	42	22.7	112	29.1
Post Graduation	123	61.5	125	67.6	248	64.4
Doctorate	-	-	1	0.5	1	0.3
Others	3	1.5	11	6.0	14	3.6
Total	200	100.0	185	100.0	385	100.0

schools (61.5 per cent) where as percentage of Graduate respondents was more in rural schools (35.0 per cent) than in urban schools (22.7 per cent). Majority of the Technical /Vocational teachers (6.0 per cent) were posted in urban schools.

In the study of Gupta and Rani (1988) the percentage of Graduate or Post Graduate teachers was more (51.1 per cent) in rural schools than in urban schools (40.0 per cent) where as percentage of Under Graduate teachers was more (41.0 per cent) in urban schools than in rural schools (33.0 per cent). Percentage of Art and Craft or Physical Education teachers was more in rural schools (10.2 per cent) than in urban schools. In Wadhawan's (1980) work the percentage of Post Graduate teachers were less (39.2 per cent) than Trained Graduate Teachers (60.8 per cent).

The findings of Gupta and Rani (1988) are similar to this sample regarding the qualification of teachers. The number of teachers with Graduation and Post Graduation are more in rural schools as compared to urban schools. Under Graduate teachers are more in urban schools. But in Art and Craft or Physical Education teachers or other Technical Teachers our findings are opposite to that of Gupta and Rani. Wadhawan (1980) found Post Graduate Teachers were less than Trained Graduate Teachers, but in this sample Post Graduate Teacher were more than Trained Graduate Teachers.

2.7 Place of Origin and Rearing

The geographical environment of an individual does influence his/ her social outlook and life chances. It is a common assumption that urban set-up provides better place for avenues/life chances for mobility of an individual than a rural set-up. These differences can be ascertained in terms of habitation and schooling. Place of rearing of public and private school respondents is presented in Table 2.16. The table shows that majority of the respondents (63.6 per cent) had their childhood schooling in urban areas and remaining (36.4 per cent) were brought up in rural environment. The percentage of respondents teaching in public schools that had their upbringing in urban set-up was more (65.1 per cent) than their private school counterparts (62.6 per cent). In terms of rural upbringing, percentage of respondents teaching in private schools was more (37.9 per cent) than those of teaching in public schools (34.9 per cent).

Table 2.16: Distribution of Respondents According to the Type of School and their Schooling in Childhood

Childhood Schooling	Type of School				Total	
	Public		Private			
	No.	Percentage	No.	Percentage	No.	Percentage
Urban	127	65.1	118	62.6	245	63.6
Rural	68	34.9	72	37.9	140	36.4
Total	195	100.0	190	100.0	385	100.0

Place of rearing of male and female respondents are presented in Table 2.17. Among the major part of the respondents in the sample who were brought up in the urban setting, a close to four fifth of them were female and 46.3 per cent were male. Those who were brought up in the rural environment, 53.7 per cent were male and 21.6 were female. This shows that female respondents in the sample availed better opportunities for the choice of the profession as compared to their male counterparts. Limited working hours and home posting make school teaching profession attractive to females in supplementing family income in addition to looking after family.

Table 2.17: Distribution of Respondents According to Sex and their Schooling in Childhood

Childhood Schooling	Sex				Total	
	Male		Female			
	No.	Percentage	No.	Percentage	No.	Percentage
Urban	82	46.3	163	78.4	245	63.6
Rural	95	53.7	45	21.6	140	36.4
Total	177	100.0	208	100.0	385	100.0

The distribution of respondents according to childhood nurturing and place of posting is presented in Table 2.18. The table portrays that percentage of respondents, with rural background was more in urban schools (47.6 per cent) than in rural schools (26.0 per cent). Where as the percentage of respondents with urban background was more in rural schools (74.0 per cent) than in urban (52.4 percent) schools. This may be due to the fact that those teachers who were brought in the rural environment always had the desire to serve in the urban schools and nurture their children for better avenues. While those respondents who were brought up in the urban set up did not mind serving in the rural schools due to higher pay in the form of rural allowance and at the same time nurturing their children in the urban set up. So desire to avail better opportunities of urban settings was always there among the respondents even if they had to serve in the rural schools. It is evident from the fact that students living in the adjoining villages to the city prefer urban schools though they have schools in their villages.

Table 2.18: Distribution of Respondents According to Place of Employment and their Schooling in Childhood

Childhood Schooling	Place of Employment				Total	
	Rural		Urban			
	No.	Percentage	No.	Percentage	No.	Percentage
Urban	148	74.0	97	52.4	245	63.6
Rural	52	26.0	88	47.6	140	36.4
Total	200	100.0	185	100.0	385	100.0

2.8 Educational Attainment in the Previous Generation

Bowles and Gintis (1975) found that there are social class variations in child rearing practices and occupational accomplishment. Middle-class parents, tend to encourage curiosity, initiative, and independence. Working and lower class parents tend to encourage obedience, neatness, honesty, and docility. As Hasley (1977a) points out, factors of both ascription (family background) and achievement (education) are operative in the acquisition of occupational status or mobility, although education has become increasingly the mediator of transmission of social status (or inter-generational mobility). "Institutionally, education is the principal agent of achievement. But at the same time the inter-generational process over which it exercises increasing sway is just as importantly one in which ascriptive forces find ways of expressing themselves as 'achievement'. Moreover our path analysis has also shown that social origin or 'ascription' has direct effects on the later career of a man, i.e. family influence does not cease after entry into the labour market".

Educational level of the father is taken as one of the ascriptive determinant of social mobility of the respondents. Responses obtained regarding the education level of their father are presented in Table

2.19. Nearly forty seven per cent of the respondents revealed Senior Secondary, 27.3 per cent as Graduation and 11.9 per cent Post Graduation as the level of education of their father. Remaining 13.5 per cent of the respondents were reluctant to reveal the education level of their father or had illiterate father. The percentage of private school respondents, who had education level of their father up to Senior Secondary, was more (52.6 per cent) than public school respondents (42.1 per cent). On the contrary the percentage of respondents, who had Graduate or Post Graduate father, was more (41.5 per cent) in public schools than in private schools (36.9 per cent). It may be due to the fact that public school teachers had been educated and well off parents which helped them to secure government jobs. On the other hand, private school teachers were younger and their parents were not well educated to guide them for better avenues and serving in private schools.

Table 2.19: Distribution of Respondents According to the Type of School and their Father's Educational Level

Educational Level	Type of the School				Total	
	Public		Private			
	No.	Percentage	No.	Percentage	No.	Percentage
High/Hr. Sec./ Sr. Sec.	82	42.1	100	52.6	182	47.3
Graduation	57	29.2	48	25.3	105	27.3
Post Graduation	24	12.3	22	11.6	46	11.9
Others	32	16.4	20	10.5	52	13.5
Total	195	100.0	190	100.0	385	100.0

Responses of male and female teachers regarding the educational level of their father are presented in Table 2.20. The table depicts that percentage of female respondents was more (45.7 per cent) who had Graduate and Post Graduate fathers, than male respondents (31.6 per cent). On the other hand percentage of male respondents was more (48.6 per cent) than female respondents (39.6 per cent) who had father with educational level up to Senior Secondary. This shows that female teachers had better educated families to guide them in securing the job in teaching profession as compared to their male counterparts. Even male teachers were more in number coming from illiterate families.

Table 2.20: Distribution of Respondents According to Sex and their Father's Educational Level

Educational Level	Sex				Total	
	Male		Female			
	No.	Percentage	No.	Percentage	No.	Percentage
High/Hr. Sec./ Sr. Sec.	86	48.6	96	46.1	182	47.3
Graduation	36	20.3	69	33.2	105	27.3
Post Graduation	20	11.3	26	12.5	46	11.9
Others	35	19.8	17	8.2	52	13.5
Total	177	100.0	208	100.0	385	100.0

Distribution of respondents teaching in rural and urban schools according to the educational level of their father is presented in Table 2.21. The table shows that percentage of rural school respondents was slightly more (48.5 per cent) than their urban counterparts (45.9 per cent), whose fathers had their educational qualifications up to Senior Secondary. Respondents with Graduate and Post Graduate father were almost equally distributed in the sample with respect to their posting in rural (39.0 per cent) and urban (39.5 per cent) schools.

Table 2.21: Distribution of Respondents According to Place of Employment and their Father's Educational Level

Educational Level	Place of Employment				Total	
	Rural		Urban			
	No.	Percentage	No.	Percentage	No.	Percentage
High/Hr. Sec./ Sr.Sec.	97	48.5	85	45.9	182	47.3
Graduation	54	27.0	51	27.6	105	27.3
Post Graduation	24	12.0	22	11.9	46	11.9
Others	25	12.5	27	14.6	52	13.5
Total	200	100.0	185	100.0	385	100.0

2.9 Inter-generational Occupational Mobility

According to Parelious and Parelious (1978) teaching, at any level, is considered unambiguously a middle-class occupation. Yet, many individuals who enter teaching are from working-class backgrounds. These individuals are mobile: their parents worked in blue-collar occupations and, for the most part, did not have a college education. Occupation of the parents of the respondents in our sample is exhibited in Table 2.22. The table shows that 44.4 per cent of the respondents came from the background where occupation of the father was some government service and a close to 32.0 per cent said that their fathers were doing farming/ business or having some industry. One ninth of the respondents disclosed that the occupation of their father was teaching and 6.5 per cent said that their father was doing some non government job. The percentage of respondents who did not want to disclose the occupation of the father was 3.4 per cent and another 2.9 per cent came from other petty occupational backgrounds. The percentage of public school respondents was little more (45.1 per cent) as compared to private school respondents (43.7 per cent) with fathers being in government services. On the contrary, the percentage of private school respondents was more (35.8 per cent) than public school respondents (28.2 per cent), who came from farming, business or industrial background. The percentage of respondents coming from teaching background was more (13.3 per cent) in public schools as compared to private schools (8.4 per cent). A little less than half of the respondents have shown the occupational change in the generation from farming/business/industry or some petty private job to teaching profession. It is observed a little more among private school respondents.

Table 2.22: Distribution of Respondents According to the Type of School and their Father's Occupation

Occupation of Father	Type of the School				Total	
	Public		Private			
	No.	Percentage	No.	Percentage	No.	Percentage
Govt. service (civil/military)	88	45.1	83	43.7	171	44.4
Farming/ Business/Industry	55	28.2	68	35.8	123	31.9
Profession (teaching)	26	13.3	16	8.4	42	10.9
Profession (non-teaching)	13	6.7	12	6.3	25	6.5
Others	7	3.6	4	2.1	11	2.9
No response	6	3.1	7	3.7	13	3.4
Total	195	100.0	190	190	385	100.0

Occupational mobility among male and female respondents is shown in Table 2.23. The table reveals that 44.0 per cent of male and 44.7 per cent of female respondents were coming from families where occupation of the father was some government service. A close to twelve per cent of male and 10.1 per cent of female respondents were having fathers in teaching profession. Forty four per cent of the male respondents and 45.2 per cent of female respondents were coming from families involved in farming/business/industry or some petty private occupation. There is little sign of occupational mobility among teachers in terms of gender difference.

Table 2.23: Distribution of Respondents According to Sex and their Father's Occupation

Occupation of Father	Sex				Total	
	Male		Female			
	No.	Percentage	No.	Percentage	No.	Percentage
Govt. service (civil/military)	78	44.0	93	44.7	171	44.4
Farming / Business/Industry	54	30.5	69	33.1	123	31.9
Profession (teaching)	21	11.9	21	10.1	42	10.9
Profession (non-teaching)	9	5.1	16	7.7	25	6.5
Others	8	4.5	3	1.5	11	2.9
No response	7	4.0	6	2.9	13	3.4
Total	177	100.0	208	100.0	385	100.0

Similar observations were noticed among the urban and rural school respondents that are presented in Table 2.24. Fifty six per cent of the respondents teaching in rural schools and 54.6 per cent of the respondents teaching in urban schools came from the families where occupation of the father was government service or teaching profession. Forty four per cent of the respondents teaching in rural schools and 45.4 per cent of the respondents teaching in urban schools came from the families doing farming/business or having some industry or doing some petty private service.

Table 2.24: Distribution of Respondents According to Place of Employment and their Father's Occupation

Occupation of Father	Place of Employment				Total	
	Rural		Urban			
	No.	Percentage	No.	Percentage	No.	Percentage
Govt. service (civil/military)	89	44.5	82	44.3	171	44.4
Farming/ Business/Industry	62	31.0	61	32.9	123	31.9
Profession (teaching)	23	11.5	19	10.3	42	10.9
Profession (non-teaching)	13	6.5	12	6.5	25	6.5
Others	6	3.0	5	2.7	11	2.9
No response	7	3.5	6	3.3	13	3.4
Total	200	100.0	185	100.0	385	100.0

2.10 Income of the Family While Joining Teaching Profession

School teaching can be distinguished from many professional occupations in terms of the relative ease with which it can be entered. The financial investment necessary to become a teacher is therefore considerably lower than for many professions. People from a variety of life-cycle stages and a variety of socio-economic conditions can 'make it' into teaching, when the entry into other professions would be impossible. In Lortie's (1975) study, approximately three-quarters of respondents had considered an alternative occupation before entering teaching. Financial obstacles were the most frequently mentioned blocks in Lortie's sample. People, who preferred medicine, but who could not afford medical school, became biology teachers.

Table 2.25 shows that nearly half of the respondents in the sample revealed the income of the family below Rs. 10,000 per month while joining teaching profession and other 39.0 per cent gave it between Rs.10,000 to 20,000 per month. Remaining 12.2 per cent disclosed their family income above Rs.20,000 per month. This shows that the majority of the respondents had limited resources when they joined the teaching profession. Type of school, in which they were posted, did not make much difference in the economic condition of the family while joining teaching profession. The average income of the family at the time of becoming a public school teacher was Rs. 12440.3 per month and that of a private school teacher was Rs. 11483.9 per month.

Table 2.25: Distribution of Respondents According to the Type of School and their Family Income While Joining Teaching Profession

Income (rupees/month)	Type of School				Total	
	Public		Private			
	No.	Percentage	No.	Percentage	No.	Percentage
	90	46.2	98	51.6	188	48.8
10,000 to 20,000	81	41.5	69	36.3	150	39.0
20,000 to 30,000	15	7.7	18	9.5	33	8.6
30,000 to 40,000	3	1.5	2	1.0	5	1.3
Above 40,000	6	3.1	3	1.6	9	2.3
Total	195	100.0	190	100.0	385	100.0
Mean income	12440.3	-	11483.9	-	11968.3	-

Table 2.26 reveals that percentage of female respondents was more (43.7 per cent) than male respondents (33.5 per cent) who had their family income more than Rs. 10,000 and less than Rs.20,000 per month while joining teaching profession. The percentage of male respondents having family income less than Rs. 10,000 per month was more (56.5 per cent) than female respondents (42.3 per cent) when they thought of becoming a schoolteacher. This shows that female respondents came from economically better families than their male counterparts.

Table 2.26: Distribution of Respondents According to Sex and their Family Income While Joining Teaching Profession

Income (rupees/month)	Sex				Total	
	Male		Female			
	No.	Percentage	No.	Percentage	No.	Percentage
Below 10,000	100	56.5	88	42.3	188	48.8
10,000 to 20,000	59	33.3	91	43.7	150	39.0
20,000 to 30,000	11	6.2	22	10.6	33	8.6
30,000 to 40,000	1	0.6	4	2.0	5	1.3
Above 40,000	6	3.4	3	1.4	9	2.3
Total	177	100.0	208	100.0	385	100.0
Mean income	11728.5	-	12172.4	-	11968.3	-

Table 2.27 indicates that percentage of urban school respondents was slightly more (40.0 per cent) than rural school respondents (38.0 per cent) having family income more than Rs. 10,000 and less than Rs.20,000 per month at the time of teaching profession. The percentage of rural school respondents was (49.0 per cent) and that of urban school respondents (48.7 per cent) who had family income less than Rs. 10,000 per month while joining teaching profession. There was no visible difference in the economic condition of the family of urban and rural school respondents at the time of joining teaching profession.

Table 2.27: Distribution of Respondents According to Place of Employment and their Family Income While Joining Teaching Profession

Income (rupees/month)	Place of Employment				Total	
	Rural		Urban			
	No.	Percentage	No.	Percentage	No.	Percentage
Below 10,000	98	49.0	90	48.7	188	48.8
10,000 to 20,000	76	38.0	74	40.0	150	39.0
20,000 to 30,000	21	10.5	12	6.5	33	8.6
30,000 to 40,000	2	1.0	3	1.6	5	1.3
Above 40,000	3	1.5	6	3.2	9	2.3
Total	200	100.0	185	100.0	385	100.0
Mean income	11715.3	-	12241.9	-	11968.3	-

Table 2.19 reveals that more than three fifth of the respondents came from the families where education level of the father was up to Senior Secondary. Fathers of a little less than four fifth of the respondents were in some government service including teaching and rest of them were involved in some private service and doing some business (Table 2.22). This shows that low socio-economic conditions of the family could be some good reasons to believe, for many of them to join teaching profession or the transition profession for better avenues.

These findings support the findings of the study conducted by Wadhawan (1980) on the school teachers of Delhi. He found a relationship between the teaching profession and lower-middle-class background of the respondents. It was found that 46.4 per cent respondents belonged to the income group of Rs.3000-7200 per annum. Social background of female respondents was better than male respondents.

2.11 Type and Size of the Family

Indian society is broadly divided into two basic units of living namely nuclear and joint or extended. When head and spouse, head and spouse with unmarried children, and head without spouse but with unmarried children, are living under one roof, it is called nuclear family. When nuclear units are supplemented with other relations from upper, same, and lower generation then they are termed as extended families.

According to Parsons (2007) due to high rate of geographical mobility in industrial society, the family is characterised by the separation of nuclear family from the pre-industrial joint family. According to Parsons, families are factories which produce human personalities and keep them stabilised by providing warmth, security and mutual support, through close-knit kinship ties. In modern industrial society the family is largely isolated from the kin. In their isolation, Leach (2007) observed, the family members expect and demand too much from each. The result is conflict and the problems are not confined to the family. The tension and hostility produced within the family find expression through the society. The privatised family breeds fear and violence against the men who are not like us. Only when the individual can break out of the prison of nuclear family, rejoin their fellows, and give and receive support will the ills of the society begin to diminish.

Respondents living in nuclear and extended families are presented in Table 2.28. Table portrays that percentage of respondents was more (58.0 per cent) living in nuclear family than those (42.0 per cent) living in extended family. Percentage of public school respondents was more (60.0 per cent) than their public school counterparts (55.8 per cent) living in nuclear family. On the contrary, percentage of private school respondents was more (44.2 per cent) than their public school counterparts (40.0 per cent) living in extended family. This shows that private school teachers were unmarried youngsters living with the parents and even with grandparents made it to the sample. On the other hand public, school respondents were in their middle age and living with their unmarried children.

Table 2.28: Distribution of Respondents According to the Type of School and the Type of Family

Type of Family	Type of School				Total	
	Public		Private			
	No.	Percentage	No.	Percentage	No.	Percentage
Nuclear	117	60.0	106	55.8	223	58.0
Extended	78	40.0	84	44.2	162	42.0
Total	195	100.0	190	100.0	385	100.0

Table 2.29 shows that percentage of female respondents was more (60.1 per cent) than male respondents (55.4 per cent) who were living in nuclear families. Whereas, percentage of male respondents was more (44.6 per cent) than their female counterparts (39.9 per cent) living in extended families.

Table 2.29: Distribution of Respondents According to Sex and the Type of Family

Type of Family	Sex				Total	
	Male		Female			
	No.	Percentage	No.	Percentage	No.	Percentage
Nuclear	98	55.4	125	60.1	223	58.0
Extended	79	44.6	83	39.9	162	42.0
Total	177	100.0	208	100.0	385	100.0

Table 2.30 reveals that percentage of urban respondents was more (60.5 per cent) than their rural counterparts (55.5 per cent) living in nuclear families. On the contrary, percentage of respondents teaching in rural schools was more (44.5 per cent) than those teaching in urban schools (39.5 per cent) living in extended families.

Table 2.30: Distribution of Respondents According to Place of Employment and the Type of Family

Type of Family	Place of Employment				Total	
	Rural		Urban			
	No.	Percentage	No.	Percentage	No.	Percentage
Nuclear	111	55.5	112	60.5	223	58.0
Extended	89	44.5	73	39.5	162	42.0
Total	200	100.0	185	100.0	385	100.0

To know the size of the family of the teachers, they were divided into three groups according to the number of family members. When the members in the family did not exceed three it was termed as small size family. When members in the family were between four to six it was called medium size family and when the members in a family were seven and more then it was named as a large size family. The table 2.31 reveals that a majority (69.9 per cent) of the respondents were living in medium sized family. Only 13.0 per cent were living in large sized family and the remaining 17.1 per cent were living in small sized family. The average size of the family was 1.98 ± 0.62. Negligible difference was noticed from the table, among public and private school respondents who were living in medium sized family. However, percentage of public school respondents was more (19.5 per cent) than private school respondents (14.7 per cent) living in small sized family. Whereas, percentage of private school respondents was more (15.3 per cent) than public school respondents living in large sized family. Average size of family was slightly more (2.03 ± 0.62) among private school respondents as compared to their public school counterparts (1.94 ± 0.61).

Table 2.31: Distribution of Respondents According to the Type of School and Family Size

Size of Family	Type of School				Total	
	Public		Private			
	No.	Percentage	No.	Percentage	No.	Percentage
Small	38	19.5	28	14.7	66	17.1
Medium	136	69.7	133	70.0	269	69.9
Large	21	10.8	29	15.3	50	13.0
Total	195	100.0	190	100.0	385	100.0
Mean Size	1.94	-	2.03	-	1.98	-
S.D.*	0.61	-	0.62	-	0.62	-

* Standard Deviation

Table 2.32 indicates that percentage of female respondents was more (72.6 per cent) than those of male respondents (66.7 per cent) living in medium sized family. On the contrary, percentage of male respondents was more (20.3 per cent) than female respondents (14.4 per cent) living in small sized family. Male and female respondents were almost equally distributed in the sample that was living in large sized family.

Table 2.32: Distribution of Respondents According to Sex and Family Size

Size of the Family	Sex				Total	
	Male		Female			
	No.	Percentage	No.	Percentage	No.	Percentage
Small	36	20.3	30	14.4	66	17.1
Medium	118	66.7	151	72.6	269	69.9
Large	23	13.0	27	13.0	50	13.0
Total	177	100.0	208	100.0	385	100.0
Mean Size	1.95	-	2.00	-	1.98	-
S.D.*	0.65	-	0.59	-	0.62	-

* Standard Deviation

Table 2.33 depicts that percentage of respondents teaching in rural schools was more (71.5 per cent) than those teaching in urban schools (68.1 per cent) that were living in medium sized family. However, percentage of urban respondents was more (19.5 per cent) than rural respondents (15.0 per cent) living in small sized family. A meager difference was visible from the table among urban and rural respondents living in large sized family. Average size of the family was more (2.02 ± 0.63) among rural respondents than urban respondents (1.95 ± 0.61). No visible difference was noticed in family size deviations among rural and urban respondents.

Table 2.33: Distribution of Respondents According to Place of Employment and Family Size

Size of Family	Place of Employment				Total	
	Rural		Urban			
	No.	Percentage	No.	Percentage	No.	Percentage
Small	30	15.0	36	19.5	66	17.1
Medium	143	71.5	126	68.1	269	69.9
Large	27	13.5	23	12.4	50	13.0
Total	200	100.0	185	100.0	385	100.0
Mean Size	2.02	-	1.95	-	1.98	-
S.D.*	0.63	-	0.61		0.62	-

* Standard Deviation

2.12 Present Income of the Family

Income of the family is another determinant to know the social class of a person besides education. Income of the family from all sources is presented in Table 2.34. The table indicates that thirty one per cent respondents gave their family income below Rs. 20,000 per month. Another 31.9 per cent gave their family income in between Rs. 20,000 to 30,000 per month. A little more than one third of the respondents had their family income above Rs. 30,000 per month. The percentage of public school respondents was considerably high (80.5 per cent) than private school respondents (57.4 per cent), who had family, income more than Rs. 20,000 per month. On the contrary, the percentage of private school respondents was more than double (42.6 per cent) than public school respondents (19.5 per cent), whose family income was below Rs. 20,000 per month. This clearly shows that public school respondents were economically better than their private school counterparts. This is due to the reason that teachers in the public schools are appointed on regular pay scales in different hierarchies. But this could be a thing of the past according to the new state policy to appoint teachers on a fixed pay. Recently appointed computer teachers are an example of this policy. This indicates that the case of public school teachers will not be different in future, in terms of salary exploitation, from their private school counterparts who are exploited by the management. The average income of the public school respondents was Rs. 33458.5 per month and that of private school respondents was Rs. 27520.9 per month.

Table 2.34: Distribution of Respondents According to the Type of School and their Family Income

Income (rupees/month)	Type of School				Total	
	Public		Private			
	No.	Percentage	No.	Percentage	No.	Percentage
Below 20,000	38	19.5	81	42.6	119	31.0
20,000 to 30,000	68	34.9	55	29.0	123	31.9
30,000 to 40,000	42	21.5	24	12.6	66	17.1
Above 40,000	47	24.1	30	15.8	77	20.0
Total	195	100.0	190	100.0	385	100.0
Mean income	33458.5	-	27520.9	-	30528.2	-

Table 2.35 shows that percentage of female respondents was more than double (49.0 per cent) than male respondents (23.2 per cent) who had family income above Rs. 30,000 per month. On the other side the percentage of male respondents was substantially more (76.8 per cent) than female (51.0 per cent) respondents, who had family income below Rs. 30,000 per month. This shows that female respondents belonged to upper income group than their male counterparts. Average income of the family per month of the female respondents was more (Rs. 32611.5) than their male (Rs. 28080.1) colleagues.

Table 2.35: Distribution of Respondents According to Sex and their Family Income

Income (rupees/month)	Sex				Total	
	Male		Female			
	No.	Percentage	No.	Percentage	No.	Percentage
Below 20,000	67	37.8	52	25.0	119	31.0
20,000 to 30,000	69	39.0	54	26.0	123	31.9
30,000 to 40,000	21	11.9	45	21.6	66	17.1
Above 40,000	20	11.3	57	27.4	77	20.0
Total	177	100.0	208	100.0	385	100.0
Mean income	28080.1	-	32611.5	-	30528.2	-

A similar trend was found from Table 2.36 among rural and urban school respondents. The percentage of urban school respondents was more (43.2 per cent) than rural school respondents (31.5 per cent) who had family income of more than Rs. 30,000 per month. Whereas the percentage of rural school respondents was more (68.5 per cent) than urban school respondents (56.8 per cent) having family income less than Rs. 30,000 per month. This reveals that urban school respondents belonged to upper economic group than their rural school counterparts. Average income of the family of urban school respondents was also more (Rs. 32692.8 per month) than rural school respondents (Rs. 28526.0 per month). The average income of family in the sample was Rs. 30528.2 per month.

Table 2.36: Distribution of Respondents According to Place of Employment and their Family Income

Income (rupees/month)	Place of Employment				Total	
	Rural		Urban			
	No.	Percentage	No.	Percentage	No.	Percentage
Below 20,000	70	35.0	49	26.5	119	31.0
20,000 to 30,000	67	33.5	56	30.3	123	31.9
30,000 to 40,000	31	15.5	35	18.9	66	17.1
Above 40,000	32	16.0	45	24.3	77	20.0
Total	200	100.0	185	100.0	385	100.0
Mean income	28526.0	-	32692.8	-	30528.2	-

2.13 Occupational Preference

The different views of scholars - some calling teaching a profession, others not - put us in a paradox. Some term it a noble profession and the mother of all other professions. Others call it a semi-profession due to easy entry, with limited or no professional training. The teaching profession at any level, which is generally considered a middle-class occupation, sometime serves as a stepping stone to enter more remunerative professions. Sometimes, final choices are made not so much in terms of the positive attractions of certain possibilities as in terms of the lack of available alternatives. In Lortie's (1975) study, approximately three-quarters of the respondents had considered an alternative occupation before entering teaching. His data suggest that many decided on teaching because their alternative choices were not viable. Approximately one-third of the respondents in his sample said "they had wanted to go into another line of work but were unable to do so because of external constraints". For many of these, "teaching 'came close' to a primary, but blocked aspiration".

When respondents in our sample were asked to reveal aspirations in life, 60.3 per cent said they wanted to become schoolteachers. Only 14.3 per cent aspired to become engineers/doctors/lawyers and 7.5 per cent wanted to join civil/defence services. Nearly 9.0 per cent wanted to go abroad and those doing some sort of business were most disliked aspirations among the respondents. Of the whole sample, 7.8 per cent declined to reveal their primary aspirations or had aspirations which were not included in the question. Among the schoolteacher aspirants, the percentage of private school respondents was more (67.3 per cent) than public school respondents (53.3 per cent). The percentage of public school respondents was more (19.5 per cent) than their private school counterparts (9.0 per cent) for those who wanted to become engineer/doctor/lawyer. There was no visible difference in the percentages of public and private school respondents who aspired to go abroad or join some government/civil service. Data reveals that public school teachers had higher aspirations to join some other established professions but practically settled with school teaching. Private school teachers had great aspirations to become school teachers but in the absence of appointments in the public schools they had to settle in private schools (Table 2.37).

Table 2.37: Distribution of Respondents According to the Type of School and Aim in Life

Aim in Life	Type of School				Total	
	Public		Private			
	No.	Percentage	No.	Percentage	No.	Percentage
School teacher	104	53.3	128	67.3	232	60.3
Engineer/doctor/ lawyer	38	19.5	17	9.0	55	14.3
Go abroad	17	8.7	18	9.4	35	9.1
Civil/defence service	14	7.2	15	8.0	29	7.5
Businessman	3	1.5	1	0.5	4	1.0
Others	19	9.8	11	5.8	30	7.8
Total	195	100.0	190	100.0	385	100.0

Table 2.38 indicates that school teaching was a preferred aspiration among the females (67.3 per cent) in the sample than their male counterparts (52.0 per cent). To become an engineer/doctor/lawyer or to join some civil/defence service were preferred aspirations among male respondents (31.6 per cent) than their female colleagues (13.4 per cent).The percentage of female respondents was more (11.1 per cent) than male respondents who desired to go abroad. School teaching, by and large, is a profession dominated by females. In public schools, fifty per cent posts are reserved for females. Due to limited working hours there is ample time to look after family besides supplementing family income. Scope for home posting sooner or later attracts females to this profession. Private schools are favourite for unmarried female teachers looking for government service or marital settlement.

Table 2.38: Distribution of Respondents According to Sex and Aim in Life

Aim in Life	Sex				Total	
	Male		Female			
	No.	Percentage	No.	Percentage	No.	Percentage
School teacher	92	52.0	140	67.3	232	60.3
Engineer/ doctor/lawyer	35	19.8	20	9.6	55	14.3
Go abroad	12	6.8	23	11.1	35	9.1
Civil/defence service	21	11.8	8	3.8	29	7.5
Businessman	2	1.1	2	1.0	4	1.0
Others	15	8.5	15	7.2	30	7.8
Total	177	100.0	208	100.0	385	100.0

Table 2.39 shows that percentage of urban school respondents was more (20.5 per cent) than rural respondents (8.5 per cent) that aspired to become engineer/doctor/lawyer whereas percentage of rural respondents was more (62.5 per cent) than urban school respondents (57.8 per cent), who aspired to become school teachers. Rural school respondents had a high desire to go abroad and to join civil/defence service than their urban counterparts.

Table 2.39: Distribution of Respondents According to Place of Employment and Aim in Life

Aim in Life	Place of Employment				Total	
	Rural		Urban			
	No.	Percentage	No.	Percentage	No.	Percentage
School teacher	125	62.5	107	57.8	232	60.3
Engineer/ doctor/lawyer	17	8.5	38	20.5	55	14.3
Go abroad	21	10.5	14	7.6	35	9.1
Civil/defence service	18	9.0	11	6.0	29	7.5
Businessman	2	1.0	2	1.1	4	1.0
Others	17	8.5	13	7.0	30	7.8
Total	200	100.0	185	100.0	385	100.0

In the sample of Gupta and Rani (1988), 73.2 per cent wanted to remain as schoolteachers, of whom 52.0 per cent were urban and 48.0 per cent rural school teachers. Among those who had other aspirations, 25.7 per cent wanted to join some government service or become an engineer or doctor and one or two gave preference to business. In this sample the percentage of respondents who aspired to become school teachers was less (60.3 per cent) than in the study of Gupta and Rani (73.2 per cent). Rural school respondents were more (62.5 per cent) than urban school respondents (57.8 per cent) similar to in the sample of Gupta and Rani who aspired to become school teachers. In this sample 17.5 per cent wanted to join some government service or become doctor/engineer/lawyer, less than in the study of Gupta and Rani where the percentage was 25.7 per cent. Doing business was the least preferred avenue similar to in the sample of Gupta and Rani.

2.14 Age at Which First Thought of Becoming a School Teacher Came in Mind

Ginsberg (1951) was of the opinion that choice of an occupation is a complex phenomenon and takes place over a period of time. Ginsberg divides this period into three specific stages.

1. Fantasy Stage: When a young child begins dreaming of his future, and is unable to assess his capabilities. It starts at the age of six.
2. Tentative Stage: When the desired future satisfaction gets an edge over existing one. It starts between the age of ten and twelve.
3. Realistic Stage: When he makes compromises between his individual wants and actual opportunity exists for him. It starts between the age of sixteen and eighteen.

An attempt was made to classify the school respondents in various stages specified by Ginsberg by asking the respondents to recall the tentative age at which the first thought of becoming a school teacher came to their mind. All the respondents of the sample could make to the last two stages specified by Ginsberg.

Table 2.40 shows that a vast majority (79.0 per cent) of the respondents considered to become a school teacher at realistic stage, when fantasies were compromised by realities. The remaining twenty-one per cent described it as the tentative age when they were in schools and were inspired by their teachers to become schoolteachers.

The percentage of public school respondents was more (83.0 per cent) than private school respondents (74.7 per cent), who conceived to become schoolteachers at the realistic stage. Whereas percentage of private school respondents was more (25.3 per cent) than public school respondents (17.0 per cent) who desired to become schoolteachers. The differences in the percentages were cognizable. The average age at which the idea of becoming a schoolteacher came in mind of public school respondents was 20.7 ± 4.0 years and that of private school respondents was 19.5 ± 4.8 years. Similarity in the average ages shows that both public and private school respondents first thought of becoming a schoolteacher in the realistic stage. The average age for the first thought of becoming a schoolteacher in the sample was 20.1 ± 4.5 years.

Table 2.40: Distribution of Respondents According to the Type of School and Age at Which First Thought of Becoming a School Teacher Came in Mind

Age in Years	Type of School				Total	
	Public		Private			
	No.	Percentage	No.	Percentage	No.	Percentage
10 – 16	33	17.0	48	25.3	81	21.0
16 – 22	101	51.8	105	55.3	206	53.5
22 – 28	56	28.7	31	16.3	87	22.6
28 onwards	5	2.5	6	3.1	11	2.9
Total	195	100.0	190	100.0	385	100.0
Mean age	20.7	-	19.5	-	20.1	-
S.D.*	4.0	-	4.8	-	4.5	-

* Standard Deviation

Table 2.41 indicates that percentage of female respondents was more (25.5 per cent) than their male counterparts (15.8 per cent) who conceived to become schoolteachers at the tentative stage. Male respondents outnumbered (84.2 per cent) their female counterparts (74.5 per cent), who thought of becoming schoolteachers at realistic stage. The difference in percentages was noticeable. This shows that female teachers were comparatively more inclined to join teaching profession in the early age of their life. The school teachers might have been their role models. However, there was not much difference in the average ages of male and female respondents when the idea of becoming a schoolteacher first came in mind.

Table 2.41: Distribution of Respondents According to Sex and Age at Which First Thought of Becoming a School Teacher Came in Mind

Age in Years	Sex				Total	
	Male		Female			
	No.	Percentage	No.	Percentage	No.	Percentage
10 - 16	28	15.8	53	25.5	81	21.0
17 - 22	100	56.5	106	51.0	206	53.5
23 - 28	43	24.3	44	21.1	87	22.6
28 onwards	6	3.4	5	2.4	11	2.9
Total	177	100.0	208	100.0	385	100.0
Mean age	20.6	-	19.6	-	20.1	-
S.D.*	4.3	-	4.5	-	4.5	-

* Standard Deviation

It is clear from Table 2.42 that rural and urban school respondents were very closely distributed when they first conceived to become schoolteachers. The percentage of rural and urban school respondents was 21.5 per cent and 20.5 per cent respectively, who conceived the idea of becoming a schoolteacher at tentative stage. At realistic stage the percentage of rural respondents was 78.5 per cent and that of urban school respondents was 79.5 per cent. The average ages of rural and urban school respondents were 20.1 years and 20.0 years, when the idea of becoming a schoolteacher first came in mind.

Table 2.42: Distribution of Respondents According to Place of Employment and Age at Which First Thought of Becoming a School Teacher Came in Mind

Age in years	Place of Employment				Total	
	Rural		Urban			
	No.	Percentage	No.	Percentage	No.	Percentage
10 - 16	43	21.5	38	20.5	81	21.0
16 - 22	102	51.0	104	56.2	206	53.5
22 - 28	50	25.0	37	20.0	87	22.6
28 onwards	5	2.5	6	3.3	11	2.9
Total	200	100.0	185	100.0	385	100.0
Mean age	20.1	-	20.0	-	20.1	-
S.D.*	4.5	-	4.5	-	4.5	-

* Standard Deviation

2.15 Career Decision Makers

Generally it is cumbersome for a school going student to decide about his future career realistically. His decision may not effectively be translated into action for want of required resources at his disposal. His family may take a decision for him. Miller and Form (1951) are of the view that rational occupational choice is rare. According to them, in most cases, accident is the deciding factor. Blau (1956) and his associates maintain that lack of information concerning real opportunities restricts choosing an occupation. Rosenberg (1957) views the process of occupational choice as series of progressive delimitations of alternatives. Lortie (1975) found that some of the attractions teaching had for a number of people, were that it enabled them to continue their association with the schools or with particularly inspirational teachers, pulled them back into the schools as adults.

Only the respondents could throw light on the agents influencing their choice of profession. Table 2.43 shows that a close to two fifth of the respondents made self-judgment in the choice of teaching as profession. Father had greater influence (24.9 per cent) as compared to mother (10.6 per cent) in the choice of the profession. Brother or sister had a little influence (4.1 per cent) in the choice of teaching profession. Influence of their schoolteachers was 6.8 per cent as disclosed by the respondents. Close relatives had influenced 5.5 per cent of the respondents and 8.3 per cent described the role of more than one agent in the choice of the profession. The percentage of private school respondents was more (42.6 per cent) than public school respondents (37.0 per cent) who decided themselves to become schoolteachers. Little difference in the percentages was found in public (35.9 per cent) and private school respondents (35.3 per cent), whose parents decided for them to choose a career. Close relatives had greater influence on public school respondents (10.2 per cent) as compared to their private school counterparts (0.5 per cent) in career decision-making. Schoolteachers put greater impact on private school respondents (9.0 per cent) than public school respondents (4.6 per cent) in the choice of the profession.

Table 2.43: Distribution of Respondents According to the Type of School and Role of Career Decision Makers

Career Decision Makers	Type of School				Total	
	Public		Private			
	No.	Percentage	No.	Percentage	No.	Percentage
Self	72	37.0	81	42.6	153	39.8
Father	52	26.7	44	23.2	96	24.9
Mother	18	9.2	23	12.1	41	10.6
Teacher	9	4.6	17	9.0	26	6.8
Close relatives	20	10.2	1	0.5	21	5.5
Brother	6	3.1	6	3.1	12	3.1
Sister	3	1.5	1	0.5	4	1.0
Two or more	15	7.7	17	9.0	32	8.3
Total	195	100.0	190	100.0	385	100.0

It is clear from Table 2.44 that male respondents outnumbered (47.4 per cent) their female counterparts (33.1 per cent) who decided themselves in the choice of the profession. Parents took decision in the choice of the profession, in large percentage of female respondents (41.4 per cent) than male respondents (26.8 per cent). There was not much difference in the percentages of those male and female respondents, for whom other agents helped them to decide their future.

Table 2.44: Distribution of Respondents According to Sex and Role of Career Decision Makers

Career Decision Makers	Sex				Total	
	Male		Female			
	No.	Percentage	No.	Percentage	No.	Percentage
Self	84	47.4	69	33.1	153	39.8
Father	41	21.2	55	26.4	96	24.9
Mother	10	5.6	31	15.0	41	10.6
Teacher	14	8.0	12	5.7	26	6.8
Close relatives	6	3.4	15	7.2	21	5.5
Brother	8	4.5	4	2.0	12	3.1
Sister	2	1.1	2	1.0	4	1.0
Two or more	12	6.8	20	9.6	32	8.3
Total	177	100.0	208	100.0	385	100.0

Table 2.45 shows that influence of parents was more in rural respondents (40.0 per cent) as compared to urban respondents (30.8 per cent), in the choice of the profession. Percentage of rural respondents was a little more (41.5 per cent) than their urban counterparts (30.8 per cent), who decided their future themselves. Teachers had more influence on urban school respondents (9.7 per cent) as compared to rural school respondents (4.0 per cent). Urban school respondents were more influenced (13.0 per cent) by brother, sister and other close relatives than rural school respondents (6.5 per cent) while taking decision to choose teaching as a profession.

Table 2.45: Distribution of Respondents According to Place of Employment and Role of Career Decision Makers

Career Decision Makers	Place of Employment				Total	
	Rural		Urban			
	No.	Percentage	No.	Percentage	No.	Percentage
Self	83	41.5	70	37.8	153	39.8
Father	52	26.0	44	23.8	96	24.9
Mother	28	14.0	13	7.0	41	10.6
Teacher	8	4.0	18	9.7	26	6.8
Close relatives	8	4.0	13	7.0	21	5.5
Brother	4	2.0	8	4.4	12	3.1
Sister	1	0.5	3	1.6	4	1.0
Two or more	16	8.0	16	8.7	32	8.3
Total	200	100.0	185	100.0	385	100.0

2.16 Length of Service

While going through the career pattern of the school teachers it was found that 40.5 per cent of the respondents had less than five years of service and 25.2 per cent had between five to ten years of service. This shows that two third of the respondents had their service less than ten years of service. Another 13.5 per cent had between 10 to 15 years of service and remaining 20.8 per cent had more than 25 years of service. The average length of the service was 10.28 years. The percentage of private school respondents was more (48.4 per cent) than private school respondents (32.8 per cent) having service less than five years. There was negligible difference in the percentages of public (38.5 per cent) and private (39.0 per cent) school respondents whose length of service was between 5 to 20 years. But there was considerable difference in the percentage of public (28.7 per cent) and private (12.6 per cent) school respondents whose length of the service was more than 20 years. Public school respondents had more average length of service (12.4 years) than private school respondents (8.2 years) (Table 2.46).

Table 2.46: Distribution of Respondents According to the Type of school and Length of Service

Length of Service in Years	Type of School				Total	
	Public		Private			
	No.	Percentage	No.	Percentage	No.	Percentage
Less than 5	64	32.8	92	48.4	156	40.5
5 – 10	48	24.6	49	25.8	97	25.2
11 – 15	17	8.7	14	7.4	31	8.0
16 – 20	10	5.2	11	5.8	21	5.5
21 – 25	24	12.3	12	6.3	36	9.4
26 or more	32	16.4	12	6.3	44	11.4
Total	195	100.0	190	100.0	385	100.0
Mean Length	12.4	-	8.2	-	10.3	-

It is clear from Table 2.47 that percentage of male respondents was more (45.2 per cent), whose service length was less than five years than private school respondents (36.5 per cent). However, on the other side, percentage of female respondents was more (48.6 per cent) than male respondents (27.7 per cent) whose length of service was between 5 to 20 years. Again public school respondents were on the positive side in the percentage (27.7 per cent) than private school

Table 2.47: Distribution of Respondents According to Sex and Length of Service

Length of Service in Years	Sex				Total	
	Male		Female			
	No.	Percentage	No.	Percentage	No.	Percentage
Less than 5	80	45.2	76	36.5	156	40.5
6 – 10	32	18.1	65	31.3	97	25.2
11 – 15	8	4.5	23	11.0	31	8.0
16 – 20	8	4.5	13	6.3	21	5.5
21 – 25	20	11.3	16	7.7	36	9.4
26 or more	29	16.4	15	7.2	44	11.4
Total	177	100.0	208	100.0	385	100.0
Mean Length	11.2	-	9.5	-	10.3	-

respondents (12.6 per cent), whose service length was more than 20 years. On the average male respondents were more experienced (11.2 years) than female respondents (9.5 years).

Looking into the service pattern of school respondents, it was found that percentage of rural school respondents was more than double (54.0 per cent) than urban school respondents (26.0 per cent), having teaching experience of less than five years. On the contrary, percentage of urban school respondents was again double (33.5 per cent) than their rural school counterparts (17.5 per cent), having teaching experience between 5 to 10 years. There was no considerable difference in the percentages of rural and urban school respondents having teaching experience between 10 to 20 years. However, there were noticeable variations in the percentages of rural (13.5 per cent) and urban school respondents (28.6 per cent), who had teaching experience of more than 20 years. On the average, urban school respondents were more experienced (12.5 years) than their rural counterparts (8.3 years). There were no perceptible deviations in the length of service among rural and urban school respondents (Table 2.48).

Table 2.48: Distribution of Respondents According to Place of Employment and Length of Service

Length of Service in Years	Place of Employment				Total	
	Rural		Urban			
	No.	Percentage	No.	Percentage	No.	Percentage
Less than 5	108	54.0	48	26.0	156	40.5
5 - 10	35	17.5	62	33.5	97	25.2
11 - 15	19	9.5	12	6.5	31	8.0
16 - 20	11	5.5	10	5.4	21	5.5
21 - 25	10	5.0	26	14.0	36	9.4
26 or more	17	8.5	27	14.6	44	11.4
Total	200	100.0	185	100.0	385	100.0
Mean Length	8.3	-	12.5	-	10.3	-

2.17 Conclusions

Data was collected from 385 teachers of Roopnagar district of the state of Punjab. Of the total respondents, 195 were teaching in public schools and 190 in private schools. The number of male respondents in the sample was 177 and that of female respondents was 208. Two hundred respondents were included in the sample from rural schools and 185 from urban schools. A vast majority of the respondents that made to the sample were young. Private school respondents were younger than their public school counterparts. Male and female respondents were almost of the same average age but average age of urban school respondents was more. More than two-third of the respondents were married. Among the married more than three-fourth were public school teachers. The sample had equal dominance of both Hindus and Sikhs. Other religions were marginally represented in the sample. More than three-fourth of the respondents that made to the sample were from General Castes. Schedule Caste respondents outnumbered from Other Backward Castes.

A little more than three-fifth of the respondents were Post Graduates. Among the Post Graduates, the number of male, urban and public school respondents was more than their counterparts. A great majority of the respondents were brought up in urban environment. Female respondents and those teaching in urban schools were on the positive side in numbers. A great deal of inter-generational mobility could be seen from the time of father to the present incumbent. Private school respondents were numerically in preponderant position in inter-generational mobility. Nearly three-fifth of the respondents were living in nuclear families. Average size of the family was 1.98 ± 0.62. Minor variations were noticed in type and size of the family in terms of type of the school, gender and place of posting. Average income of the family was Rs. 30528.2 per month. Public school respondents were leading their private school counterparts in terms of family income. Female respondents and those posted in urban schools were in better financial position than their counterparts. While revealing their ambition in life, three-fifth of the respondents wanted to become school teachers. Female and private school respondents were numerically in preponderant position. Nearly four-fifth of the respondents recalled the first thought to become a school teacher at realistic stage. Two-fifth of the respondents decided themselves to become school teachers and other one-third revealed that their parents took decision for them. Influence of parents was more on female respondents in the choice of their career.

3

Prevalence of Unprofessional Practices Among Teachers

3.1 Introduction

Education exists in human society as a system of social relationships among various status-role holders. Social relationship is a human action in a context that is socially defined. In such a situation various status-role holders are expected to act as per socially set norms or standards. The socially set norms for various status-role holders in social institution are termed as status-role definitions. The status-role definitions for various status-role holders in a social institution are governed by other social institutions in the society in different contexts. The basis for various status-role definitions in social institutions is the values that are a part of the culture of plurality of individuals or groups. Anything that is considered to be desirable or to have some worth of its own is a value. Some of the values may form the basic principle of human living and social interaction, such as truth, justice, equality, humanism, tolerance, peace, etc. Some others are qualities that are considered desirable such as excellence, commitment, studiousness, honesty, empathy, etc. Despite socially defined context for interaction provided by social institutions, not all the individuals in a group accept the social status-role definitions or act as per role expectations. Such deviance from the social role expectations is generally controlled with sanctions of various types. Deviance on a large scale may lead to modifications in the structure of status-role definitions or change in social institutions. Social institutions may undergo changes in order to meet the demands of the different social situations in terms of time and space (Aikara 2004). Sometimes the change may also influence the value system, such as;

mundane values like social position, power, wealth, material possessions, etc. take preference over the basic and desirable values. This change in the value system may also influence the status-role definitions of various status-role holders in the social institutions like education.

Durkheim (1973) was of the opinion that excessive individualism in education can lead to personal defeat and social chaos. For him, education is above all a social means to a social end - the means by which a society guarantees its own survival. The teacher is society's agent, the critical link in cultural transmission. It is his task to create a social and a moral being. Through him, society creates man in its image. "That," says Durkheim, "is the task and glory of education". It is not merely a matter of allowing an individual to develop in accordance with his nature, disclosing what ever hidden capacities lie there only waiting to be revealed. Education creates a new being. For Durkheim, school had a crucial and clearly specified function: to create a new being, shaped according to the needs of the society. While this might seem restrictive and repressive to child-centered educators, Durkheim argues that the very reverse is true. Only by imposing limits can the child be liberated from the inevitable frustrations of incessant striving. Only as the child is systematically exposed to his country's cultural heritage can he achieve a sense of identity and personal fulfilment. Only as he is conscious of his implication in a society to which he is bound by duty and desire can he become a moral being. Durkheim eliminates the church because a sound morality must be founded in reason, not revelation. The family is out since the indulgent warmth of kinship ties is incompatible with the sterner demands of morality. If the family, small and intimate as it has become, can provide emotional support and tension release, it is not setting for cultivating the abstract idea of duty. On the other hand, moral education cannot be deferred until adulthood, nor it can be entrusted to adult agencies whose demands are excessive for a young child. So the task of moral education devolves upon the school (Durkheim 1973).

The shift from twentieth to twenty-first century is witnessed as the transition phase of science and technology to information and communication technology. Extensive use of communication technology has made the world a globalised village. According to

Giddens, "the driving force of the new globalisation is the communication revolution", and beyond its effects on the individual, this revolution is fundamentally altering the way public institutions interact (Giddens 2000). Giddens talk of the nation, the family, work, tradition, nature, as if they were all the same as in the past. They are not. They are institutions that have become inadequate to the tasks they are called upon to perform. The pessimistic view of globalisation would see it as destroying local culture, widening world inequalities and worsening the lot of impoverished, in the developing societies. Globalisation, creates a world of winners and losers, a few on the fast track to prosperity, the majority condemned to a life of misery and despair (Giddens 1999). Neo-liberal political philosophy of the world nations have too much dominance by the marketplace over the effective modes of active governments and a more effective global civil society, thus leading to all troubles (Giddens 2000). Education, a public institution, is not an exception in the globalised world. The beneficiaries of the globalised world are those who have access to or are a part of the knowledge-based society. That is to say, those who have access to globalised educational institutions, not those who are devoid of these institutions. The role of the welfare-state is either intentional or ineffective, in creating inequalities in this public institution.

It is obvious from this discussion that education is a virtuous institution for the survival of society. The teacher is the representative of society for the production of worthy social beings. The conduct of the teacher is based on the value system laid down by the plurality of the individuals or groups. Some values are basic for all the individuals in the society and some others are desirable from different status-role holders. School is the context for the transmission of value system. The conduct for a teacher may have cultural variations, nevertheless a common minimum is the same for the all. National Education Association of the United States have laid down a code of ethics and all members of the profession have a moral duty to abide by the code of ethics which is based on the following five principles.

3.2 A Code of Ethics for American School Teachers

FIRST PRINCIPLE : The primary obligation of the teaching profession is to guide children, youth, and adults in the pursuit of knowledge and skills, to prepare them in the ways of democracy, and to help them to become happy, useful, self-supporting citizens. The ultimate strength of the nation lies in the social responsibility, economic competence, and moral strength of the individual American.

In fulfilling the obligations of this first principle the teacher will-

1. Deal justly and impartially with students regardless of their physical, mental, emotional, political, economic, social, racial, or religious characteristics;
2. Recognize the differences among students and seek to meet their individual needs;
3. Encourage students to formulate and work for high individual goals in the development of their physical, intellectual, creative, and spiritual endowments;
4. Aid students to develop an understanding and appreciation not only of the opportunities and benefits of American democracy but of their obligations to it;
5. Respect the right of every student to have confidential information about himself withheld except when its release is to authorized agencies or is required by law;
6. Accept no remuneration for tutoring except in accordance with approved policies of the governing board.

SECOND PRINCIPLE: The members of the teaching profession share with parents the task of shaping each student's purposes and acts toward socially acceptable ends. The effectiveness of many methods of teaching is dependent upon cooperative relationships with the home.

In fulfilling the obligations of this second principle the teacher will-

1. Respect the basic responsibility of parents for their children;
2. Seek to establish friendly and cooperative relationships with the home;
3. Help to increase the student's confidence in his own home and avoid disparaging remarks which might undermine that confidence;

4. Provide parents with information that will serve the best interests of their children, and be discreet with information received from parents;
5. Keep parents informed about the progress of their children as interpreted in terms of the purposes of school.

THIRD PRINCIPLE: The teaching profession occupies a position of public trust involving not only the individual teacher's personal conduct, but also the interaction of the school and the community. Education is most effective when these many relationships operate in a friendly, cooperative, and constructive manner.

In fulfilling the obligations of this third principle the teacher will-

1. Adhere to any reasonable pattern of behavior accepted by the community for professional persons;
2. Perform the duties of citizenship, and participate in community activities with due consideration for his obligations to his students, his family and himself;
3. Discuss controversial issues from an objective point of view, there by keeping his class free from partisan opinions;
4. Recognize that the public schools belong to the people of community, encourage lay participation in shaping the purposes of the school, and strive to keep the public informed of the educational program which is being provided;
5. Respect the community in which he is employed and be loyal to school system, community, state, and nation;
6. Work to improve education in the community and to strengthen the community's moral, spiritual, and intellectual life.

FOURTH PRINCIPLE: The members of the teaching profession have inescapable obligations with respect to employment. These obligations are nearly always shared employer-employee responsibilities based upon mutual respect and good faith.

In fulfilling the obligations of this Fourth principle the teacher will-

1. Conduct professional business thru the proper channels;
2. Refrain from discussing confidential and official information with unauthorized persons;
3. Apply for employment on the basis of competence only, and avoid asking for a specific position known to be filled by another teacher;
4. Seek employment in a professional manner, avoiding such practices as the indiscriminate distribution of applications;
5. Refuse to accept a position when the vacancy has been created through unprofessional activity or pending controversy over professional policy or the application of unjust personnel practices and procedures;
6. Adhere to the conditions of a contract until service there under has been performed, the contract has been terminated by mutual consent, or the contract has otherwise been legally terminated;
7. Give and expect due notice before a change of position is to be made;
8. Be fair in all recommendations that are given concerning the work of other teachers;
9. Accept no compensation from producers of instructional supplies when one's recommendations affect the local purchase or use of such teaching aids;
10. Engage in no gainful employment, outside of his contract, where the employment affects adversely his professional status or impairs his standing with students, associates, and the community;
11. Cooperate in the development of school policies and assume one's professional obligations thereby incurred;
12. Accept one's obligation to the employing board for maintaining a professional level of service.

FIFTH PRINCIPLE: The teaching profession is distinguished from many other occupations by the uniqueness and quality of the professional relationships among all teachers. Community support and respect are influenced by the standards of teachers and their attitudes towards teaching and other teachers.

In fulfilling the obligations of this fifth principle the teacher will-

1. Deal with other members of the profession in the same manner as he himself wishes to be treated;
2. Stand by other teachers who have acted on his behalf and at his request;
3. Speak constructively of other teachers, but report honestly to responsible persons in matters involving welfare of students, the school system, and the profession;
4. Maintain active membership in professional organizations and, thru participation, strive to attain the objectives that justify such organized groups;
5. Seek to make professional growth continuous by such procedures as study, research, travel, conferences, and attendance at professional meetings;
6. Make the teaching profession so attractive in ideals and practices that sincere and young people will want to enter it.

3.3 A Code of Professional Ethics for Indian School Teachers

The draft of the Code of Professional Ethics for Indian school teachers, developed earlier in 1988, was reviewed in a national workshop held in NCERT, with a view to evolving a fresh Code of Professional Ethics for Teachers in the light of changing role of teachers. Five major areas of professional activities which encompass the work of a teacher were selected.

1. Teacher in relation to pupils.
2. Teacher in relation to parents/guardians.
3. Teacher in relation to society and the nature.
4. Teacher in relation to profession, colleagues and professional organization.
5. Teacher in relation to management/administration.

The basis of the principles laid down for American and Indian school teachers are the same. The core of the guidelines for teachers is based on the relationships between various actors in education. If actors involved act as per value based rules laid for their actions then the outcome of the education in the larger society is well served.

The first most significant relationship in education is that of teacher with the student. If the teacher is in the possession of the basic values of human living and the knowledge of various disciplines, and is committed to transfer them to the student in the formal setting. On the other side, the student is anxious to accept the knowledge and the basic values of human living, then that relationship is said to be fruitful. The other actors in the education are parents or guardians, who have to provide the support system to the student for acquisition of values and knowledge. They have to interact with the teacher and other actors in education to facilitate the teaching-learning process. They are also the beneficiaries of the outcome of the teacher-student relationship besides the student.

Community or the larger society is both, the beneficiaries and the investors, of education through its individual and societal functions. Social change, division of labour, social stratification, social cohesion etc. are some benefits of education for society. Qualitative and quantitative improvements in education are some investments of society in education. Teacher in the possession of professional values is also contributing to education. If he has cordial and supportive role towards the colleagues them he is contributing to education and the formal institution of education. By becoming the member of a professional organisation, he is serving the profession as well as protecting his own interests. Another relationship in education is that of the teacher with the administrator or management. Administration or management provides the formal setting and guidelines for the teaching learning activity. It monitors the actors and coordinates between the actors in education. It also constructs policies and evaluates the existing policies for the improvement in education. If all actors involved in education act as per the rules laid for them the larger functions of education are well served in society. For each of these areas, certain ethical principles were chosen to serve as guidelines for ethical practices of a teacher and other actors in education.

In the light of the aforesaid ethics, change in the status-role definitions of various status-role holders highlighted by various studies, and changes in various social institutions, the conduct of the school teachers deserve to be looked into. For this endeavour six unprofessional practices have been identified and defined among school teachers.

3.4 Unprofessional Practices Defined

Absenteeism: People are not going to work or school when they should be going. Teachers are away from school during their duty hours. Those who have equation with the principal are adjusted with non-teaching duties out of the school. Others take the advantage of higher bureaucratic and political connections in abstaining from school. Kin of the members of the management in private schools, working as teachers in the school, misuse their connections in abstaining from school.

Dereliction of Duty: Dereliction of duty is the failure on the part of the people to do something that they have to do because it is the part of their job. While in the school, teachers do not teach during their teaching hours. Other leisure activities like gossiping, sitting idle in the classroom or in school canteen etc. take priority over teaching.

Lack of Responsibility: People do not have a sense of being accountable for the work or job that is necessary or wanted. School teachers are supposed to possess the knowledge and desired skill to impart that knowledge to the students. Besides transmission of knowledge, they are expected to reconstitute personalities and create productive, moral and responsible social beings. On the contrary, they lack the required zeal and commitment to do this.

Discrimination: To treat a person or a group of people differently on the basis of their skin colour, caste, class, race, religion, sex etc. A sense of universalism is lacking in the teachers. Personal whims do play a role while doing one's duties. Students are not treated without the distinction of caste, class and creed.

Authoritarianism: A manner in which total acquiescence is demanded and there is no freedom for the people to act as they wish. Total obedience is expected from the students and there is no space for empathetic understanding of their feelings.

Commercial Venality: A corrupt practice that is connected with, profit, and not quality or morality. Public funding funds the professional knowledge and skill acquired by the teachers. This knowledge should be used for the welfare of the society and students, but on the contrary it is used for individual welfare and self-development of the teachers through private tutoring.

3.5 Prevalence of Unprofessional Practices

Responses obtained for various unprofessional practices are tabulated in terms of percentages and mean values on a five point scale. It is clear from Table 3.1 that discrimination against the students was the most prevailed (19.2 per cent) unprofessional practice (UPP) and authoritarianism (13.9 per cent) was the least prevailed UPP among the teachers. Nearly eighteen percent teachers admitted the prevalence of commercial venality. Lack of responsibility (16.9 per cent) and dereliction of duty (16.8 per cent) were closely tied UPPs. Fifteen and half per cent teachers admitted the prevalence of absenteeism as an UPP. Shah (1970) in his study of secondary school teachers found that everybody rejected the authoritarian role of a school teacher. Except commercial venality which was the leading UPP among private school teachers, public school teachers were leaders in all other five UPPs. Dutt (1970) in her work, while comparing school teachers with other white-collar professionals, found school teachers lacking in code of professional ethics. In this study the absenteeism among the school teachers was 15.5 per cent but in World Bank report authored by Chand and Mishra (2004) it was found to be 36.0 per cent on one day. In UNESCO's International Institute of Educational Planning study (2007), the school teacher absenteeism was found to be 25.0 per cent, second highest in the world. Commercial venality or private tutoring, which was second highly prevailing (17.7 per cent) UPP among school teachers in this study, was termed by UNESCO as unethical practice that does not complement learning rather leads to corruption. Sen (2008) in his observation blamed school teacher absenteeism, delayed arrival of teachers in schools and private tutoring, as the key factors for the poor condition of Indian public school system.

Tapodhan in his study (1991) found that private school teachers of secondary schools had more favourable professional attitudes towards their work as compared to their public school counterparts. But in Chauhan's work (1995) type of school had no bearing on professional responsibility of high school teachers of Haryana. However, he found that in terms of attitude towards teaching, public school teachers were lagging behind, than their private school counterparts.

Table 3.1: Prevalence of Unprofessional Practices among Public and Private School Teachers

Unprofessional Practice	Public		Private		Total	
	No.	Percentage	No.	Percentage	No.	Percentage
Discrimination	57	52.3	52	47.7	109	19.2 (100.0)
Commercial Venality	39	39.0	61	61.0	100	17.7 (100.0)
Lack of Responsibility	52	54.2	44	45.8	96	16.9 (100.0)
Dereliction of Duty	62	65.3	33	34.7	95	16.8 (100.0)
Absenteeism	57	64.8	31	35.2	88	15.5 (100.0)
Authoritarianism	47	59.5	32	40.5	79	13.9 (100.0)
Total	314	-	253	-	567	100

* Totals vary due to multiple responses

To see the relative prevalence of six identified UPP among school teachers a five point scale was also used. On the scale magnitude of the response was taken as '5' for Strongly Agree, '4' for Fairly Agree, '3' for Agree, '2' Disagree and '1' for Strongly Disagree for six identified UPP among school teachers. Then mean values of all responses were calculated for each UPP. Responses obtained about the relative prevalence of various UPPs among public and private school teachers and their mean values are enlisted in Table 3.2. Except commercial venality which was the leading UPP among private school teachers, public school teachers were quite ahead in remaining UPPs. Noticeable differences in the mean values for absenteeism and dereliction of duty reveal that these UPPs were more prevalent in magnitude among public school teachers. In lack of responsibility

Table 3.2: Relative Prevalence of Unprofessional Practices Among Public and Private School Teachers on a Five Point Scale

Unprofessional Practice	Public (Mean Value)	Private (Mean Value)	Total (Mean Value)
Authoritarianism	2.16	2.08	2.12
Lack of Responsibility	2.15	1.99	2.07
Absenteeism	2.19	1.87	2.03
Dereliction of Duty	2.11	1.88	2.00
Commercial Venality	1.61	1.71	1.66
Discrimination	1.72	1.58	1.65

and discrimination against students, private school teachers were leading but in authoritarian outlook they were closely tied with their public school colleagues.

Table 3.3 shows that male teachers were ahead than their female counterparts in absenteeism and dereliction of duty whereas female teachers were leaders in authoritarianism and discrimination against students, commercial venality and lack of responsibility. In Wadhawan's work (1980) on school teachers of Delhi, male teachers were found to be more professional than female teachers. In terms of other variables studied, school teachers were generally found to be less professional. But in the study of Tapodhan (1991) in the state of Gujarat, female school teachers had more favourable professional attitudes than male teachers. In the study of Chauhan (1995) in the state of Haryana, gender did not have any bearing on professional responsibility and teaching attitude of school teachers.

Table 3.3: Prevalence of Unprofessional Practices Among Male and Female Teachers

Unprofessional Practice	Male		Female		Total	
	No.	Percentage	No.	Percentage	No.	Percentage
Discrimination	38	34.9	71	65.1	109	19.2 (100.0)
Commercial Venality	45	45.0	55	55.0	100	17.7 (100.0)
Lack of Responsibility	45	46.9	51	53.1	96	16.9 (100.0)
Dereliction of Duty	49	51.6	46	48.4	95	16.8 (100.0)
Absenteeism	48	54.5	40	45.5	88	15.5 (100.0)
Authoritarianism	30	38.0	49	62.0	79	13.9 (100.0)
Total	255	-	312	-	567	100

* Totals vary due to multiple responses

Responses obtained on a five point scale for the relative prevalence of UPPs among male and female teachers are grouped in Table 3.4. In absenteeism, dereliction of duty, authoritarianism and lack of responsibility, male teachers were on the higher side than their female colleagues. Meagre difference was found in the mean values in commercial venality but in discrimination against students, female teachers were on the higher side than their male counterparts.

Table 3.4: Relative Prevalence of Unprofessional Practices Among Male and Female Teachers on a Five Point Scale

Unprofessional Practice	Male (Mean Value)	Female (Mean Value)	Total (Mean Value)
Authoritarianism	2.19	2.05	2.12
Lack of Responsibility	2.18	1.96	2.07
Absenteeism	2.21	1.85	2.03
Dereliction of Duty	2.12	1.88	2.00
Commercial Venality	1.69	1.63	1.66
Discrimination	1.60	1.70	1.65

Rural and urban variations among the teachers regarding various UPPs are enlisted in Table 3.5. In absenteeism, discrimination against students, and commercial venality, rural teachers were ahead of their urban counterparts. Negligible difference was found in the percentage of teachers in terms of lack of responsibility and authoritarian outlook. In the study of Gupta and Rani (1988) on the school teachers of Samana town in Punjab, it was found that urban teachers were more committed towards their profession as compared to their rural counterparts. The male teachers from rural and urban areas were more committed than female teachers. Among the females, urban teachers were more committed. Similar observations were noticed in the study of Tapodhan (1991) of 480 Gujarati speaking secondary school teachers, that urban school teachers had more favourable professional attitudes than rural teachers.

Table 3.5: Prevalence of Unprofessional Practices Among Rural and Urban School Teachers

Unprofessional Practice	Rural		Urban		Total	
	No.	Percentage	No.	Percentage	No.	Percentage
Discrimination	57	52.3	52	47.7	109	19.2 (100.0)
Commercial Venality	58	58.0	42	42.0	100	17.7 (100.0)
Lack of Responsibility	48	50.0	48	50.0	96	16.9 (100.0)
Dereliction of Duty	41	43.2	54	56.8	95	16.8 (100.0)
Absenteeism	47	53.4	41	46.6	88	15.5 (100.0)
Authoritarianism	40	50.6	39	49.4	79	13.9 (100.0)
Total	291	-	276	-	567	100.0

* Totals vary due to multiple responses

Variations in the place of their posting in terms of mean values on the five point scale are classified in Table 3.6. Unprofessional practices like absenteeism, lack of responsibility, and commercial venality were more prevalent among rural teachers. Small differences were found in mean values in rural and urban teachers in terms of discrimination against students. In authoritarian outlook and dereliction of duty, rural teachers were leaders though the differences in the mean values were small.

Table 3.6: Relative Prevalence of Unprofessional Practices Among Rural and Urban School Teachers on a Five Point Scale

Unprofessional Practice	Rural (Mean Value)	Urban (Mean Value)	Total (Mean Value)
Authoritarianism	2.17	2.07	2.12
Lack of Responsibility	2.17	1.97	2.07
Absenteeism	2.11	1.95	2.03
Dereliction of Duty	2.04	1.96	2.00
Commercial Venality	1.74	1.58	1.66
Discrimination	1.67	1.63	1.65

3.6 Conclusions

The six unprofessional practices identified and defined among the teachers were analysed against the type of the institution, gender, and location of the institution. Before drawing conclusions based on the responses, magnitude of each UPP was analysed. It was found that discrimination against the students, commercial venality, and lack of responsibility were leading UPPs among the teachers. Dereliction of duty, absenteeism, and authoritarianism were next less prevalent UPPs among the teachers.

Absenteeism, dereliction of duty, discrimination against students and authoritarianism were the leading UPPs among the public school teachers. Commercial venality was the most reported UPP among private school teachers. Shah (1970) in his study of secondary school teachers also found that authoritarian role of a school teacher was no more acceptable. Dutt (1970) in her comparative study found that school teachers did not adhere to professional code of ethics. Chand and Mishra (2004) in their World Bank report found that the problem of teacher absenteeism in public schools was more than double than that of, in this study. In UNESCO's study (2007) the problem of teacher absenteeism in Indian schools was 25.0 per cent, second highest in the World. Sen (2008) in his observation termed absenteeism, delayed arrival of teachers in schools and private tutoring as the key factors that were taking a toll of Indian public school system. Similar findings were noticed in the study of Tapodhan (1991), that teachers of private secondary schools had more favourable professional attitudes towards their work as compared to their public school counterparts. Chauhan (1995) in his work though found that type of school had no bearing on the professional responsibility of high school teachers of Haryana but in terms of attitude towards teaching, public school teachers were lagging behind their private school counterparts.

Absenteeism and dereliction of duty were the leading UPPs among male teachers whereas discrimination against students, authoritarianism, commercial venality and lack of responsibility were the most prevailed UPPs among female teachers. Similar observations were noticed in the work of Wadhawan (1980) on school teachers of Delhi. Though male teachers were more professional than female teachers but on the whole school teachers were found to less professional. On the contrary Tapodhan (1991) in his study of Gujarati speaking school teachers found that female teachers were having more favourable professional attitudes towards work as compared to male teachers. Chauhan (1995) found that gender did not have any bearing on professional responsibility and teaching attitude among school teachers of Haryana.

Rural teachers were far ahead in absenteeism, discrimination, and commercial venality. On the other hand, urban teachers were leaders in dereliction of duty. Both rural and urban teachers were closely tied in lack of responsibility and authoritarianism. Gupta and Rani (1988) in their study of school teachers of Samana in Punjab, found male teachers from rural and urban areas were more committed than female teachers. Among the females, urban teachers were more committed. But on the whole, urban teachers were more committed towards their profession as compared to their rural counterparts. Tapodhan (1991) in his study of 480 Gujarati speaking secondary school teachers also found that urban school teachers had more favourable professional attitudes than rural teachers.

4

Correlates of Unprofessional Practices

4.1 Introduction

In the previous chapter an attempt was made to see the variance in various unprofessional practices (UPPs) among the teachers in terms of type of the institution, gender and location of the institution. This chapter is an endeavour to see the relationship between various UPPs and socio-economic factors like age, marital status, religion, caste, designation, place of nurturing, education of the father, occupation of the father, income of the family while joining teaching profession, age at which first thought of becoming a school teacher came in mind, career decision makers, and length of service among the teachers.

4.2 Age and Unprofessional Practices

A relationship between age and various UPPs among the teachers is shown in Table 4.1. The table portrays that teachers were heavily concentrated in the age group of 21 - 30 years with respect to all UPPs. Four seventh of the teachers were indulging in private tutoring to make easy money, discrimination against students (46.8 per cent) and absenteeism (45.5 per cent) were some other highly responded UPPs among this group of young teachers. Dereliction of duty was next less prevailed (34.7 per cent) UPP, lack of responsibility (42.7 per cent) and authoritarianism (43.0 per cent) were next closely tied UPPs among the youngest group of teachers. High responses for various UPPs were also noticed in other higher age groups but approximated just to the half as compared to the youngest age group of teachers. Negligible variance was noticed from the table regarding relative prevalence of various UPPs except commercial venality in higher age group of teachers. Commercial venality was most prevalent

UPP among the youngest group of teachers out of lust for making money. Private school teachers represented the youngest group of teachers indulging in private tutoring due to marginal salaries. A reciprocal relationship was noticed in the age of teachers and prevalence of various UPPs. With the increase in the age of the teachers there was a decrease in the prevalence of various UPPs. It can be concluded that younger teachers were more involved in various UPPs as compared to older one, hence less professional as school teachers.

A similar trend was noticed in the study conducted by Gupta and Rani (1988) in a small town of Samana in Punjab, that the higher the age more was the commitment towards profession. But in the study of Tapodhan (1991) based on 480 Gujarati speaking secondary school teachers of Gujarat, it was found that age had no bearing on the professional attitude of teachers.

4.3 Marital Status and Unprofessional Practices

Prevalence of various UPPs among the teachers according to their marital status is presented in Table 4.2. Two third of the teachers that made to the sample were married. Various UPPs were highly distributed towards married teachers. In the married group, dereliction of duty (74.7 per cent), lack of responsibility (68.8 per cent) and discrimination against students (68.8 per cent) were some widely prevalent UPPs. Authoritarianism (65.8 per cent) and absenteeism (63.6 per cent) were next less prevalent UPPs and indulgence in private tutoring (57.0 per cent) was least prevalent UPP. Reverse was the trend among unmarried teachers who had inclination towards private tutoring. Unmarried teachers were generally private school teachers and young computer teachers of public schools. Desire for lavish living and limited salaries forced them in indulging in private tutoring instead of teaching during school hours. Most off them have established private academies which guarantee passing the board examinations in lieu of money. They were not dependent on their jobs in the schools rather they were working there for the advertisement of their academies to get students from the schools. On the other hand, majority of the married teachers were public school teachers having UPPs among them that were the result of poor management of the schools. Similar observations were noticed in Table 3.1 of chapter 3, that dereliction of duty, absenteeism and authoritarianism were the leading UPPs

Table 4.1: Distribution of Respondents According to Age and UPPs

Age in Years	UPP											
	Absenteeism		Dereliction of Duty		Lack of Responsibility		Discrimination		Authoritarianism		Commercial Venality	
	No.	%age	No.	%age	No.	%age	No.	%age	No.	%age	No.	%age
21-30	40	45.5	33	34.7	41	42.7	51	46.8	34	43.0	57	57.0
31-40	21	23.9	25	26.3	24	25.0	28	25.7	20	25.3	17	17.0
41-50	19	21.6	23	24.2	20	20.8	25	22.9	18	22.8	17	17.0
51-60	8	9.1	14	14.7	11	11.5	5	4.6	7	8.9	9	9.0
Total	88	100.0	95	100.0	96	100.0	109	100.0	79	100.0	100	100.0

Table 4.2: Distribution of Respondents According to Marital Status and UPPs

Marital Status	UPP											
	Absenteeism		Dereliction of Duty		Lack of Responsibility		Discrimination		Authoritarianism		Commercial Venality	
	No.	%age	No.	%age	No.	%age	No.	%age	No.	%age	No.	%age
Married	56	63.6	71	74.7	66	68.8	73	67.0	52	65.8	57	57.0
Unmarried	30	34.1	23	24.2	28	29.2	34	31.2	27	34.2	40	40.0
Widowed	1	1.1	1	1.1	1	1.0	1	0.9	0	0.0	1	1.0
Separated/ Divorced	1	1.1	0	0.0	1	1.0	1	0.9	0	0.0	2	2.0
Total	88	100.0	95	100.0	96	100.0	109	100.0	79	100.0	100	100.0

among public school teachers caused by poor monitoring system. But in the study of Tapodhan (1991) marital status had no effect on the professional attitude of Gujarati speaking secondary school teachers.

4.4 Religion and Unprofessional Practices

The sample was almost equally represented by the teachers belonging to both Hindu and Sikh religions. Table 4.3 throws light in variations in UPPs according to religion. Authoritarian attitude towards the students was the most prevalent (54.4 per cent) and private tutoring was the least prevalent (44.0 per cent), UPP among Hindu teachers. Little variations were noticed among Hindu teachers in terms of other UPPs. Indulgence in private tutoring was the most responded to (56.0 per cent) followed by discrimination against students (53.2 per cent) and authoritarian outlook (44.3 per cent) was the least prevalent UPP among Sikh teachers. On the average variations in other UPPs were not visible among Sikh teachers. The only Jain respondent in the sample opted for dereliction of duty and other lone respondent who did not want to disclose his/her religion responded to absenteeism and authoritarianism. It can be concluded that Hindu teachers were less responsible towards their duties and less sincere towards their students and believed in authoritarian nature of a school teacher. Sikh teachers were found to be discriminating against the students and believed in private tutoring.

4.5 Caste and Unprofessional Practices

Variations in various UPPs according to three major Caste groupings in the sample are shown in Table 4.5. Among the General Caste teachers, absenteeism was most prevalent (85.2 per cent) and private tutoring (75.0 per cent) was the least prevalent UPP. Lack of responsibility (81.3 per cent) and dereliction of duty (81.1 per cent) were next closely tied UPP among teachers belonging to General Castes. Authoritarianism (79.7 per cent) and discrimination against the students (78.9 per cent) were some other less prevalent UPPs among General Caste teachers. A reverse trend was noticed among Scheduled Caste teachers. Indulgence in private tutoring (17.0 per cent) followed by authoritarian outlook (15.2 per cent), were the most prevalent and absenteeism (9.1 per cent) was the least prevalent UPP among the teachers belonging to Scheduled Castes.

Table 4.3: Distribution of Respondents According to Religion and UPPs

Religion	UPP											
	Absenteeism		Dereliction of Duty		Lack of Responsibility		Discrimination		Authoritarianism		Commercial Venality	
	No.	%age	No.	%age	No.	%age	No.	%age	No.	%age	No.	%age
Hindu	44	50.0	48	50.5	49	51.0	51	46.8	43	54.4	44	44.0
Sikh	43	48.9	46	48.4	47	49.0	58	53.2	35	44.3	56	56.0
Others	1	1.1	1	1.1	-	-	-	-	1	1.3	-	-
Total	88	98.9	95	100.0	96	100.0	109	100.0	79	100.0	100	100.0

Table 4.4: Distribution of Respondents According to Caste and UPPs

Caste	UPP											
	Absenteeism		Dereliction of Duty		Lack of Responsibility		Discrimination		Authoritarianism		Commercial Venality	
	No.	%age	No.	%age	No.	%age	No.	%age	No.	%age	No.	%age
General	75	85.2	77	81.1	78	81.3	86	78.9	63	79.7	75	75.0
SC	8	9.1	13	13.7	12	12.5	14	12.8	12	15.2	17	17.0
OBC	5	5.7	5	5.3	6	6.3	9	8.3	4	5.1	8	8.0
Total	88	100.0	95	100.0	96	100.0	109	100.0	79	100.0	100	100.0

Discrimination against students (8.3 per cent) followed by private tutoring (8.0 per cent), were the most prevalent and authoritarian outlook was the least prevalent (5.1 per cent), UPP among the teachers belonging to Other Backward Castes. Absenteeism, dereliction of duty, and lack of responsibility were prominent UPPs among the teachers belonging to General Castes whereas commercial venality, authoritarianism, discrimination against students were leading UPPs among the teachers belonging to Scheduled Castes and Other Backward Castes. On the whole UPPs were more prevalent among teachers belonging to General Castes and least among the Other Backward Castes. An analogous observation was noticed in the study of Tapodhan (1991) that Gujarati school teachers belonging to Other Backward Castes were had more favourable professional attitudes as compared to teachers belonging to other castes.

4.6 Designation and Unprofessional Practices

School teachers are generally divided into three categories according to educational qualifications and classes to be taught. The basic qualification for a teacher designate is High/Higher Secondary/ Senior Secondary and one year Diploma in respective discipline. The teacher designate is supposed to teach Middle school classes. Master/ Mistress designates are Graduates in respective discipline with Bachelor of Education and teach High school classes. Lecturers are Post Graduates with Bachelor of Education and teach Senior Secondary classes.

A relationship between classes being taught by the teachers according to their designation and prevalence of various UPPs are shown in Table 4.5. Absenteeism (51.1 per cent), lack of responsibility (51.0 per cent) and discrimination against the students (50.5 per cent) were some prominent UPPs among the teachers whose designation was Teacher (Art and Craft/ Physical Education/ Language/ Computer). Dereliction of duty (48.4 per cent) and commercial venality (48.0 per cent) were less prevalent and authoritarianism (46.8 per cent) was the least prevalent UPP among the teachers that had their designation as Teacher. Authoritarian attitude towards the students (35.4 per cent), discrimination against the students (33.9 per cent) and dereliction of duty were some prominent UPP prevalent among the teachers whose designation was Master or Mistress. Lack of responsibility (31.3 per cent) and absenteeism (27.3 per cent) were other less prevalent and commercial venality was least prevalent (24.0 per cent) UPP among Masters or Mistresses. Commercial venality (28.0 per cent), absenteeism (21.6 per cent) and dereliction of duty (17.9 per cent) were some leading UPPs among Lecturers. Lack of responsibility (17.7 per cent) and authoritarianism (17.7) were equally prevalent and discrimination against the students (15.6 per cent) was least prevalent UPP among the Lecturer designates. It is clear from the table that various UPPs were most prevalent among teachers followed by Maters or Mistresses and least prevalent among the Lecturers. It can be concluded that direct correlation is found between the designation and professionalisation of school teachers. Higher educational level and the higher classes being taught could be the probable reasons for high professionalisation of school teachers.

4.7 Schooling in Childhood and Unprofessional Practices

To see the relationship between place of childhood nurturing and various UPPs, the responses of the teachers are presented in Table 4.6. Those who were brought up in the urban environment, commercial venality (80.0 per cent), lack of responsibility (76.0 per cent) and absenteeism (75.0 per cent) were some leading UPPs. Dereliction of duty (74.7 per cent) and discrimination against students (74.3 per cent) were some other less prevalent and authoritarian attitude (72.2 per cent) was least prevalent UPP among the teachers who were brought up in urban environment. Authoritarianism (27.8 per cent), discrimination against the students (25.7 per cent) and dereliction of duty (25.3 per cent) were some prominent UPPs prevalent among the teachers who were brought up in rural environment. Absenteeism (25.0 per cent) and lack of responsibility (24.0 per cent) were less prevalent and commercial venality (20.0 per cent) was the least prevalent UPP among the teachers who had their upbringing in the rural environment. It is clear from the table that place of origin and nurturing has an impact in the prevalence of UPPs among the teachers. It was found that the prevalence of various UPPs were almost three times more among those who were brought up in the urban environment as compared to those nourished in the rural settings. That meant urban nourishing restricted them in inculcating the basic values of human living and desired professional values.

Table 4.5: Distribution of Respondents According to the Designation and UPPs

Designation	UPP											
	Absenteeism		Dereliction of Duty		Lack of Responsibility		Discrimination		Authoritarianism		Commercial Venality	
	No.	%age	No.	%age	No.	%age	No.	%age	No.	%age	No.	%age
Teacher	45	51.1	46	48.4	49	51.0	55	50.5	37	46.8	48	48.0
Master/Mistress	24	27.3	32	33.7	30	31.3	37	33.9	28	35.4	24	24.0
Lecturer	19	21.6	17	17.9	17	17.7	17	15.6	14	17.7	28	28.0
Total	88	100.0	95	100.0	96	100.0	109	100.0	79	100.0	100	100.0

Table 4.6: Distribution of Respondents According to Childhood Schooling and UPPs

Childhood Schooling	UPP											
	Absenteeism		Dereliction of Duty		Lack of Responsibility		Discrimination		Authoritarianism		Commercial Venality	
	No.	%age	No.	%age	No.	%age	No.	%age	No.	%age	No.	%age
Urban Area	66	75.0	71	74.7	73	76.0	81	74.3	57	72.2	80	80.0
Rural Area	22	25.0	24	25.3	23	24.0	28	25.7	20	27.8	20	20.0
Total	88	100.0	95	100.0	96	100.0	109	100.0	79	100.0	100	100.0

4.8 Educational Level of the Father and Unprofessional Practices

The correlation between the education level of the father and various UPPs is presented in the Table 4.7. Indulgence in private tutoring (50.0 per cent), discrimination against the students (47.7 per cent), and dereliction of the duty (46.3 per cent), were some leading UPPs among the teachers whose father had education up to Senior Secondary. Lack of responsibility (41.6 per cent), absenteeism (40.9 per cent) and authoritarian attitude (39.3 per cent) were some other less prevalent UPPs among this group of teachers. Authoritarianism (31.6 per cent), absenteeism (28.4 per cent) and discrimination against the students (26.6 per cent) were some prominent UPPs among the teachers who had Graduate fathers. Those teachers who had Post Graduate fathers, authoritarianism (19.0 per cent) followed by absenteeism (17.0 per cent) were some leading UPPs. The 'Others', category in the table included the respondents who had illiterate fathers. Lack of responsibility (21.9 per cent) followed by dereliction of duty (16.8 per cent) were some leading UPPs among teachers who had illiterate fathers. It is clear from the table that there was a reciprocal relationship between education level of the father and prevalence of various UPPs. With the increase in the educational level of the father there was a decrease in the prevalence of various UPPs among the teachers.

4.9 Occupation of the Father and Unprofessional Practices

Relationship between the occupation of the father and prevalence of various UPPs is shown in Table 4.8. Commercial venality (50.0 per cent), absenteeism (48.9 per cent) and dereliction of duty (47.4 per cent) were some leading UPPs among the teachers coming from the background of some type of government service. Close to half of the teachers were from this group of respondents. Commercial venality (33.0 per cent), dereliction of duty (32.6 per cent) and authoritarianism (30.4 per cent) were some prominent UPPs among the teachers hailing from farming/business/industry background. On the average, a close to one third of the respondents was from this group of teachers. Those who were from teaching background discrimination against the students (14.7 per cent), lack of responsibility (12.5 per cent), absenteeism (11.4 per cent) and authoritarianism (11.4 per cent) were the prominent UPPs. A meager number of teachers came from the families doing some petty jobs and had idle fathers. This means government service background had a direct correlation with un-professionalism among the school teachers. A similar trend but in less degree was noticed among the teachers coming from farming/ business/industry background. The teachers coming from teaching and non-teaching occupational background were more professional.

4.10 Income of the Family While Joining Teaching Profession and Unprofessional Practices

A relationship between the income of the family, while joining teaching profession and prevalence of various UPPs is given in Table 4.9. Authoritarianism (60.8 percent), lack of responsibility (53.1 per cent) and commercial venality (53.0 per cent) were some leading UPPs among the teachers who had family income below Rs. 10,000 per month while joining teaching profession. Discrimination against the students (32.1 per cent), commercial venality (31.0 per cent) and dereliction of duty (29.5 per cent) were some prominent UPPs among the teachers having family income between Rs. 10,000 and Rs. 20,000 per month at the time of joining teaching profession. The table establishes a relationship between the lower income of the family at the time of joining teaching profession and higher prevalence of various UPPs among the teachers. On the average more than half of the teachers came from lower income families.

4.11 Present Income of the Family and Unprofessional Practices

Relationship between the present income of the family and the prevalence of various UPPs is presented in Table 4.10. Commercial venality (41.0 per cent), discrimination against the students (33.0 per cent) and authoritarianism (32.9 per cent) were some prominent UPPs among the teachers with family income below Rs. 20,000 per month. Authoritarianism (36.7 per cent), lack of responsibility (34.4 per cent) and absenteeism (33.0 per cent) were leading UPPs among the teachers having family income between Rs. 20,000 to Rs. 30,000 per month. Absenteeism (37.5 per cent), lack of responsibility (37.5 per cent) and dereliction of duty (36.9 per cent) were the most prevalent UPPs among the teachers with family income more than Rs. 30,000 per month. The table shows that commercial venality was associated with lower income of the family whereas absenteeism, lack of responsibility and dereliction of duty were associated with higher income of the family.

Table 4.7: Distribution of Respondents According to Education Level of the Father and UPPs

Education of the Father	UPP											
	Absenteeism		Dereliction of Duty		Lack of Responsibility		Discrimination		Authoritarianism		Commercial Venality	
	No.	%age	No.	%age	No.	%age	No.	%age	No.	%age	No.	%age
High/Higher or Senior Secondary	36	40.9	44	46.3	40	41.6	52	47.7	31	39.3	50	50.0
Graduation	25	28.4	21	22.1	22	22.9	29	26.6	25	31.6	26	26.0
Post Graduation	15	17.0	14	14.7	13	13.5	11	10.1	15	19.0	15	15.0
Others	12	13.6	16	16.8	21	21.9	17	15.6	8	10.1	9	9.0
Total	88	100.0	95	100.0	96	100.0	109	100.0	79	100.0	100	100.0

Table 4.8: Distribution of Respondents According to Occupation of the Father and UPPs

Occupation of Father	UPP											
	Absenteeism		Dereliction of Duty		Lack of Responsibility		Discrimination		Authoritarianism		Commercial Venality	
	No.	%age	No.	%age	No.	%age	No.	%age	No.	%age	No.	%age
Govt. Service (Civil/Military)	43	48.9	45	47.4	45	46.9	47	43.1	35	44.3	50	50.0
Farming/ Business/ Industry	26	29.5	31	32.6	29	30.2	32	29.4	24	30.4	33	33.0
Profession (Teaching)	10	11.4	9	9.5	12	12.5	16	14.7	9	11.4	8	8.0
Profession (Non-Teaching)	3	3.4	1	1.1	3	3.1	5	4.6	5	6.3	4	4.0
Others	2	2.3	3	3.2	2	2.1	4	3.7	3	3.8	1	1.0
No Response	4	4.5	6	6.3	5	5.2	5	4.6	3	3.8	4	4.0
Total	88	100.0	95	100.0	96	100.0	109	100.0	79	100.0	100	100.0

Table 4.9: Distribution of Respondents According to the Income of the Family While Joining Teaching Profession and UPPs

Income of the Family	UPP											
	Absenteeism		Dereliction of Duty		Lack of Responsibility		Discrimination		Authoritarianism		Commercial Venality	
	No.	%age	No.	%age	No.	%age	No.	%age	No.	%age	No.	%age
Below 10,000	44	50.0	49	51.6	51	53.1	50	45.9	48	60.8	53	53.0
10,000 to 20,000	25	28.4	28	29.5	27	28.1	35	32.1	22	27.8	31	31.0
20,000 to 30,000	12	13.6	13	13.7	12	12.5	16	14.7	6	7.6	12	12.0
30,000 to 40,000	5	5.7	4	4.2	4	4.2	4	3.7	2	2.5	2	2.0
Above 40,000	2	2.3	1	1.1	2	2.1	4	3.7	1	1.3	2	2.0
Total	88	100.0	95	100.0	96	100.0	109	100.0	79	100.0	100	100.0

Table 4.10: Distribution of Respondents According to Present Income of the Family and UPPs

Income of the Family	UPP											
	Absenteeism		Dereliction of Duty		Lack of Responsibility		Discrimination		Authoritarianism		Commercial Venality	
	No.	%age	No.	%age	No.	%age	No.	%age	No.	%age	No.	%age
Below 20,000	26	29.5	30	31.6	27	28.1	36	33.0	26	32.9	41	41.0
20,000 to 30,000	29	33.0	30	31.6	33	34.4	34	31.2	29	36.7	25	25.0
30,000 to 40,000	17	19.3	13	13.7	15	15.6	23	21.1	9	11.4	16	16.0
Above 40,000	16	18.2	22	23.2	21	21.9	16	14.7	15	19.0	18	18.0
Total	88	100.0	95	100.0	96	100.0	109	100.0	79	100.0	100	100.0

In the study of Wadhawan (1980) on school teachers of Delhi, it was found that low socio-economic background was associated with poor professional commitment. Ramana (1986) in her study of women school teachers also found their role performance was associated with socio-economic background. In the study of Saroha (1995) of school teachers of Faridabad district in Haryana, an association was found between socio-economic status, self-concept and social adjustment in terms of male and female as well as achieved and ascribed. Kapoor in his study (2000) found the effect of socio-economic background towards the acquisition of environmental education and attitude towards environment awareness among school teachers of Arunachal Pradesh.

4.12 Aim in Life and Unprofessional Practices

Social psychologists are of the view that fulfillment of one's aim in life to enter a profession is related to the adjustment in the profession. The relationship between aim in life and prevalence of various UPPs is shown in Table 4.11. Commercial venality (65.0 per cent), dereliction of duty (56.8 per cent) and lack of responsibility (56.3 per cent) were some noted UPPs among the teachers who disclosed their aim of life to become a teacher. Authoritarianism (25.3 per cent), dereliction of duty (24.2 per cent) and discrimination against students (22.9 per cent) were notable UPPs among the teachers who wanted to become an engineer, doctor or lawyer. Absenteeism (10.2 per cent) was most prevalent and dereliction of duty (3.2 per cent) was least prevalent UPP among the teachers who had their aim in life to join some civil or defence service. Dereliction of duty (9.5 per cent), discrimination against students (8.3 per cent) and absenteeism (8.0 per cent) were notable UPPs among the teachers who were aimless or could not recall their aim in life.

The table reveals that first getting the label of a teacher and later making good money by indulging in private tutoring attracted the youngsters to become school teachers. Making easy money without taking pains for the duties and responsibilities attracted many youngsters to the profession. Persons having higher aspirations in life have lower level of UPPs as compared to those who aspired to become teachers very early in their life. Ramana also found in her study (1986) that professional aspirations are associated with role performance of school teachers. Raju (1992) in his study of senior secondary school teachers of Delhi, found that professional choice satisfaction more or less contribute towards professional commitment.

4.13 Age at Which the First Thought of Becoming a School Teacher Came in Mind and Unprofessional Practices

The responses obtained for the relationship between the first thought of becoming a school teacher came in mind and the prevalence of various UPPs is presented in Table 4.12. Authoritarianism (21.5 per cent), commercial venality (18.0 per cent) and discrimination against the students (16.5 per cent) were some prominent UPPs among the teachers who thought to become school teachers at the fantasy and tentative stage. Absenteeism, lack of responsibility and dereliction of duty were some other less prevalent UPPs among this group of teachers. Dereliction of duty (87.4 per cent), lack of responsibility (86.5 per cent) and absenteeism (85.2 per cent) were some leading UPPs among the teachers who thought of becoming school teachers at realistic stage when individual makes compromise between wants and actual opportunity exists for him. Discrimination against students, commercial venality and authoritarianism were other less prevalent UPPs among this group of teachers. The prominent UPPs among this group of teachers were the result of poor monitoring system and lack of commitment towards the profession.

4.14 Career Decision Makers and Unprofessional Practices

A relationship between career decision makers and the prevalence of various UPPs is given in Table 4.13. Table shows that commercial venality (41.0 per cent), authoritarianism (40.5 per cent) and discrimination against students (40.4 per cent) were some widely prevalent UPPs among the teachers who took decision for themselves to become school teachers. Among the teachers whose fathers took the decision for them, commercial venality (25.0 per cent), lack of responsibility (24.0 per cent) and dereliction of duty (22.7 per cent) were leading UPPs. Authoritarianism (19.0 per cent), discrimination against the students (18.3 per cent) and dereliction of duty (17.9 per cent) were widely prevailed UPPs for whom their mother decided that they should join teaching profession. For those, inspired by their teacher to join teaching profession, discrimination against students (8.3 per cent), absenteeism (8.0 per cent) and commercial venality (7.0 per cent) were highly prevalent UPP.

4.15 Length of Service and Unprofessional Practices

Relationship between length of service and prevalence of various UPPs among the teachers is given in Table 4.14. The table shows that commercial venality (41.0 per cent), authoritarianism (40.5 per cent) and discrimination against students (40.4 per cent) were some prominent UPPs among the youngsters who had less than 5 years of service. Among the teachers with the length of service between 5 to 10 years, lack of responsibility (22.9 per cent), dereliction of duty (22.1 per cent) and authoritarian attitude (21.5 per cent) were widely prevalent UPPs. Commercial venality (14.0 per cent), dereliction of duty (13.7 per cent) and discrimination against the students (12.8 per cent) were leading UPPs among the teachers with the length of service between 10 to 15 years. Among the teachers with service of more than 25 years, absenteeism (14.8 per cent), discrimination against the students (13.8 per cent) and lack of responsibility (13.5 per cent) were highly prevalent UPPs. The table reveals the UPPs that are related with personal value system like commercial venality, authoritarianism, discrimination etc. were more prevalent among the young teachers whereas UPP which are related to professional value system like absenteeism, dereliction of duty, lack of responsibility etc. were more prominent among the experienced teachers.

Table 4.11:Distribution of Respondents According to the Aim in Life and UPPs

Aim in Life	UPP											
	Absenteeism		Dereliction of Duty		Lack of Responsibility		Discrimination		Authoritarianism		Commercial Venality	
	No.	%age	No.	%age	No.	%age	No.	%age	No.	%age	No.	%age
School Teacher	47	53.4	54	56.8	54	56.3	55	50.5	44	55.7	65	65.0
Engineer/ Doctor/ lawyer	16	18.2	23	24.2	21	21.9	25	22.9	20	25.3	14	14.0
Civil /Defense Service	9	10.2	3	3.2	8	8.3	10	9.2	7	8.9	8	8.0
To Go Abroad	8	9.1	6	6.3	7	7.3	9	8.3	3	3.8	9	9.0
Businessman	1	1.1	0	0.0	0	0.0	1	0.9	0	0.0	0	0.0
Others	7	8.0	9	9.5	6	6.3	9	8.3	5	6.3	4	4.0
Total	88	100.0	95	100.0	96	100.0	109	100.0	79	100.0	100	100.0

Table 4.12: Distribution of Respondents According to the Age at which First Thought of Becoming a School Teacher Came in Mind and UPP

Age in Years	UPP											
	Absenteeism		Dereliction of Duty		Lack of Responsibility		Discrimination		Authoritarianism		Commercial Venality	
	No.	%age	No.	%age	No.	%age	No.	%age	No.	%age	No.	%age
Less than 16	13	14.8	12	12.6	13	13.5	18	16.5	17	21.5	18	18.0
16 - 22	50	56.8	62	65.3	59	61.5	66	60.6	47	59.5	59	59.0
22 - 28	21	23.9	19	20.0	20	20.8	23	21.1	12	15.2	20	20.0
28 Onwards	4	4.5	2	2.1	4	4.2	2	1.8	3	3.8	3	3.0
Total	88	100.0	95	100.0	96	100.0	109	100.0	79	100.0	100	100.0

Table 4.13: Distribution of Respondents According to the Career Decision Makers and UPP

Career Decision Makers	UPP											
	Absenteeism		Dereliction of Duty		Lack of Responsibility		Discrimination		Authoritarianism		Commercial Venality	
	No.	%age	No.	%age	No.	%age	No.	%age	No.	%age	No.	%age
Self	31	35.2	35	36.8	34	35.4	44	40.4	32	40.5	41	41.0
Father	20	22.7	22	23.2	23	24.0	20	18.3	17	21.5	25	25.0
Mother	12	13.6	17	17.9	15	15.6	20	18.3	15	19.0	11	11.0
Two or more	10	11.4	8	8.4	9	9.4	8	7.3	8	10.1	7	7.0
Teacher	7	8.0	2	2.1	5	5.2	9	8.3	2	2.5	7	7.0
Close Relatives	8	9.1	11	11.6	10	10.5	8	7.3	5	6.3	9	9.0
Total	88	100.0	95	100.0	96	100.0	109	100.0	79	100.0	100	100.0

Table 4.14: Distribution of Respondents According to the Length of Service and UPP

Length of Service in Years	Absenteeism		Dereliction of Duty		Lack of Responsibility		D iscrimination		Authoritarianism		Commercial Venality	
	No.	%age	No.	%age	No.	%age	No.	%age	No.	%age	No.	%age
5 and Less than 5	31	35.2	35	36.8	34	35.4	44	40.4	32	40.5	41	41.0
6 to 10	18	20.5	21	22.1	22	22.9	20	18.3	17	21.5	20	20.0
11 to 15	10	11.4	13	13.7	11	11.5	14	12.8	9	11.4	14	14.0
16 to 20	7	8.0	9	9.5	8	8.3	6	5.5	6	7.6	4	4.0
21 or more	22	25.0	17	17.9	21	21.8	25	23.0	15	19.0	21	21.0
Total	88	100.0	95	100.0	96	100.0	109	100.0	79	100.0	100	100.0

4.16 Conclusions

Commercial venality was most prevalent UPP among the youngest group of teachers out of lust for making money. Mostly private school teachers represented the youngest group of teachers indulging in private tutoring due to limited salaries. With the increase in the age of the teachers there was a decrease in the prevalence of various UPPs. Gupta and Rani (1988) also found in their study of school teachers of Samana town of Punjab that professional commitment increased with the increase in age of teachers. But Tapodhan (1991) in his study of Gujarati speaking school teachers found that age had no bearing on the professional attitude of teachers. Unmarried teachers were generally private school teachers and young computer teachers teaching in public schools had inclination towards private tutoring. Desire for lavish living and limited salaries forced them to indulge in private tutoring instead of teaching during school hours. Most of them had established private academies that guaranteed passing the board examinations in lieu of money. They were not dependent on their jobs in the schools, rather they were working there for the promotion of their academies to get students from the schools. On the other hand, majority of the married teachers were public school teachers having those UPPs among them caused by the poor management of the schools. Tapodhan (1991) in his study of school teachers of Gujarat found that marital status had no effect on the professional attitude of teachers.

Absenteeism, dereliction of duty, and lack of responsibility were prominent UPPs among the teachers belonging to General Castes whereas commercial venality, authoritarianism, discrimination against students were leading UPPs among the teachers belonging to Scheduled Castes and Other Backward Castes. Tapodhan (1991) in his study found that Gujarati speaking school teachers belonging to Other Backward Castes had more favourable professional attitudes as compared to teachers who belonged to other castes. The investigated UPPs were most prevalent among teachers teaching Middle standard classes followed by Maters/Mistresses teaching High standard classes and least prevalent among the Lecturers teaching Senior Secondary classes.

The prevalence of various types of UPPs was on the average three times more among the teachers who were brought up in the urban environment than their rural counterparts. With the increase in the educational level of the father there was a decrease in the prevalence of various UPPs among the school teachers. There was a relationship between the lower income of the family at the time of joining teaching profession and higher prevalence of various UPPs among the teachers because on the average more than half of the respondents came from low income families. Commercial venality was associated with lower income of the family whereas absenteeism, lack of responsibility and dereliction of duty were associated with higher income of the family. Wadhawan (1980) in his study of school teachers of Delhi found that low socio-economic background was associated with poor professional commitment. Ramana (1986) in her study of women school teachers found an association between socio-economic background and their role performance. Saroha (1995) in her study of school teachers of Haryana found an association between achieved and ascribed socio-economic status and, self-concept and social adjustment, among male and female teachers. Kapoor (2000) in his study also found a correlation between socio-economic background and, acquisition of environment education and attitude toward environment awareness, among school teachers of Arunachal Pradesh.

Getting the status of a teacher by joining teaching profession and later making good money by indulging in private tutoring attracted the youngsters to become school teachers. Making easy money without taking pains for the duties and responsibilities attracted many youngsters to the profession. The teachers in the profession who had high aspirations in life had lower level of UPPs as compared to those who aspired to become school teachers. Ramana (1986) also found a correlation between professional aspirations and role performance of school teachers. Raju (1992) in his study of school teachers of Delhi found that professional choice satisfaction contributed towards professional commitment of teachers. Those UPPs which were related with basic value system like commercial venality, authoritarianism, discrimination were more prevalent among the young teachers where as UPPs which were related to professional value system like absenteeism, dereliction of duty, lack of responsibility were more prominent among the experienced teachers.

5

Reasons and Remedies for Unprofessional Practices

5.1 Introduction

Anticipating the poor response in admitting to the prevalence of various unprofessional practices among their fraternity by the school teacher respondents, an attempt was made by asking the teachers to state reasons and remedies for various UPPs, to judge the grimness of the problem as highlighted by other similar studies. Wadhawan (1980) in his study found that school teachers of Delhi were less professional and less satisfied with school teaching as their career. Raju (1992) in his extensive study of school teachers from Delhi advocated that the professional development among teachers is possible if right people join the profession. Chauhan (1995) concluded, in his work on school teachers of the state of Haryana, that lack of teaching attitude and poor organisational climate contribute towards making them irresponsible about their duties. Word Bank report authored by Chand and Mishra (2004) reveal that 36 per cent of primary school teachers are absent from school on one day in the state of Punjab. An IIM-A study (2006) blamed poor quality of teaching and supporting staff and ineffective monitoring system, for dismal condition of primary public schools in the state of Punjab. The UNESCO's International Institute of Educational Planning study (2007) on corruption in education identified 25.0 per cent absenteeism in India, the second highest in the world, private tutoring an unethical practice, and involvement of teachers in mismanagement of schools, as some grey areas in Indian educational system. Sen (2008) while talking about a just society in reality blamed the broken down inspection system of Indian public schools, teacher absenteeism, delayed arrival of teachers in schools and private tutoring, for widening the divide between privileged and unprivileged in the era of globalisation. Another study (2006) conducted by PRATHAM made dereliction of duty among primary schools teachers for poor outcome of public school students in backward border districts of state of Punjab.

After studying the prevalence of six identified unprofessional practices among the school teachers and analysing their correlates with other variables, an attempt was made to ascertain the reasons for various UPPs. In this chapter the reasons for various UPPs are classified according to the type of school, gender and place of posting. The possible corrective measures to each UPP are also presented after giving the reasons. The corrective measures are also outlined according to the type of school, gender and place of posting for each UPP.

5.2 Absenteeism

5.2.1 Reasons for Absenteeism

After admitting the prevalence of absenteeism among the school teachers, the respondents were asked to give the reasons for this practice. The reasons given by the teachers for absenteeism are presented in Table 5.1. The table shows that one sixth of the teachers gave adjustment with the principal and more than one seventh of them revealed the lack of monitoring as the leading reasons for absenteeism. Another thirteen per cent pointed out job security and 11.6 per cent of them gave engaged in non-teaching activities as some other reasons for teacher absenteeism. One ninth pointed out the distant posting and one eleventh gave doing side business to enhance earnings as some other reasons for teacher absenteeism. Abuse of high connections, bad school atmosphere and poor relations with colleagues were some more reasons revealed by the teachers though less in magnitude. The others category in the table was included to get the supplementary responses that were not part of the table to enhance findings of the study.

The responses of public school teachers on the average were three to four times more than their private school counterparts though the number in the sample was 195 and 190 respectively. This indicates that the public schools were the grim area for absenteeism. Both public and private school teachers - shared non-cordial teacher-teacher relationship - the reason for absenteeism.

To see the difference in opinion for absenteeism among male and female teachers, the responses are presented in Table 5.2. The table reveals that abuse of high connections (97.4 per cent), adjustment with the principal (88.6 per cent), non-cordial teacher-teacher relationship (71.4 per cent) and others are not attending (66.7 per cent), were some highly stated reasons by female teachers for absenteeism. Job security and non-conducive school atmosphere were other less responded reasons given by the same group of teachers for keeping teachers away from school. Engaged in non-teaching activities (56.0 per cent) and poor monitoring system (51.5 per cent) were a little more stipulated reasons given by male teachers. Doing side business and distant posting were two equally acknowledged reasons for absenteeism, by both male and female teachers. The table indicates that female teachers viewed the bureaucratic or political power and theory of populism as the main causes for keeping teachers away from teaching institutions. In the present context no institution escapes from direct political interference which erodes its working discipline. School environment also suffers from this practice. When school principals feel helpless in accommodating the erratic teachers, they are threatened to face the wrath of local politicians or bureaucrats. A majority of the teachers working in the private schools are kin and kith of the school management and principals have to approach its members-who are generally local politicians- through these teachers for major decisions. The principals of private schools have little autonomy to run the schools. Conflict in the teaching community and following the bad practices of colleagues were some other means for abstaining teachers from the schools. Most of the teachers always keep vigil on their colleagues for the favours they get from the principal and then they blackmail them for their quota/ share.

Table 5.1: Distribution of Respondents According to Reasons for Absenteeism and the Type of School

Reasons	Type of School				Total	
	Public		Private			
	No.	Percentage	No.	Percentage	No.	Percentage
Adjustment with principal	26	74.3	9	25.7	35	16.3 (100.0)
Lack of check on attendance	24	72.7	9	27.3	33	15.3 (100.0)
Job security	18	64.3	10	35.7	28	13.0 (100.0)
Engaged in non-teaching activities	17	68.0	8	32.0	25	11.6 (100.0)
Posted away from home	19	79.2	5	20.8	24	11.2 (100.0)
Doing side business	13	65.0	7	35.0	20	9.3 (100.0)
Abuse of high connections	15	83.3	3	16.7	18	8.4 (100.0)
School atmosphere is not good	10	71.4	4	28.6	14	6.5 (100.0)
Teacher-teacher relationship is not good	4	57.1	3	42.9	7	3.3 (100.0)
Others are not attending	3	50.0	3	50.0	6	2.8 (100.0)
Others	3	60.0	2	40.0	5	2.3 (100.0)
Total*	152	-	53	-	215	100.0

* Totals vary due to multiple responses.

Table 5.2: Distribution of Respondents According to Reasons for Absenteeism and Sex

Reasons	Sex				Total	
	Male		Female			
	No.	Percentage	No.	Percentage	No.	Percentage
Adjustment with principal	4	11.4	31	88.6	35	16.3 (100.0)
Lack of check on attendance	17	51.5	16	48.5	33	15.3 (100.0)
Job security	12	42.8	16	57.2	28	13.0 (100.0)
Engaged in non-teaching activities	14	56.0	11	44.0	25	11.6 (100.0)
Posted away from home	12	50.0	12	50.0	24	11.2 (100.0)
Doing side business	10	50.0	10	50.0	20	9.3 (100.0)
Abuse of high connections	1	5.6	17	97.4	18	8.4 (100.0)
School atmosphere is not good	6	42.9	8	57.1	14	6.5 (100.0)
Teacher-teacher relationship is not good	2	28.6	5	71.4	7	3.3 (100.0)
Others are not attending	2	33.3	4	66.7	6	2.8 (100.0)
Others	3	60.0	2	40.0	5	2.3 (100.0)
Total*	83	-	132	-	215	100.0

* Totals vary due to multiple responses.

The responses given for the reasons of absenteeism by rural and urban teachers are exhibited in Table 5.3. The table indicates that urban teachers asserted themselves three to four times over rural counterparts in terms giving reasons for absenteeism among the school teachers. Non congenial school atmosphere (92.9 per cent), non cordial teacher-teacher relationship (85.7 per cent), and job security (82.1 per cent) were the most talked reasons given by urban teachers for absenteeism. Adjustment with the principal, distant posting, and abuse of high connections were other reasons for absenteeism brought forward by same group of teachers. Poor monitoring system, engaged in non teaching activities and following bad practices of colleagues were less stated reasons put forward by urban teachers for absenteeism.

5.2.2 Corrective Measures to Contain Absenteeism

When teachers were asked, "how this can be controlled?". The responses given by them are presented in Table 5.4. A close to sixteen per cent suggested teacher motivation through rewards and fifteen percent opined effective monitoring system as the measures to contain absenteeism. One seventh of them advocated abstaining teachers from non-teaching duties and 11.6 per cent gave ideal role of principal to control absenteeism. Posting near homes, use of Annual Confidential Reports (ACR), strict role of Parent Teacher Association (PTA) or Village Education Development Committees (VEDC), and role of students were some other measures suggested by the teachers to control absenteeism among school teachers.

It is clear from the table that absenteeism was more prevalent in public schools due to ineffective monitoring system and the prevailing practice of populism that was not the case in private schools. Abstaining teachers from non-teaching duties like Census, health surveys and other similar jobs can make them present in the school. Lack of appreciation for punctual teachers make others feel disenchanted to become regular. Monitoring only by the head was not considered sufficient rather the involvement of stakeholders like community and students was also felt desirable to put things in order. Sen (2008) also blamed the broken down inspection system of Indian public schools for teacher absenteeism and delayed arrival in the

Table 5.3: Distribution of Respondents According to Reasons for Absenteeism and Place of Employment

Reasons	Place of Employment				Total	
	Rural		Urban			
	No.	Percentage	No.	Percentage	No.	Percentage
Adjustment with principal	7	20.0	28	80.0	35	16.3 (100.0)
Lack of check on attendance	8	24.2	25	75.8	33	15.3 (100.0)
Job security	5	17.9	23	82.1	28	13.0 (100.0)
Engaged in non-teaching activities	8	32.0	17	68.0	25	11.6 (100.0)
Posted away from home	5	20.8	19	79.2	24	11.2 (100.0)
Doing side business	6	30.0	14	70.0	20	9.3 (100.0)
Abuse of high connections	4	22.2	14	77.8	18	8.4 (100.0)
School atmosphere is not good	1	7.1	13	92.9	14	6.5 (100.0)
Teacher-teacher relationship is not good	1	14.3	6	85.7	7	3.3 (100.0)
Others are not attending	2	33.3	4	66.7	6	2.8 (100.0)
Others	1	20.0	4	80.0	5	2.3 (100.0)
Total*	48	-	167	-	215	100.0

* Totals vary due to multiple responses.

Table 5.4: Distribution of Respondents According to Remedies for Absenteeism and the Type of School

Remedies	Type of School				Total	
	Public		Private			
	No.	Percentage	No.	Percentage	No.	Percentage
Rewarding teachers with high attendance	102	51.8	95	48.2	197	15.8 (100.0)
Periodical and surprise check	99	53.2	87	46.8	186	15.0 (100.0)
Abstaining from non-teaching duties	107	61.8	66	38.2	173	13.9 (100.0)
Principal becoming the role model	76	52.8	68	47.2	144	11.6 (100.0)
Posting teachers in the vicinity of homes	87	66.9	43	33.1	130	10.4 (100.0)
Affecting ACRs for absenteeism	67	56.8	51	43.2	118	10.4 (100.0)
Greater role of PTA/VEDC	43	44.8	53	55.2	96	7.7 (100.0)
Greater role of students	44	60.3	29	39.7	73	5.9 (100.0)
Greater role of fellow teachers	35	54.7	29	45.3	64	5.1 (100.0)
Increasing casual leave of teachers	22	51.2	21	48.8	43	3.5 (100.0)
Others	11	58.0	8	42.0	19	1.5 (100.0)
Total*	693	-	550	-	1243	100.0

* Totals vary due to multiple responses.

Table 5.5: Distribution of Respondents According to Remedies for Absenteeism and Sex

Remedies	Sex				Total	
	Male		Female			
	No.	Percentage	No.	Percentage	No.	Percentage
Rewarding teachers with high attendance	78	39.6	119	60.4	197	15.8 (100.0)
Periodical and surprise check	90	48.4	96	51.6	186	15.0 (100.0)
Abstaining from non-teaching duties	85	49.1	88	50.9	173	13.9 (100.0)
Principal becoming the role model	75	52.1	69	47.9	144	11.6 (100.0)
Posting teachers in the vicinity of homes	56	43.1	74	56.9	130	10.4 (100.0)
Affecting ACRs for absenteeism	60	50.8	58	49.1	118	10.4 (100.0)
Greater role of PTA/VEDC	45	46.9	51	53.1	96	7.7 (100.0)
Greater role of students	37	50.7	36	49.3	73	5.9 (100.0)
Greater role of fellow teachers	31	48.4	33	51.6	64	5.1 (100.0)
Increasing casual leave of teachers	18	41.9	25	58.1	43	3.5 (100.0)
Others	14	73.7	5	26.3	19	1.5 (100.0)
Total*	589	-	654	-	1243	100.0

* Totals vary due to multiple responses.

schools. The World Bank report authored by Chand and Mishra (2004) also reveals the gloomy dimension of public primary schools in the state of Punjab due to 36.0 per cent teacher absenteeism. A survey report (2008) brought out by a daily about Tarn Taran, a border district reveal that the inspection system is totally shattered due to the non-availability of vehicles and financial resources to maintain and ply them.

In suggesting measures to contain absenteeism the responses are exhibited in Table 5.5. Rewarding teachers with high attendance (60.4 per cent), increasing casual leave (58.1 per cent), and posting teachers in the vicinity (56.9 per cent) were some highly asserted measures suggested by female teachers to contain absenteeism. Other measures were shared by male and female teachers to control absenteeism among the school teachers.

The responses of teachers from rural and urban schools are shown in Table 5.6. The table reveals that teachers of urban schools were two to three times more vocal in suggesting measures to contain absenteeism. Posting teachers in the vicinity of their homes (81.5 per cent), abstaining teachers from non teaching duties (78.0 per cent), and affecting ACRs (76.3 per cent) were some highly acknowledged remedies suggested by urban school teachers to contain absenteeism. Effective monitoring system, role of fellow teachers and ideal principal were some other measures suggested by urban school teachers, though less in magnitude, to contain absenteeism.

5.3 Dereliction of Duty

5.3.1 Reasons for Dereliction of Duty

When teachers were asked to give reasons for this UPP, their responses are exhibited in Table 5.7. The table brought forward that burdened by non-teaching duties in the school (17.7 per cent) and lack of appreciation for efficient teachers (15.2 per cent) were some predominant reasons for abstaining teachers from classes. One eighth of the teachers gave lack of monitoring with in the school and ineffective officiating principal (15.5 per cent), some other reasons for dereliction of duty. Lack of sincerity among the students, equation with the principal, lack of teaching-learning material, bad school atmosphere and low intelligence level of the students, were many other reasons stated by the teachers of dereliction of duty. Except low pay as the reason for dereliction of duty among the private school teachers, for all other reasons; the responses of public school teachers were three to four times more than their private school counterparts. This shows that problem of dereliction of duty is grimmer in public schools as compared to private schools. Poor socio-economic condition of the students, ineffective monitoring system due to officiating principal and practice of populism were some predominant causes found for dereliction of duty among teaching fraternity of public schools. Voluntary or forced involvement in non teaching duties, disinterestedness among students and lack of monitoring of schools by higher officials were other reasons given by public school teachers for dereliction of duty. An analytical report of education indicators by National University of Educational Planning and Administration (NUEPA) for (2005-06) revealed the fact that the teachers were not only to blame for this, sometime they were working as paramedic, enumerator and election staff at the cost of children and teaching.

Responses according to the gender for the reasons of dereliction of duty among teachers are presented in Table 5.8. Non-congenial school atmosphere (72.7 per cent), non availability of teaching-learning material (68.2 per cent), and ineffective monitoring by officiating principal (60.0 per cent) were some leading reasons given by male teachers for dereliction of duty. Equation with the principal (56.5 per cent) and poor socio-economic condition of the students (55.5 per cent) were prominent reasons given by female teachers for dereliction of duty. For other reasons responses were shared by male as well as female teachers.

Table 5.6: Distribution of Respondents According to Remedies for Absenteeism and Place of Employment

Remedies	Place of Employment				Total	
	Rural		Urban			
	No.	Percentage	No.	Percentage	No.	Percentage
Rewarding teachers with high attendance	60	30.5	137	69.5	197	15.8 (100.0)
Periodical and surprise check	45	24.2	141	75.8	186	15.0 (100.0)
Abstaining from non-teaching duties	38	22.0	135	78.0	173	13.9 (100.0)
Principal becoming the role model	42	29.2	102	70.8	144	11.6 (100.0)
Posting teachers in the vicinity of homes	24	18.5	106	81.5	130	10.4 (100.0)
Affecting ACRs for absenteeism	28	23.7	90	76.3	118	10.4 (100.0)
Greater role of PTA/VEDC	34	35.4	62	64.6	96	7.7 (100.0)
Greater role of students	27	37.0	46	63.0	73	5.9 (100.0)
Greater role of fellow teachers	17	26.6	47	73.4	64	5.1 (100.0)
Increasing casual leave of teachers	13	30.2	30	69.8	43	3.5 (100.0)
Others	5	26.3	14	73.7	19	1.5 (100.0)
Total*	333	-	910	-	1243	100.0

* Totals vary due to multiple responses.

Table 5.7: Distribution of Respondents According to Reasons for Dereliction of Duty and the Type of School

Reasons	Type of School				Total	
	Public		Private			
	No.	Percentage	No.	Percentage	No.	Percentage
Burdened by non-teaching duties in school	47	79.7	12	20.3	59	17.7 (100.0)
No appreciation for efficient teachers	37	72.2	14	27.5	51	15.3 (100.0)
Lack of monitoring	31	73.8	11	26.2	42	12.6 (100.0)
Officiating principal not effective	30	85.7	5	14.3	35	10.5 (100.0)
Students are not serious in studies	19	76.0	6	24.0	25	7.5 (100.0)
Equation with the principal	19	82.6	4	17.4	23	6.9 (100.0)
Lack of teaching-learning material	15	68.2	7	31.8	22	6.6 (100.0)
School atmosphere is not good	16	72.7	6	27.3	22	6.6 (100.0)
Intelligence level of students is low	16	88.9	2	11.1	18	5.4 (100.0)
Other teachers are not attending classes	12	70.6	5	29.6	17	5.1 (100.0)
Not paid adequately	7	46.7	8	53.3	15	4.5 (100.0)
Others	4	80.0	1	20.0	5	1.5 (100.0)
Total*	253	-	81	-	334	100.0

* Totals vary due to multiple responses

Table 5.8: Distribution of Respondents According to Reasons for Dereliction of Duty and Sex

Reasons	Sex				Total	
	Male		Female			
	No.	Percentage	No.	Percentage	No.	Percentage
Burdened by non-teaching duties	30	50.8	29	49.2	59	17.7 (100.0)
No appreciation for efficient teachers	28	54.9	23	45.1	51	15.3 (100.0)
Lack of governance	24	57.1	18	42.9	42	12.6 (100.0)
Officiating principle not effective	21	60.0	14	40.0	35	10.5 (100.0)
Students are not serious in studies	13	52.0	12	48.0	25	7.5 (100.0)
Equation with the principal	10	43.5	13	56.5	23	6.9 (100.0)
Lack of teaching-learning material	15	68.2	7	31.8	22	6.6 (100.0)
School atmosphere is not good	16	72.7	6	27.3	22	6.6 (100.0)
Intelligence level of students is low	8	44.5	10	55.5	18	5.4 (100.0)
Other teachers are not attending classes	9	52.9	8	47.1	17	5.1 (100.0)
Not paid adequately	9	60.0	6	40.0	15	4.5 (100.0)
Others	4	80.0	1	20.0	5	1.5 (100.0)
Total*	187	-	147	-	334	100.0

* Totals vary due to multiple responses.

Reasons for dereliction of duty given by rural and urban teachers are presented in Table 5.9. Equation with the principal (87.0 per cent), ineffective officiating principal in monitoring (85.7 per cent) and burdened by non-teaching duties (81.4 per cent) were predominant reasons given by urban teachers for dereliction of duty. No appreciation for efficient teachers, lack of monitoring by higher officials, and limited salary were some other reasons given by urban teachers for dereliction of duty. Non seriousness among the students was the only reason highly opined by the rural teachers for dereliction of duty among the teachers. Urban teachers were three to four times more assertive for giving reasons for dereliction of duty.

5.3.2 Corrective Measures to Contain Dereliction of Duty

After knowing reasons for dereliction of duty the teachers were asked, "how can it be curbed?". Their responses are depicted in Table 5.10. One sixth of the teachers suggested, restraining teachers from non-teaching work and regular monitoring (15.7 per cent), measures to contain dereliction of duty among school teachers. One seventh of teachers advocated teacher motivation through in-service seminars and one eighth spelled out consensual role of principal in running school affairs, were some other remedies put forward to make the teachers dutiful. Teacher autonomy, evaluation of attitude towards work and active role of PTA/VEDC were some other measures revealed by the teachers though less in magnitude. While giving the remedies for dereliction of duty little differences in the percentages were noticed among public and private school teachers except restraining from non-teaching duties which was a preponderating practice in public schools.

Most of the public schools in the district sans fulltime principals due to lack of regular promotion policy, rather senior teacher of the school are given the responsibility to run the school. Even in Punjab out of total 1293 posts of principals in public schools, 1150 have been lying vacant for several years. In spite of enjoying the legitimate powers of fulltime principal, nevertheless officiating principal is unable to use strict measures against staff to contain UPP like dereliction of duty due to the apprehension of marginalisation after the term. Some times the officiating duties pass on to junior teachers when some senior teachers, particularly female teachers refuse to take the responsibility of officiating principal which further undermines the authority of the principal. Due to non-availability and incompetency of supporting staff, all the non-teaching duties within the school, like maintenance of records, preparing pay-rolls, carrying reports to the district offices etc., rests on the teachers at the cost of teaching. Department of school education have made compulsory for all teachers to attend in-service seminars to reinvent the lost glory of professionalism among them, for last several years. Some senior fellow teachers are chosen as resource persons in the seminars. Sometimes they may not be able to add to the knowledge and skills of the seminarians due to lack of knowledge of the subject related pedagogic practices and professional ethics. Lack of any provision of resource persons from the fields of psychology, sociology, education etc. put a question mark on the fruitfulness of in-service seminars though teachers are ready to add to their knowledge and skills. Autocratic style of officiating principal sometimes further polarise the school staff to take part in day-to-day functioning of the school thus further deteriorating the school atmosphere.

Wadhawan's work (1980) on school teachers of Delhi found that teachers hardly tried to enhance their subject knowledge and expressed no utility of in-service training programs. An IIM-A study (2006) of 400 districts of 13 states, have found that Sarva Shiksha Abhiyan, the Centre's flagship scheme to improve primary education, is a success in numbers. The study explains that more than 50.0 per cent of Indian children are dependent on private schools, among the highest in the world, due to the failure of state-run schools to provide quality education. The study suggests that quality can be assured if besides infrastructure, teaching staff, support staff and monitoring system, are in place. Involvement of communities, in the running of state schools, say parent-teacher associations, has had significant impact in Kerala and Nagaland.

Table 5.9: Distribution of Respondents According to Reasons for Dereliction of Duty and Place of Employment

Reasons	Place of Employment				Total	
	Rural		Urban			
	No.	Percentage	No.	Percentage	No.	Percentage
Burdened by non-teaching duties	11	18.6	48	81.4	59	17.7 (100.0)
No appreciation for efficient teachers	10	19.6	41	80.4	51	15.3 (100.0)
Lack of governance	11	26.2	31	73.8	42	12.6 (100.0)
Officiating principle not effective	5	14.3	30	85.7	35	10.5 (100.0)
Students are not serious in studies	23	92.0	2	8.0	25	7.5 (100.0)
Equation with the principal	3	13.0	20	87.0	23	6.9 (100.0)
Intelligence level of students is low	5	27.8	13	72.2	18	6.6 (100.0)
Other teachers are not attending classes	5	29.4	12	70.6	17	6.6 (100.0)
Not paid adequately	4	26.7	11	73.3	15	5.4 (100.0)
Lack of teaching-learning material	5	22.7	17	77.3	22	5.1 (100.0)
School atmosphere is not good	6	27.3	16	72.7	22	4.5 (100.0)
Others	1	20.0	4	80.0	5	1.5 (100.0)
Total*	89	-	245	-	334	100.0

* Totals vary due to multiple responses.

Table 5.10: Distribution of Respondents According to Remedies for Dereliction of Duty and the Type of School

Remedies	Type of School				Total	
	Public		Private			
	No.	Percentage	No.	Percentage	No.	Percentage
Restrain from non-teaching work	137	64.3	76	35.7	213	61.5 (100.0)
Regular and surprise check of classrooms	94	46.8	107	53.2	201	15.7 (100.0)
Teacher motivation through seminars	88	46.3	102	53.7	190	14.8 (100.0)
Consensual role of principal	84	53.2	74	46.8	158	12.3 (100.0)
Class autonomy to the teacher	75	54.7	62	45.3	137	10.7 (100.0)
Evaluation of attitude toward work	67	51.1	64	48.9	131	10.2 (100.0)
Greater role of PTA/VEDC	67	54.5	56	45.5	123	9.6 (100.0)
Through greater role of students	57	49.1	59	50.9	116	9.0 (100.0)
Others	8	61.5	5	38.5	13	1.0 (100.0)
Total*	677	-	605	-	1282	100.0

* Totals vary due to multiple responses.

The responses to remedies suggested by male and female teachers to contain dereliction of duty among the teachers are shown in Table 5.11. Evaluation of attitude towards work (57.3 per cent), teacher motivation through in-service seminars (56.8 per cent) and monitoring of classroom activity by higher officials (54.7 per cent) were some highly advocated measures to contain this practice by female teachers. Greater role of students, restraining from non-teaching work and class autonomy to the teacher were some other less responded practices given by the teachers to contain dereliction of duty. Greater role of PTA/VEDC (52.8 per cent) was the predominantly suggested measure by male teachers to contain this practice. The table reveals that female teachers were more vocal in giving the remedies to contain this practice as compared to their male counterparts.

Views of rural and urban teachers are presented in Table 5.12. Restraining teachers from non teaching duties (77.5 per cent), class autonomy to the teacher (73.0 per cent) and role of students (70.7 per cent) were highly suggested measures by urban teachers to contain this practice among the school teachers. Non autocratic style of functioning of principal, role of PTA/VEDC and monitoring of classroom activity by higher officials were other measures advocated by urban teachers to contain this practice. Use of teacher motivation seminars was a measure highly asserted by rural teachers to contain dereliction of duty. Urban teachers were two times more vocal than their rural counterparts in giving most of the remedies to control dereliction of duty among teachers.

Table 5.11: Distribution of Respondents According to Remedies for Dereliction of Duty and Sex

Remedies	Sex				Total	
	Male		Female			
	No.	Percentage	No.	Percentage	No.	Percentage
Restrain from non-teaching work	98	46.0	115	54.0	213	61.5 (100.0)
Regular and surprise check of classrooms	91	45.3	110	54.7	201	15.7 (100.0)
Teacher motivation through seminars	82	43.2	108	56.8	190	14.8 (100.0)
Role of principal through teamwork	71	45.0	87	55.0	158	12.3 (100.0)
Class autonomy to the teacher	67	49.0	70	51.0	137	10.7 (100.0)
Evaluation of attitude toward work	56	42.7	75	57.3	131	10.2 (100.0)
Greater role of PTA/VEDC	65	52.8	58	47.2	123	9.6 (100.0)
Through greater role of students	53	45.7	63	54.3	116	9.0 (100.0)
Others	9	69.2	4	30.8	13	1.0 (100.0)
Total*	592	-	690	-	1282	100.0

* Totals vary due to multiple responses.

Table 5.12: Distribution of Respondents According to Remedies for Dereliction of Duty and Place of Employment

Remedies	Place of Employment				Total	
	Rural		Urban			
	No.	Percentage	No.	Percentage	No.	Percentage
Restrain from non-teaching work	48	22.5	165	77.5	213	61.5 (100.0)
Regular and surprise check of classrooms	63	31.3	138	68.7	201	15.7 (100.0)
Teacher motivation through seminars	120	63.2	70	36.8	190	14.8 (100.0)
Role of principal through teamwork	48	30.4	110	69.6	158	12.3 (100.0)
Class autonomy to the teacher	37	27.0	100	73.0	137	10.7 (100.0)
Evaluation of attitude toward work	44	33.6	87	66.4	131	10.2 (100.0)
Greater role of PTA/VEDC	38	30.9	85	69.1	123	9.6 (100.0)
Through greater role of students	34	29.3	82	70.7	116	9.0 (100.0)
Others	5	61.5	8	38.5	13	1.0 (100.0)
Total*	437	-	845	-	1282	100.0

* Totals vary due to multiple responses.

5.4 Lack of Responsibility

5.4.1 Reasons for Lack of Responsibility

Responses obtained for various reasons stated for lack of responsibility are shown in Table 5.13. The table indicates that ignorance about the importance of their role towards students (15.2 per cent) and lack of active role of parents (14.2 per cent) were the prominent reasons given by the teachers for lack of responsibility towards their students. Nearly one seventh of the teachers stated that job security make them irresponsible and another 13.1 per cent said irresponsible students makes them irresponsible towards their duties. Preferences to other leisure activities, low pay and burdened by personal problems in the school were some other less responded reasons for lack of responsibility among the teachers.

Preferences to other leisure activities (85.2 per cent), who indulge in non-teaching activities, are appreciated (73.7 per cent), and transmission of knowledge is the only duty of a teacher (72.2 per cent) were highly propounded reasons given by public school teachers for lack of responsibility among school teachers. Private school teachers gave low pay and irresponsible colleagues as the dominant reasons for this practice. In most of the reasons for lack of responsibility public school teachers were two to three time more vocal as compared to their private counterparts.

Various reasons given by male and female teachers for lack of a sense of responsibility towards their duties are shown in Table 5.14. Irresponsible colleagues to follow (60.0 per cent), ignorant of their role for students (59.1 per cent) and burdened by personal problems in school (57.1 per cent) were some prominent reasons given by female teachers for this practice. Low pay (62.0 per cent), irresponsible students (57.9 per cent), transmission of knowledge is the only duty of a teacher (55.6 per cent) were highly advocated reasons given by male teachers for this practice. Female teachers were comparatively more vocal in giving the reasons than their male colleagues in some reasons for lack of responsibility.

Table 5.13: Distribution of Respondents According to Reasons for Lack of Responsibility and the Type of School

Reasons	Type of School				Total	
	Public		Private			
	No.	Percentage	No.	Percentage	No.	Percentage
Ignorant of the importance of their role for students	24	54.5	20	45.5	44	15.2 (100.0)
Lack of parents active role	27	65.8	14	34.2	41	14.2 (100.0)
Job security make them irresponsible	28	70.0	12	30.0	40	13.9 (100.0)
Students are not responsible	23	60.5	15	39.5	38	13.1 (100.0)
Preference to other leisure activities than teaching	23	85.2	4	14.8	27	9.3 (100.0)
Teachers are not adequately paid	7	33.3	14	66.7	21	7.3 (100.0)
Burdened by personal problems in school	14	66.7	7	33.3	21	7.3 (100.0)
Who indulge in non teaching activities are appreciated	14	73.7	5	26.3	19	6.6 (100.0)
Transmission of knowledge is the only duty of teacher	13	72.2	5	27.8	18	6.2 (100.0)
Others are not responsible	5	33.3	10	66.7	15	5.2 (100.0)
Others	3	60.0	2	40.0	5	1.7 (100.0)
Total*	181	-	108	-	289	100.0

* Totals vary due to multiple responses.

Table 5.14: Distribution of Respondents According to Reasons for Lack of Responsibility and Sex

Reasons	Sex				Total	
	Male		Female			
	No.	Percentage	No.	Percentage	No.	Percentage
Ignorant of importance of their role for students	18	40.9	26	59.1	44	15.2 (100.0)
Lack of parents active role	18	44.0	23	56.0	41	14.2 (100.0)
Job security make them irresponsible	20	50.0	20	50.0	40	13.9 (100.0)
Students are not responsible	22	57.9	16	42.1	38	13.1 (100.0)
Preference to other leisure activities than teaching	15	55.6	12	44.4	27	9.3 (100.0)
Teachers are not adequately paid	13	62.0	8	38.0	21	7.3 (100.0)
Burdened by personal problems in school	9	42.9	12	57.1	21	7.3 (100.0)
Who indulge in non teaching activities are appreciated	10	52.6	9	47.4	19	6.6 (100.0)
Transmission of knowledge is the only duty of teacher	10	55.6	8	44.4	18	6.2 (100.0)
Others are not responsible	6	40.0	9	60.0	15	5.2 (100.0)
Others	2	40.0	3	60.0	5	1.7 (100.0)
Total*	143	-	146	-	289	100.0

* Totals vary due to multiple responses.

The responses of rural and urban school teachers for the reasons of lack of responsibility are exhibited in Table 5.15. Preference to other leisure activities than teaching (92.6 per cent), irresponsible students (81.6 per cent) and job security (80.0 per cent) were highly talked reasons given by the urban teachers for lack of responsibility among the teachers. Low pay, burdened by personal problems in the school and who indulge in non teaching activities are appreciated, were some other reasons specified by urban teachers for this UPP. Of all specified reasons for this practice urban teachers asserted themselves three to four times more as compared to their rural colleagues.

5.4.2 Corrective Measures to Contain Lack of Responsibility

After stating the reasons for lack of responsibility, teachers were asked to respond to the corrective measures to contain this UPP. Responses are displayed in Table 5.16. The table shows that a close to one six of the teachers suggested, the role of in-service motivational seminars and one seventh said the awareness about their rights among the students, as some prominent measures to contain this practice. More than thirteen per cent suggested the role of teacher associations and one eighth of them suggested the role PTA/VEDC and appreciation of responsible teachers, as the means to correct this measure. Teamwork, fixing the accountability and class autonomy were some other steps propagated, though less in magnitude, to check this practice. Greater role of teacher associations (55.0 per cent) was more stated corrective measure stipulated by private school teachers. Giving more class autonomy to teacher (56.9 per cent) and active participation of teachers in school affairs (54.2 per cent) were more talked remedies given by public school teachers to contain this practice. All other suggested measures were shared both by public and private school teachers.

Public schools generally cater to the needs of the students coming from lower middle class and poor families. Some of them are sometimes first generation school goers and unaware of their rights and obligations teachers owe towards them. If this is not the case, they have no courage, to raise a voice against irresponsible teachers. Similar concern was found recently in the survey conducted by People

Forum (2008) that the falling trend of students from General Castes has made the teachers in public schools irresponsible, as there is no one left, either the students or parents, in the schools to challenge irresponsible teaches. Here role of PTA/VEDC has some significance to come forward and have a say in monitoring the school affairs, though that may be unwelcome for irresponsible teachers. Role of teacher associations can also have some significance in this regard, who cater to the welfare of the teachers. Similar measures were suggested by Sen (2008) in his lecture. Involvement of responsible teachers in running the day-to-day affairs may convey some message to their irresponsible teachers. There activities can have a supportive role for the principal in mending the affairs of the school.

Measures suggested by male and female teachers to contain lack of responsibility among the school teachers are presented in Table 5.17. Honouring responsible teachers (60.1 per cent), role of teacher motivational in service seminars (60.0 per cent), and role of teacher associations (55.0 per cent) were highly opined means proposed by female teachers to contain this practice. Making students aware of their rights, teacher classroom autonomy and active participation of teachers in school affairs were other significant measures given by same group of teachers to contain this UPP. Female teachers were more assertive in expressing the corrective measures to contain this practice.

Responses of rural and urban teachers to contain lack of responsibility among teachers are displayed in Table 5.18. The table indicates that giving classroom autonomy to teachers (74.1 per cent), active participation of teachers in school affairs (74.0 per cent) and making students aware of their rights (72.2 per cent) were highly suggested measures by urban teachers to contain this practice. Role of teacher associations, through teacher and PTA/VEDC relationship, and through in service motivational seminars, were other less responded means given by same group of teachers to contain this practice. Urban teachers were two to three times more assertive in suggesting the remedial measures to contain lack of responsibility among the school teachers.

Table 5.15: Distribution of Respondents According to Reasons for Lack of Responsibility and Place of Employment

Reasons	Place of Employment				Total	
	Rural		Urban			
	No.	Percentage	No.	Percentage	No.	Percentage
Ignorant of the importance of their role for students	15	34.1	29	65.9	44	15.2 (100.0)
Lack of parents active role	14	34.1	27	65.9	41	14.2 (100.0)
Job security make them irresponsible	8	20.0	32	80.0	40	13.9 (100.0)
Students are not responsible	7	18.4	31	81.6	38	13.1 (100.0)
Preference to other leisure activities than teaching	2	7.4	25	92.6	27	9.3 (100.0)
Teachers are not adequately paid	6	28.6	15	71.4	21	7.3 (100.0)
Burdened by personal problems in school	6	28.6	15	71.4	21	7.3 (100.0)
Who indulge in non teaching activities are appreciated	6	31.6	13	68.4	19	6.6 (100.0)
Transmission of knowledge is the only duty of teacher	7	38.9	11	61.1	18	6.2 (100.0)
Others are not responsible	5	33.3	10	66.7	15	5.2 (100.0)
Others	-	-	5	100.0	5	1.7 (100.0)
Total*	76	-	213	-	289	100.0

* Totals vary due to multiple responses.

Table 5.16: Distribution of Respondents According to Remedies for Lack of Responsibility and the Type of School

Remedies	Type of School				Total	
	Public		Private			
	No.	Percentage	No.	Percentage	No.	Percentage
Through motivational in-service seminars	109	49.5	111	50.5	220	17.1 (100.0)
Making students aware of their rights	97	51.9	90	48.1	187	14.6 (100.0)
Role of teacher associations	76	45.0	93	55.0	169	13.2 (100.0)
Through teacher and PTA/VEDC relationship	82	51.2	78	48.8	160	12.5 (100.0)
Honouring responsible teachers	80	50.6	78	49.4	158	12.3 (100.0)
Active participation of teachers in school affairs	77	54.2	65	45.8	142	11.1 (100.0)
Fixing the accountability of teachers	59	50.0	59	50.0	118	9.2 (100.0)
Greater autonomy to teachers in classroom affairs	66	56.9	50	43.1	116	9.0 (100.0)
Others	9	69.2	4	30.8	13	1.0 (100.0)
Total*	655	-	628	-	1283	100.0

* Totals vary due to multiple responses.

Table 5.17: Distribution of Respondents According to Remedies for Lack of Responsibility and Sex

Remedies	Sex				Total	
	Male		Female			
	No.	Percentage	No.	Percentage	No.	Percentage
Through motivational in-service seminars	88	40.0	132	60.0	220	17.1 (100.0)
Making students aware of their rights	86	46.0	101	54.0	187	14.6 (100.0)
Role of teacher associations	76	45.0	93	55.0	169	13.2 (100.0)
Through teacher and PTA/VEDC relationship	78	48.8	82	51.2	160	12.5 (100.0)
Honouring responsible teachers	63	39.9	95	60.1	158	12.3 (100.0)
Active participation of teachers in school affairs	69	48.6	73	51.4	142	11.1 (100.0)
Fixing the accountability of teachers	60	50.8	58	49.2	118	9.2 (100.0)
Greater autonomy to teachers in classroom affairs	55	47.4	61	52.6	116	9.0 (100.0)
Others	10	77.0	3	23.0	13	1.0 (100.0)
Total*	585	-	698	-	1283	100.0

* Totals vary due to multiple responses.

Table 5.18: Distribution of Respondents According to Remedies for Lack of Responsibility and Place of Employment

Remedies	Place of Employment				Total	
	Rural		Urban			
	No.	Percentage	No.	Percentage	No.	Percentage
Through motivational in-service seminars	64	29.1	156	70.9	220	17.1 (100.0)
Making students aware of their rights	52	27.8	135	72.2	187	14.6 (100.0)
Role of teacher associations	48	28.4	121	71.6	169	13.2 (100.0)
Through teacher and PTA°/VEDC relationship	46	28.8	114	71.2	160	12.5 (100.0)
Honouring responsible teachers	47	29.7	111	70.3	158	12.3 (100.0)
Active participation of teachers in school affairs	37	26.0	105	74.0	142	11.1 (100.0)
Fixing the accountability of teachers	44	37.3	74	62.7	118	9.2 (100.0)
Greater autonomy to teachers in classroom affairs	30	25.9	86	74.1	116	9.0 (100.0)
Others	4	30.8	9	69.2	13	1.0 (100.0)
Total*	372	-	911	-	1283	100.0

* Totals vary due to multiple responses.

5.5 Discrimination

5.5.1 Reasons for Discrimination against Students

The teachers who admitted to discrimination against students gave their reasons which are given in Table 5.19. Discrimination on the basis of intelligence level of the students was the most prominent (37.5 per cent) reason stated by the teachers. Consonance to the life style of the teachers and cleanliness and personal hygiene were equally cited (14.2 percent) reasons for discrimination against the students. Discrimination on the basis of compliance to the personal whims of the teachers (11.9 per cent) and caste (8.0 percent) were some other less responded reasons given by the teachers. Discrimination on the basis of class, language, religion and province, was also responded but meager in magnitude.

Discrimination on the basis of province (75.0 per cent), on the basis of cleanliness and personal hygiene (72.4 per cent), and religion (66.7 per cent) were prominent reasons given by public school teachers for discrimination against students. Consonance to the lifestyle of the teachers, socio-economic status, and caste were other reasons given by same group of teachers for this practice. Discrimination on the basis of compliance to personal whims of the teachers (57.1 per cent) was predominant reason given by private school teachers for this UPP. In revealing the reasons for this UPP public school teachers were more vocal than their private school counterparts.

Reasons for discrimination against the students brought forward by male and female teachers are revealed in Table 5.20. Discrimination on the basis of consonance to the lifestyle of the teachers (72.4 per cent), socio-economic status (68.4 per cent) and compliance to the personal whims of the teachers (67.9 per cent) were highly acknowledged reasons pointed by female teachers for this practice. Language spoken by the students, intelligence level, and religion were other less responded reasons given by this group of teachers for discrimination against the students. Female teachers were comparatively more assertive in giving the reasons for this practice as compared to their male counterparts.

Table 5.19: Distribution of Respondents According to Reasons for Discrimination against Students and the Type of School

Reasons	Type of School				Total	
	Public		Private			
	No.	Percentage	No.	Percentage	No.	Percentage
Intelligence level of the students	45	51.1	43	48.9	88	37.5 (100.0)
Consonance to the life style of the teachers	19	65.5	10	34.5	29	12.4 (100.0)
Cleanliness and personal hygiene	21	72.4	8	27.6	29	12.4 (100.0)
Compliance to personal whims of the teachers	12	42.9	16	57.1	28	11.9 (100.0)
On the basis of caste	9	60.0	6	40.0	15	8.0 (100.0)
Social class of the students	12	63.4	7	36.6	19	6.4 (100.0)
On the basis of language they speak	5	50.0	5	50.0	10	4.2 (100.0)
On the basis of religion	6	66.7	3	33.3	9	3.8 (100.0)
On the basis of the province they belong	3	75.0	1	25.0	4	1.7 (100.0)
Others	4	100.0	-	-	4	1.7 (100.0)
Total*	136	-	99	-	235	100.0

* Totals vary due to multiple responses.

Table 5.20: Distribution of Respondents According to Reasons for Discrimination against Students and Sex

Reasons	Sex				Total	
	Male		Female			
	No.	Percentage	No.	Percentage	No.	Percentage
Intelligence level of the students	36	40.9	52	59.1	88	37.5 (100.0)
Consonance to the life style of the teachers	8	27.6	21	72.4	29	12.4 (100.0)
Cleanliness and personal hygiene	13	44.8	16	55.2	29	12.4 (100.0)
Compliance to personal whims of the teachers	9	32.1	19	67.9	28	11.9 (100.0)
Social class of the students	6	31.6	13	68.4	19	8.0 (100.0)
On the basis of caste	9	60.0	6	40.0	15	6.4 (100.0)
On the basis of language they speak	4	40.0	6	60.0	10	4.2 (100.0)
On the basis of religion	4	44.4	5	56.6	9	3.8 (100.0)
On the basis of the province they belong	-	-	4	100.0	4	1.7 (100.0)
Others	2	50.0	2	50.0	4	1.7 (100.0)
Total*	91	-	144	-	235	100.0

* Totals vary due to multiple responses.

In giving the reasons for discrimination against the students the responses of rural and urban school teachers are displayed in Table 5.21. Discrimination on the basis of language spoken by students (90.0 per cent), socio-economic class of the students (79.0 per cent) and cleanliness and personal hygiene (75.9 per cent) were highly depicted reasons for this practice by urban teachers. Discrimination on the basis of province they belong to, religion and consonance to the life style of the teachers were other less replied reasons given by same group of teachers for this UPP. Urban teachers were highly assertive in giving reasons for this practice as compared to their rural colleagues.

5.5.2 Corrective Measures to Contain Discrimination against Students

The remedies suggested by the teachers to contain the practice of discrimination against students are exhibited in Table 5.22. One seventh of the teachers were of the opinion that by giving the campus a secular outlook and role of the principal in discouraging casteism (13.3 per cent) as some prominent measures given by teachers to contain discrimination against the students. Educating students about cleanliness and personal hygiene (13.0 per cent) and introduction of moral science in curriculum (13.0 per cent) were some other suggested remedies to control discrimination against students. Changing the view of teachers through in service motivational seminars and role of members of PTA/VEDC were some other measures advocated by teachers though less in magnitude to contain this practice. Educating students about cleanliness (55.6 per cent), introduction of moral science in curriculum (55.6 per cent), commendation of teachers with objective outlook through ACRs (52.2 per cent) were some prominent corrective measures suggested by public school teachers to contain discrimination against students. Role of students (56.0 per cent), role of PTA/VEDC members in maintaining a sense of universalism (53.1 per cent) and through self realisation by colleagues (52.2 per cent) were highly acknowledged means suggested by private school teachers to contain this practice. All other corrective measures were equally shared by the teachers.

Table 5.21: Distribution of Respondents According to Reasons for Discrimination against Students and Place of Employment

Reasons	Place of Employment				Total	
	Rural		Urban			
	No.	Percentage	No.	Percentage	No.	Percentage
Intelligence level of the students	26	29.5	62	70.5	88	37.5 (100.0)
Consonance to the life style of the teachers	10	34.5	19	65.5	29	12.4 (100.0)
Cleanliness and personal hygiene	7	24.1	22	75.9	29	12.4 (100.0)
Compliance to personal whims of the teachers	13	46.4	15	53.6	28	11.9 (100.0)
Social class of the students	4	21.0	15	79.0	19	8.0 (100.0)
On the basis of caste	8	53.3	7	46.7	15	6.4 (100.0)
On the basis of language they speak	1	10.0	9	90.0	10	4.2 (100.0)
On the basis of religion	3	33.3	6	66.7	9	3.8 (100.0)
On the basis of the province they belong	1	25.0	3	75.0	4	1.7 (100.0)
Others	1	25.0	3	75.0	4	1.7 (100.0)
Total*	74	-	161	-	235	100.0

* Totals vary due to multiple responses.

Table 5.22: Distribution of Respondents According to Remedies for Discrimination against Students and the Type of School

Remedies	Type of School				Total	
	Public		Private			
	No.	Percentage	No.	Percentage	No.	Percentage
Giving school campus a secular outlook	99	51.7	93	48.3	192	14.6 (100.0)
Role of principal to discourage casteism	86	49.1	89	50.9	175	13.3 (100.0)
Educating students about cleanliness	95	55.6	76	44.4	171	13.0 (100.0)
Introduction of moral science in curriculum	95	55.6	76	44.4	171	13.0 (100.0)
Changing view of teachers through seminars	80	49.4	82	50.6	162	12.3 (100.0)
Role of PTA/VEDC in creating sense of universalism	67	46.9	76	53.1	143	10.9 (100.0)
Role of students against discrimination	51	44.0	65	56.0	116	8.8 (100.0)
Through self realisation by colleagues	47	48.0	51	52.0	98	7.5 (100.0)
Commendation in ACRs who have objective outlook	41	52.2	39	48.8	80	6.1 (100.0)
Others	4	51.1	3	42.9	7	0.5 (100.0)
Total*	665	-	650	-	1315	100.0

* Totals vary due to multiple responses.

Students are discriminated on the basis of their intelligence in public schools. Ordinary students are sometimes not promoted to the next class with the fear of spoiling teacher's board result and thus undermining his performance. Those who conform to the life style of the teachers are bestowed with special privileges at the cost of the deserved ones. Students coming from poor families, who are unable to maintain cleanliness, are not attended well. Moreover, the physical education teachers hardly bother to educate students about cleanliness and personal hygiene that affect their performance. Caste based polarisation is rampant among the teachers and, is extended even to the student community. Principals make little efforts to control it and sometimes they are a part of it. Making pressure groups on the basis of caste are also in practice in many public schools.

Views of male and female teachers to contain discrimination against students are shown in Table 5.23. The table reveals that changing views of teachers through in service seminars (61.1 per cent), educating students about cleanliness (60.8 per cent), and introduction of moral science in curriculum (60.2 per cent) were highly reported remedies by female teachers to contain discrimination against students. Giving school campus a secular outlook (58.9 per cent), role of principal to discourage casteism (56.0 per cent), and role of PTA/VEDC members in creating a sense of universalism among teachers (56.0 per cent) were other less reported measures to contain this practice among school teachers. Female teachers were outnumbered than their male colleagues in giving the corrective measures to contain discrimination against the students.

Remedies acknowledged by rural and urban teachers to contain discrimination against students are exhibited in Table 5.24. The table conveys that giving school campus a secular outlook (75.0 per cent), educating students about cleanliness (74.3 per cent), and introduction of moral science in curriculum (74.3 per cent) were prominent means suggested by urban teachers to contain this practice. Role of principal to discourage casteism, commendation through ACRs that have objective outlook, changing views of teachers through in service seminars were other less asserted measures to contain discrimination against students by same group of teachers. Urban teachers were almost three times more assertive in giving the views to contain discrimination against students by school teachers.

Table 5.23: Distribution of Respondents According to Remedies for Discrimination against Students and Sex

Remedies	Sex				Total	
	Male		Female			
	No.	Percentage	No.	Percentage	No.	Percentage
Giving school campus a secular outlook	79	41.1	113	58.9	192	14.6 (100.0)
Role of principal to discourage casteism	77	44.0	98	56.0	175	13.3 (100.0)
Educating students about cleanliness	67	39.2	104	60.8	171	13.0 (100.0)
Introduction of moral science in curriculum	68	39.8	103	60.2	171	13.0 (100.0)
Changing view of teachers through seminars	63	38.9	99	61.1	162	12.3 (100.0)
Role of PTA/VEDC in creating sense of universalism	63	44.0	80	56.0	143	10.9 (100.0)
Role of students against discrimination	57	49.1	59	50.9	116	8.8 (100.0)
Through self realisation by colleagues	46	46.9	52	53.1	98	7.5 (100.0)
Commendation in ACRs who have objective outlook	43	53.7	37	46.3	80	6.1 (100.0)
Others	4	51.1	3	42.9	7	0.5 (100.0)
Total*	567	-	748	-	1315	100.0

* Totals vary due to multiple responses.

Table 5.24: Distribution of Respondents According to Remedies for Discrimination against Students and Place of Employment

Remedies	Place of Employment				Total	
	Rural		Urban			
	No.	Percentage	No.	Percentage	No.	Percentage
Giving school campus a secular outlook	48	25.0	144	75.0	192	14.6 (100.0)
Role of principal to discourage casteism	47	26.8	128	73.2	175	13.3 (100.0)
Educating students about cleanliness	44	25.7	127	74.3	171	13.0 (100.0)
Introduction of moral science in curriculum	44	25.7	127	74.3	171	13.0 (100.0)
Changing view of teachers through seminars	45	27.8	117	72.2	162	12.3 (100.0)
Role of PTA/VEDC in creating sense of universalism	41	28.7	102	71.3	143	10.9 (100.0)
Role of students against discrimination	34	29.3	82	70.7	116	8.8 (100.0)
Through self realisation by colleagues	29	29.6	69	70.4	98	7.5 (100.0)
Commendation in ACRs that have objective outlook	22	27.5	58	72.5	80	6.1 (100.0)
Others	-	-	7	100.0	7	0.5 (100.0)
Total*	354	-	961	-	1315	100.0

* Totals vary due to multiple responses.

5.6 Authoritarianism

Responses obtained for the reasons of authoritarian attitude of teachers towards their students are shown in Table 5.25. The table indicates that one sixth of the teachers stated ignorance about the empathetic attitude and one seventh said that students were not their children, as the reasons for their authoritarian attitude. More than thirteen per cent termed that it is the moral duty of students to obey their teachers and other one eighth of them reasoned that it is due to the ignorance of their rights. Authoritarian outlook is good for students and parents want teachers to be authoritative, were other reasons given by one ninth of the teachers. Teachers got authoritative attitude from their teachers and students lack the knowledge that teachers have, were some other though important but less responded reasons for authoritative attitude of the teachers.

Students are ignorant of their rights (73.1 per cent), ignorant about empathetic attitude (68.6 per cent), and students are not their own children (66.7 per cent) were highly expressed reasons by public school teachers for authoritarian attitude of teachers toward their students. Parents want teachers to be authoritative, it is moral duty of students to obey teachers, and teachers got authoritative outlook from their teachers were other reported reasons by same group of teachers for this practice. Authoritative image is good for students (65.2 per cent) were the only reason predominantly expressed by private school teachers for this practice. In expressing the reasons for authoritarian outlook of the school teachers public school teachers were two times more assertive than their private school counterparts.

5.6.1 Reasons for Authoritarianism

The responses for the reasons of authoritarian attitude of teachers towards their students by male and female teachers are presented in Table 5.26. Principal and colleagues are authoritative (90.0 per cent), teachers got authoritative outlook from their teachers (72.2 per cent), and parents want teachers to be authoritative (65.2 per cent) were eminent reasons outlined by female teachers for authoritarian outlook of the teachers. It is moral duty of students to obey their teachers, authoritative outlook is good for students, and students lack knowledge that teachers have, were other reasons given by same group of teachers for this practice. Female teachers were more vociferous in giving reasons for this practice than their male colleagues.

Table 5.25: Distribution of Respondents According to Reasons for Authoritarianism and the Type of School

Reasons	Type of School				Total	
	Public		Private			
	No.	Percentage	No.	Percentage	No.	Percentage
Ignorant about empathetic attitude	24	68.6	11	31.4	35	16.4 (100.0)
Students are not their children	20	66.7	10	33.3	30	14.0 (100.0)
Moral duty of students to obey teachers	18	62.1	11	37.9	29	13.6 (100.0)
Students are ignorant of their rights	19	73.1	7	26.9	26	12.2 (100.0)
Authoritative outlook is good for students	8	34.8	15	65.2	23	10.7 (100.0)
Parents want teachers to be authoritative	15	65.2	8	34.8	23	10.7 (100.0)
Got authoritative outlook from their teachers	11	61.1	7	38.9	18	8.4 (100.0)
Students lack knowledge that teachers have	10	58.8	7	41.2	17	7.9 (100.0)
Principal and colleagues are authoritative	6	54.5	5	45.5	11	5.1 (100.0)
Others	2	100.0	-	-	2	0.9 (100.0)
Total*	133	-	81	-	214	100.0

* Totals vary due to multiple responses.

Table 5.26: Distribution of Respondents According to Reasons for Authoritarianism and Sex

Reasons	Sex				Total	
	Male		Female			
	No.	Percentage	No.	Percentage	No.	Percentage
Ignorant about empathetic attitude	16	45.7	19	54.3	35	16.4 (100.0)
Students are not their children	14	46.7	16	53.3	30	14.0 (100.0)
Moral duty of students to obey teachers	11	37.9	18	62.1	29	13.6 (100.0)
Students are ignorant of their rights	12	46.1	14	53.9	26	12.2 (100.0)
Authoritative outlook is good for students	9	39.1	14	60.9	23	10.7 (100.0)
Parents want teachers to be authoritative	8	34.8	15	65.2	23	10.7 (100.0)
Got authoritative outlook from their teachers	5	27.8	13	72.2	18	8.4 (100.0)
Students lack knowledge that teachers have	7	41.2	10	58.8	17	7.9 (100.0)
Principal and colleagues are authoritative	1	9.1	10	90.9	11	5.1 (100.0)
Others	1	50.0	1	50.0	2	0.9 (100.0)
Total*	84	-	130	-	214	100.0

* Totals vary due to multiple responses.

Views of rural and urban school teachers for the authoritative outlook of the teachers are brought forward in Table 5.27. The table indicates that it is moral duty of students to obey their teachers (82.8 per cent), principal and colleagues are authoritative (81.8 per cent), and students are not their own children (80.0 per cent) were leading reasons expressed by urban teachers for this practice. Students are ignorant of their rights, students lack knowledge that teachers have, and parents want teachers to be authoritative were other less responded reasons stipulated by same group of teachers for this practice. Urban teachers were three to four times more communicative in giving the reasons for this practice than their rural counterparts.

5.6.2 Corrective Measures to Contain Authoritarianism

The measures suggested by the teachers to contain this practice are presented in Table 5.28. More than twenty nine per cent of the teachers suggested the role of principal for greater student-teacher interaction through co-curricular activities and twenty seven per cent spelled out the role of in service seminars in reminding the teachers about empathetic attitude and their obligations, as the course of action to contain this practice. More than eleven per cent advocated the adoption of child centered approach in schools and one tenth of them pointed out role of principal in maintaining the empathetic attitude of teachers. Role of members of PTA/VEDC, therapeutic counselling of teachers and use of ACR's were some less responded measures to contain authoritarian attitude of the teachers. Role of principal in maintaining empathetic attitude of teachers (5.0 per cent), reminding teachers of their obligations and empathetic attitude through seminars (52.4 per cent), and therapeutic counselling of teachers having authoritative outlook (52.0 per cent), were major corrective measures indicated by public school teachers to contain this practice among the teachers. Role of PTA/VEDC members in maintaining empathetic attitude of teachers (53.2 per cent) was the only remedy strongly spelled out by private school teachers to contain this practice. In all other measures to contain this practice both public and private school teachers were equally vociferous.

Table 5.27: Distribution of Respondents According to Reasons for Authoritarianism and Place of Employment

Reasons	Place of Employment				Total	
	Rural		Urban			
	No.	Percentage	No.	Percentage	No.	Percentage
Ignorant about empathetic attitude	11	31.4	24	68.6	35	16.4 (100.0)
Students are not their children	6	20.0	24	80.0	30	14.0 (100.0)
Moral duty of students to obey teachers	5	17.2	24	82.8	29	13.6 (100.0)
Students are ignorant of their rights	6	23.1	20	76.9	26	12.2 (100.0)
Authoritative outlook is good for students	10	43.5	13	56.5	23	10.7 (100.0)
Parents want teachers to be authoritative	6	26.1	17	73.9	23	10.7 (100.0)
Got authoritative outlook from their teachers	5	27.8	13	72.2	18	8.4 (100.0)
Students lack knowledge that teachers have	4	23.5	13	76.5	17	7.9 (100.0)
Principal and colleagues are authoritative	2	18.2	9	81.8	11	5.1 (100.0)
Others	-	-	2	100.0	2	0.9 (100.0)
Total*	55	-	159	-	214	100.0

* Totals vary due to multiple responses.

Table 5.28: Distribution of Respondents According to Remedies for Authoritarianism and the Type of School

Remedies	Type of School				Total	
	Public		Private			
	No.	Percentage	No.	Percentage	No.	Percentage
Role of principal for greater student-teacher interaction through co-curricular activities	201	52.0	186	48.0	387	29.3 (100.0)
Reminding their obligations and empathetic attitude through seminars	186	52.4	169	47.6	355	26.9 (100.0)
Introduction of child centered approach	84	51.1	63	42.9	147	11.1 (100.0)
Role of principal in maintaining empathetic attitude of teachers	70	53.0	62	47.0	132	10.0 (100.0)
Greater role of PTA/VEDC in maintaining empathetic attitude of teachers	58	46.8	66	53.2	124	9.4 (100.0)
Therapeutic counselling of teachers having authoritative outlook	52	52.0	48	48.0	100	7.5 (100.0)
Commendation through ACRs that have non-authoritative outlook	35	50.7	34	49.3	69	5.2 (100.0)
Others	6	60.0	4	40.0	10	0.8 (100.0)
Total*	692	-	632	-	1324	100.0

* Totals vary due to multiple responses.

The core of the teaching-learning activity is the teacher-student relationship. If teacher, is in the possession of knowledge and desired skill to impart it, and his attitude is empathetic, cooperative and supportive, and the student is ready to acquire the knowledge then the purpose of teaching-learning activity is achieved. Sometimes, authoritarian attitude of the teacher comes in the way in the formation of teacher-student relationship. The data shows that authoritarian attitude is prevalent among the teachers and is comparatively much more among public school teachers as compared to private school counterparts. Hardly any provision is available to diffuse this attitude among the teachers though legislation is there to adopt child centered approach, but nobody aware of it. In-service seminars are only subject oriented in the absence of resource persons from the fields of sociology and psychology. Generally students are treated as numbers, so many passed or failed, instead of so many personalities are made or spoiled. In practice, the morality is dictated by the teachers, rather than practiced and emulated by the student. Co-curricular activities are limited in public schools as they are taken as extra burden on teachers. In a systematic study of professional role of secondary school teachers, Shah (1970) notices considerable evidence of role consensus among various role definers in that they almost unanimously rejected the old authoritarian concept of the teacher role and, instead, conceived of it in more diffuse terms.

Views of male and female teachers to contain authoritarian outlook of teachers is submitted in Table 5.29. The table reveals that introduction of child centered approach (61.9 per cent), reminding teachers their obligations and empathetic attitude through seminars (60.0 per cent), and therapeutic counselling of teachers having authoritative attitude (59.0 per cent) were leading remedies suggested by female teachers to contain this UPP among the school teachers. Role of principal for greater student-teacher interaction through co-curricular activities, role of PTA/VEDC in maintaining empathetic attitude of teachers, and role of principal in maintaining empathetic attitude of teachers were other less talked corrective measures given by same group of teachers to contain this practice. Female teachers were more communicative in suggesting the remedies to control this practice than their male counterparts.

Table 5.29: Distribution of Respondents According to Remedies for Authoritarianism and Sex

Remedies	Sex				Total	
	Male		Female			
	No.	Percentage	No.	Percentage	No.	Percentage
Role of principal for greater student-teacher interaction through co-curricular activities	165	42.6	222	57.4	387	29.3 (100.0)
Reminding their obligations and empathetic attitude through seminars	142	40.0	213	60.0	355	26.9 (100.0)
Introduction of child centered approach	56	38.1	91	61.9	147	11.1 (100.0)
Role of principal in maintaining empathetic attitude of teachers	61	46.2	71	53.8	132	10.0 (100.0)
Greater role of PTA/VEDC in maintaining empathic attitude of teachers	57	46.0	67	54.0	124	9.4 (100.0)
Therapeutic counselling of teachers having authoritative outlook	41	41.0	59	59.0	100	7.5 (100.0)
Commendation through ACRs that have non-authoritative outlook	33	47.8	36	52.2	69	5.2 (100.0)
Others	6	60.0	4	40.0	10	0.8 (100.0)
Total*	561	-	763	-	1324	100.0

* Totals vary due to multiple responses.

In furnishing the corrective measures to contain authoritarian attitude of school teachers the responses of rural and urban school teachers are presented in Table 5.30. The table shows that introduction of child centered approach (76.2 per cent), therapeutic counselling of teachers having authoritative outlook (74.0 per cent), and reminding teachers of their obligations and empathetic attitude through seminars (73.8 per cent) were highly acknowledged measurers put forward by urban teachers to contain this practice. Role of principal for greater student-teacher interaction through co curricular activities, role of principal in maintaining empathetic attitude of teachers, and role PTA/VEDC in maintaining empathetic attitude of teachers were other remedies suggested by the same group of teachers. Urban school teachers were almost three times more communicative in reacting to the remedies than their rural colleagues to contain this practice among school teachers.

5.7 Commercial Venality

5.7.1 Reasons for Commercial Venality

Commercial venality was the last UPP investigated among the school teachers. Responses obtained for various reasons cited for commercial venality are given in Table 5.31. About thirty per cent of the teachers indicated insufficient salary to meet both ends and 11.6 per cent stated that lust for money forced them to indulge in private tutoring.

A close to ten per cent revealed that money determines social status and other 9.4 per cent stated that syllabus could not be completed in school hours, as reasons for commercial venality. One twelfth of the teachers asserted that there is no check on private tuitions and that quality of teaching was better at tuitions, and these led to unprofessional practices. Taking tuitions is a status symbol these days, professional ethics has no relevance today and everybody is indulging, were some other less responded reasons from respondents for commercial venality.

Table 5.30: Distribution of Respondents According to Remedies for Authoritarianism and Place of Employment

Remedies	Place of Employment				Total	
	Rural		Urban			
	No.	Percentage	No.	Percentage	No.	Percentage
Role of principal for greater student-teacher interaction through co-curricular activities	102	26.3	285	73.7	387	29.3 (100.0)
Reminding their obligations and empathetic attitude through seminars	93	26.2	262	73.8	355	26.9 (100.0)
Introduction of child centered approach	35	23.8	112	76.2	147	11.1 (100.0)
Role of principal in maintaining empathetic attitude of teachers	37	28.0	95	72.0	132	10.0 (100.0)
Greater role of PTA/VEDC in maintaining empathic attitude of teachers	36	29.0	88	71.0	124	9.4 (100.0)
Therapeutic counselling of teachers having authoritative outlook	26	26.0	74	74.0	100	7.5 (100.0)
Commendation through ACRs that have non-authoritative outlook	25	36.2	44	63.8	69	5.2 (100.0)
Others	2	20.0	8	80.0	10	0.8 (100.0)
Total*	356	-	968	-	1324	100.0

* Totals vary due to multiple responses.

Table 5.31: Distribution of Respondents According to Reasons for Commercial Venality and the Type of School

Reasons	Type of School				Total	
	Public		Private			
	No.	Percentage	No.	Percentage	No.	Percentage
Salary is not sufficient to meet both ends	18	26.9	49	73.1	67	29.9 (100.0)
Out of lust for money students are forced to take tuitions	12	46.2	14	53.8	26	11.6 (100.0)
Money determines the social status	11	50.0	11	50.0	22	9.8 (100.0)
Syllabus can not be completed in school hours	7	33.3	14	66.7	21	9.4 (100.0)
No check on private tuition	13	68.4	6	31.6	19	8.5 (100.0)
Quality of teaching at tuition is better than in school	9	47.4	10	52.6	19	8.5 (100.0)
Taking private tuition is a status symbol for students	6	33.3	12	66.7	18	8.0 (100.0)
Professional ethics has no relevance in present context	7	41.2	10	58.8	17	7.6 (100.0)
Because others are indulging in private tuition	7	50.0	7	50.0	14	6.3 (100.0)
Other	1	100.0	-	-	1	0.4 (100.0)
Total*	91	-	133	-	224	100.0

* Totals vary due to multiple responses.

Insufficient salary to meet the both ends (73.1 per cent), syllabus can not be completed in school hours (66.7 per cent), and taking private tuitions is a status symbol for students (66.7 per cent) were prominent reasons described by private school respondents for commercial venality. Professional ethics have no relevance in the present context, lust for money force teachers to take tuitions, and quality of private tuition is better than school classroom were other less asserted reasons outlined by private school teachers for this practice. No check on private tutoring was the only highly asserted reason revealed by public school teachers. Private school teachers were comparatively more vocal in giving the reasons for commercial venality than their public school counterparts.

Responses for the reasons of commercial venality among the school teachers conveyed by male and female teachers are shown in Table 5.32. The table points out that taking private tuitions is a status symbol (72.2 per cent), no check on private tuition (68.4 per cent) and quality of teaching at tuition is better than school (68.4 per cent) were leading reasons stated by male teachers for commercial venality. Because others are indulging in private tuitions, material possessions determine the social status, and professional ethics have no relevance in the present context were other less responded reasons put forward by male teachers for this practice. Insufficient salary to meet both ends (58.2 per cent) and lust for money force them to take tuitions (53.9 per cent) were two eminent reasons given by female teachers for commercial venality among school teachers. Male teachers were more vocal than their female counterparts in revealing the reason for this UPP.

The reasons for commercial venality among school teachers delineated by rural and urban teachers are presented in Table 5.33. The table portrays that taking private tuition is a status symbol for students (77.8 per cent), lust for money force them to take tuitions (69.2 per cent), and because others are indulging in private tuitions (64.3 per cent) were some major reasons delineated by urban teachers for commercial venality. Material possessions determine the social status, lack of check on private tuition, and quality of teaching at tuition is better than school were other less acknowledged reasons revealed by urban teachers for this UPP. Syllabus can not be completed in school hours (61.9 per cent) was the only asserted reason put forward by rural teachers for this practice. Urban teachers were comparatively more vociferous as compared to rural colleagues in responding to the reasons for commercial venality among school teachers.

5.7.2 Corrective Measures to Contain Commercial Venality

After stating various reasons for commercial venality, the teachers were asked to spell out the measures to contain this practice. Their responses are presented in Table 5.34. As is evident from the table, that enhancement of salary to fulfill the needs of the family (16.0 per cent) and role of in-service seminars (12.1 per cent) were some prominent measures suggested by the teachers. Cooperative role of students (11.8 per cent) and equality in opportunities of education (11.3 per cent) were some other remedies propagated by the teachers to check this practice. One ninth of the teachers advocated the role of members of PTA/VEDC and checks of higher authorities (10.6 per cent) can have great effect to control commercial venality. Mending stop-gap-arrangement of teachers, decentralising teaching-learning activity and using ACRs to check it were some other less responded measures to control commercial venality. Affecting ACRs of those who indulge in private tutoring (65.5 per cent), mending stop-gap arrangement of teachers (61.9 per cent), and check on private tutoring by higher authorities (58.6 per cent) were the highly expressed corrective measures by public school teachers to contain commercial venality. Equality in opportunities of education (54.4 per cent), role of students in timely completion of curriculum (53.5 per cent), and enhancement of salary to fulfill the needs of the family (51.6 per cent) was the leading remedies given by private school teachers to contain this practice. All other corrective measures were shared by both public and private school teachers.

Commercial venality was the only UPP that was heavily prevalent among private school teachers. Private schools that were philanthropic social institutions earlier have now become profit ogranisations. Though principal and members of management committee excellently govern them but there is a large gap what they charge from the students and what they pay to the teachers. Low salary force private school teachers to indulge in private tutoring, a practice declared unethical by UNESCO. When teachers ask for increment in salary they are told to give the way for others willing to work on low salary. This stop-gap-arrangement takes the toll on teaching-learning activity. There are directions of Punjab and Haryana Court to pay a minimum basic salary of Rs. 4550 for Middle school teachers and Rs. 5480 for High school teachers of private schools but they are getting Rs. 750 to Rs. 1500 per month and secure affiliation to State Education Board by submitting fake salary statements.

Moreover there is no provision of in-service seminars for private school teachers. Some teachers join private schools to acquire teaching experience for doing B.Ed. through distance education or joining government service. Very few public school teachers were indulging in private tuition due to lack of check on this practice by the authorities. Private schools are serving as the breeding grounds of teachers making education a private commodity, to make huge profits out of it. Sen (2008) while talking about a just society in reality in the era of globalisation, emphasised the indispensable role of qualitative and quantitative public school education system for the marginalised. Blaming the broken down inspection system of Indian public schools, for teacher absenteeism, delayed arrival in the school and private tutoring, that has a profound effect on the schooling of poor and underprivileged children - sometimes first-generation school goers - unsure of their rights and unable to raise their voice. He advocated the role of parents and teacher associations instead of teacher unions, in inculcating the work culture among the school teachers, in the delivery of school education.

Remedies expressed by male and female teachers to contain commercial venality are furnished in Table 5.35. Revisit to professional ethics through in-service seminars (56.2 per cent), role PTA/VEDC members (55.6 per cent), and equality in opportunities in education (54.4 per cent) were eminent corrective measures suggested by female teachers to contain this practice. Enhancement of salary to fulfill the needs of family, decentralisation of teaching-learning activity, and mending stop-gap arrangement were other remedies proposed by female teachers to contain commercial venality among school teachers. Female teachers were comparatively more vocal in suggesting the means to contain this practice.

Table 5.32: Distribution of Respondents According to Reasons for Commercial Venality and Sex

Reasons	Sex				Total	
	Male		Female			
	No.	Percentage	No.	Percentage	No.	Percentage
Salary is not sufficient to meet both ends	28	41.8	39	58.2	67	29.9 (100.0)
Out of lust for money students are forced to take tuitions	12	46.1	14	53.9	26	11.6 (100.0)
Money determines the social status	14	63.6	8	36.4	22	9.8 (100.0)
Syllabus can not be completed in school hours	11	52.4	10	47.6	21	9.4 (100.0)
No check on private tuition	13	68.4	6	31.6	19	8.5 (100.0)
Quality of teaching at tuition is better than in school	13	68.4	6	31.6	19	8.5 (100.0)
Taking private tuition is a status symbol for students	13	72.2	4	27.8	18	8.0 (100.0)
Professional ethics has no relevance in present context	10	58.8	7	41.2	17	7.6 (100.0)
Because others are indulging in private tuition	9	64.3	5	35.7	14	6.3 (100.0)
Others	1	100.0	-	-	1	0.4 (100.0)
Total*	124	-	100	-	224	100.0

* Totals vary due to multiple responses.

Table 5.33: Distribution of Respondents According to Reasons for Commercial Venality and Place of Employment

Reasons	Place of Employment				Total	
	Rural		Urban			
	No.	Percentage	No.	Percentage	No.	Percentage
Salary is not sufficient to meet both ends	27	40.3	40	59.7	67	29.9 (100.0)
Out of lust for money students are forced to take tuitions	8	30.8	18	69.2	26	11.6 (100.0)
Money determines the social status	8	36.4	14	63.6	22	9.8 (100.0)
Syllabus can not be completed in school hours	13	61.9	8	38.1	21	9.4 (100.0)
No check on private tuition	7	36.8	12	63.2	19	8.5 (100.0)
Quality of teaching at tuition is better than in school	7	36.8	12	63.2	19	8.5 (100.0)
Taking private tuition is a status symbol for students	4	22.2	14	77.8	18	8.0 (100.0)
Professional ethics has no relevance in present context	7	41.2	10	58.8	17	7.6 (100.0)
Because others are indulging in private tuition	5	35.7	9	64.3	14	6.3 (100.0)
Others	-	-	1	100.0	1	0.4 (100.0)
Total*	86	-	138	-	224	100.0

* Totals vary due to multiple responses.

Table 5.34: Distribution of Respondents According to Remedies for Commercial Venality and the Type of School

Remedies	Type of School				Total	
	Public		Private			
	No.	Percentage	No.	Percentage	No.	Percentage
Enhancement of salary to fulfill the needs of the family	93	48.4	99	51.6	192	16.0 (100.0)
Revisit to professional ethics through seminars	74	50.7	72	49.3	146	12.1(100.0)
Role of students in timely completion of curriculum	66	46.5	76	53.5	142	11.8 (100.0)
Equality in opportunities of education	62	45.6	74	54.4	136	11.3 (100.0)
Role of PTA/VEDC in containing this practice	67	50.4	66	49.6	133	11.1 (100.0)
Check on private tuitions by authorities	75	58.6	53	41.4	128	10.6 (100.0)
Mending stop-gap-arrangement of teachers	78	61.9	48	38.1	126	10.5 (100.0)
Decentralisation of teaching-learning activity	50	49.5	51	50.5	101	8.4 (100.0)
Affecting ACRs of those who indulge in private tuition	55	65.5	29	34.5	84	7.0 (100.0)
Others	4	28.6	10	71.4	14	0.1 (100.0)
Total*	624	-	578	-	1202	100.0

* Totals vary due to multiple responses.

Table 5.35: Distribution of Respondents According to Remedies for Commercial Venality and Sex

Remedies	Sex				Total	
	Male		Female			
	No.	Percentage	No.	Percentage	No.	Percentage
Enhancement of salary to fulfill the needs of the family	88	45.8	104	54.2	192	16.0 (100.0)
Revisit to professional ethics through seminars	64	43.8	82	56.2	146	12.1(100.0)
Role of students in timely completion of curriculum	69	48.6	73	51.4	142	11.8 (100.0)
Equality in opportunities of education	62	45.6	74	54.4	136	11.3 (100.0)
Role of PTA/VEDC in containing this practice	59	44.4	74	55.6	133	11.1 (100.0)
Check on private tuitions by authorities	66	51.6	62	48.4	128	10.6 (100.0)
Mending stop-gap-arrangement	60	47.6	66	52.4	126	10.5 (100.0)
Decentralisation of teaching-learning activity	48	47.5	53	52.5	101	8.4 (100.0)
Affecting ACRs of those who indulge in private tuition	45	53.6	39	46.4	84	7.0 (100.0)
Others	8	57.1	6	42.9	14	0.1 (100.0)
Total*	569	-	633	-	1202	100.0

* Totals vary due to multiple responses.

Views of rural and urban teachers to contain commercial venality among the school teachers are shown in Table 5.36. Equality in opportunities in education (76.5 per cent), mending stop-gap arrangement (75.4 per cent), and affecting ACRs of those who indulge in private tutoring (73.8 per cent) were the prominent corrective measures given by urban teachers to contain commercial venality among school teachers. Check on private tuitions by higher authorities, decentralisation of teaching-learning activity, and role of students in timely completion of curriculum were other less responded remedies given by urban teachers to contain this practice. Urban teachers were three times more vociferous in revealing the corrective measures to contain this practice as compared to their rural counterparts.

Table 5.36: Distribution of Respondents According to Remedies for Commercial Venality and Place of Employment

Remedies	Place of Employment				Total	
	Rural		Urban			
	No.	Percentage	No.	Percentage	No.	Percentage
Enhancement of salary to fulfill the needs of the family	53	27.6	139	72.4	192	16.0 (100.0)
Revisit to professional ethics through seminars	41	28.1	105	71.9	146	12.1(100.0)
Role students in timely completion of curriculum	38	26.8	104	73.2	142	11.8 (100.0)
Equality in opportunities of education	32	23.5	104	76.5	136	11.3 (100.0)
Role of PTA/VEDC in containing this practice	43	32.3	90	67.7	133	11.1 (100.0)
Check on private tuitions by authorities	34	26.6	94	73.4	128	10.6 (100.0)
Mending stop-gap-arrangement	31	24.6	95	75.4	126	10.5 (100.0)
Decentralisation of teaching-learning activity	27	26.7	74	73.3	101	8.4 (100.0)
Affecting ACRs of those who indulge in private tuition	22	26.2	62	73.8	84	7.0 (100.0)
Others	1	7.1	13	92.9	14	0.1 (100.0)
Total*	322	-	880	-	1202	100.0

* Totals vary due to multiple responses.

5.8 Conclusions

From the above analysis, it can be concluded that absenteeism, the first UPP studied among the school teachers was more prevalent in public schools due to ineffective monitoring system and the prevailing practice of populism that was not the case in private schools. The common belief in the administrative bureaucracy, that teaching profession is a leisurely profession and teachers are competent enough to provide better field data as compared to personnel from other non-teaching departments. They put them on non-teaching duties like Census, health surveys and other similar jobs at the cost of teaching. Lack of appreciation for punctual and efficient teachers makes them and others feel discouraged to be efficient. Supportive monitoring system by other stakeholders like community and students was also felt desirable to put things in order. Most of the public schools in the district are without fulltime principals due to lack of regular promotion policy, rather senior teacher of the school are given the responsibility to run the school. Firstly, he is sidelined from his teaching duties for running the school; secondly he has to seek the assurance for support in managing the administrative activities from teaching as well as non-teaching staff rather to exercise legitimate monitoring authority. In this way, individual limitations and virtual authority render him to maintain the required discipline. In the department of school education there have been no appointments of competent non-teaching supportive staff rather all posts are filled on compassionate grounds. Either they are incompetent or are problem creators for the officiating principals. The obvious solution for an officiating principal is to get non-teaching work done from teachers at the cost of teaching.

Autocratic style of officiating principal sometimes further polarise the school staff to take part in day-to-day functioning of the school thus deteriorating the school atmosphere. Public schools generally cater to the needs of the students coming from lower middle class and poor families. Some of them are sometimes first generation school goers and unaware of their rights and obligations that teachers owe towards them. If this is not the case, they have no courage, to raise a voice against irresponsible teachers. Here role of PTA/VEDC members, the ultimate beneficiaries of education system, have been advocated in monitoring the school affairs, though that may be unwelcome for irresponsible teachers. Role of teacher associations to monitor the conduct of their members can also have some significance in this regard, who cater to the welfare of the teachers. Involvement of responsible teachers in running the day-to-day affairs may convey some message to their irresponsible colleagues. These activities can have a supportive role for the principal in mending the affairs of the school.

Students are discriminated on the basis of their socio-economic conditions in public schools. Ordinary students are sometimes not promoted to the next class with the fear of spoiling teacher's board result and thus undermining his performance. Those who conform to the life style of the teachers are bestowed with special privileges at the cost of the deserved ones. Students coming from poor families, who are unable to maintain cleanliness, are not given much attention. Moreover, physical education teachers hardly bother to educate students about cleanliness and personal hygiene that affect their performance. Caste based polarisation is prevalent among the teachers and, is extended even to the student community. Principals make little efforts to control it and sometimes they are a part of it. Making pressure groups on the basis of caste are also prevalent in many public schools.

An IIM-A study (2006) of 400 districts in 13 states has found that more than 50 per cent of Indian children are subscribing to private schools - the highest in the world - due to poor quality of education in public schools. The study has found that involvement of communities like parent-teacher associations in running the state schools, have had a great effect in improving the quality of education in Kerala and Nagaland. The study has suggested that sufficient teaching and supporting staff and good monitoring system are indispensable for maintaining the quality of education. A survey report (2008) brought out by a daily about Tarn Taran a border district in state of Punjab, has blamed the shattered inspection system due to non availability of vehicles and financial resources to maintain and ply them, for the poor quality of education in state run schools. Sen (2008) in his observation also blamed the broken down inspection system for teacher absenteeism, delayed arrival in school and private tuition, for poor quality of education in Indian public schools. He advocated the role of parents and teacher associations in inculcating the work culture among school teachers, in the delivery of school education. The UNESCO's International Institute of Educational Planning study (2007) revealed that 25 per cent absenteeism among school teachers is the second highest in the world and is draining 22.5 per cent funds in India. It also found the practice of ghost teachers and involvement of teachers in mismanagement of the schools as other grey areas of Indian school education system.

The core of the teaching-learning activity is the teacher-student relationship. If teacher, is in the possession of knowledge and desired skill to impart it, and his attitude is empathetic, cooperative and supportive, and the student is ready to acquire the knowledge then the purpose of teaching-learning activity is achieved. Sometimes, authoritarian attitude of the teacher comes in the way in the formation of teacher-student relationship. The data shows that authoritarian attitude is prevalent among the teachers and is comparatively much more among public school teachers as compared to private school counterparts. Hardly any provision is available to diffuse this attitude among the teachers though legislation is there to adopt child centered approach, but there is lack of awareness about it. In-service seminars are considered fruitless as they are only subject oriented and lack teacher motivation and skill enhancement. In the age of materialism and self oriented approach to life, there is hardly a feeling of empathy towards students; rather they are treated as numbers - so many passed or failed - instead of so many personalities made or marred. In practice, the morality is forced on the student community; rather reflected in the teacher and copied by the student. Co-curricular activities are limited in public schools - as they are taken by teachers as extra burden - to convey a feeling of self worth among student community. Shah (1970) in his study found that there was a consensus among various role definers of a school teacher role and they almost unanimously rejected the old authoritarian concept of a teacher role.

6

Summary and Conclusions

6.1 Introduction

Education is considered to have the potential to maintain a social order that is considered desirable in the modern civilised societies through its individual and societal functions. Therefore qualitative, egalitarian and universal educational system at different levels (school, college and university) holds the key to have a dream of that social order in the society. Education, a social institution, has its impact on various social institutions like stratification, polity, economy and religion and is constantly affected by them. Social change, one of the societal functions of education, is the large scale change in the value system of the society. Sometimes undesirable or mundane values take preference over desirable or essential values of human living, in the course of time and space, especially among those, who are made responsible by the society to transmit desirable values across generations, like teachers.

Numerous studies like Chand and Mishra (2004); NUEPA (2005-06); IIM-A (2006); Ghuman (2006); PRATHAM ASER (rural) (2006); UNESCO's IIEP (2007); Punjab Education Development (amendment) Bill (2007); Public Interest Litigation (2007); People Forum (2008); Sen (2008) and Survey Report (2008) have highlighted the plight of school education and, a deviation from basic and desirable professional values among school teachers.

What would be the situation if the deviation from the desirable professional values is among the school teachers, the founder professionals of the entire educational system?

In the light of these observations, the present study was planned to investigate the prevalence of various types of unprofessional practices.

The aims and objectives of the study are:

1. To investigate the role of socio-economic and demographic profile of school teachers in the prevalence of unprofessional practices.
2. To examine the role of the type of the institution in the prevalence of unprofessional practices in school teachers.
3. To learn the status-role of the administrator (officials in the upper hierarchy or management) in the prevalence of unprofessional practices among school teachers.
4. To understand the status-role of students in the prevalence of unprofessional practices among the school teachers.
5. To investigate the status-role of the parents in the prevalence of unprofessional practices among school teachers.
6. To explore the importance of the role of the community (members of parent-teacher association and village educational development committee) in the school system in containing the prevalence of unprofessional practices in school teachers.

The primary objectives of this study were to examine the prevalence of unprofessional practices among the school teachers. Six unprofessional practices investigated are:

Absenteeism: People are not going to work or school when they should be going. Teachers are away from school during their duty hours. Those who have equation with the principal are adjusted with non-teaching duties out of the school. Others take the advantage of higher bureaucratic and political connections in abstaining from school. Kin of the members of the management in private schools, working as teachers in the school, misuse their connections in abstaining from school.

Dereliction of Duty: Dereliction of duty is the failure on the part of the people to do something that they have to do because it is the part of their job. While in the school, teachers do not teach during their teaching hours. Other leisure activities like gossiping, sitting idle in the classroom or in school canteen etc. take priority over teaching.

Lack of Responsibility: People do not have a sense of being accountable for the work or job that is necessary or wanted. School teachers are supposed to possess the knowledge and desired skill to impart that knowledge to the students. Besides transmission of knowledge, they are expected to reconstitute personalities and create productive, moral and responsible social beings. On the contrary, they lack the required zeal and commitment to do this.

Discrimination: To treat a person or a group of people differently on the basis of their skin colour, caste, class, race, religion, sex etc. A sense of universalism is lacking in the teachers. Personal whims do play a role while doing one's duties. Students are not treated without the distinction of caste, class and creed.

Authoritarianism: A manner in which total acquiescence is demanded and there is no freedom for the people to act as they wish. Total obedience is expected from the students and there is no space for empathetic understanding of their feelings.

Commercial Venality: Commercial venality is a corrupt practice that is connected with, profit, and not quality or morality. Public funding, funds, the professional knowledge and skill acquired by the teachers. This knowledge should be used for the welfare of the society and students, but on the contrary it is used for individual welfare and self-development of the teachers through private tutoring.

6.2 Method of Research

In the present study an attempt has been made to learn the deviation from the desirable values called the unprofessional practices among the school teachers followed by the reasons and remedies for each unprofessional practice. The universe of the study was Roopnagar district school teachers. Three hundred and eighty five teachers were included in the sample and 195 teachers were from public schools and 190 were from private schools. Further, 177 male and 208 female teachers were interviewed. Rural and urban differences in the prevalence of UPPs were analysed by interviewing two hundred teachers from rural schools and 185 from urban schools. Case studies were conducted with the other respondents like students, administrators or members of school management, and parents to supplement the findings.

6.3 Major Findings of the Study

Major findings of the study were presented in the preceding chapters. Chapter second presents socio-economic profile of the teachers in the light of the variables like age, marital status, religion, caste, educational attainment, place of origin and rearing, educational level of the previous generation, occupational mobility, family income at the time of joining teaching profession, type and size of the family, family income, occupational preference, age at which first thought of becoming a school teacher came in mind, career decision makers, and length of service. In the third chapter prevalence of six UPPs viz. absenteeism, dereliction of duty, lack of responsibility, discrimination, authoritarianism and commercial venality, were lineated against the type of the institution, sex and place of posting. Fourth chapter was an endeavour to see the relationship between six UPPs and socio-economic factors like age, marital status, religion, caste, designation, place of nurturing, education of the father, occupation of the father, income of the family while joining teaching profession, age at which first thought of becoming a school teacher came in mind, career decision makers, and length of service among the teachers. An attempt was made to ascertain the reasons and corrective measures for six UPPs in chapter five. The reasons and remedies for six UPP were studied according to the type of school, gender and place of posting. The summary and conclusions of these chapters are presented in the following paragraphs.

6.3.1 Socio-economic Profile of the Teachers

A vast majority of the teachers were young. Private school teachers were younger than their public school counterparts. Male and female teachers were almost of the same average age but average age of urban school teachers was more than the rural school teachers. More than two-third of the teachers were married. Among the married more than three-fourth were public school teachers. The sample had equal dominance of teachers belonging to both Hindu and Sikhs religions. Other religions were marginally represented in the sample. More than three-fourth of the teachers were from General Castes. Scheduled Caste teachers outnumbered the Other Backward Castes.

A little more than three-fifth of the teachers were Post Graduates. Among the Post Graduates, urban male teachers teaching in public schools were more than their counterparts. A great majority of the teachers were brought up in an urban environment. Female teachers outnumbered in urban schools as compared to rural schools. A great deal of inter-generational mobility could be seen from the time of father to the present incumbent. Private school teachers were numerically in preponderant position in inter-generational mobility. Nearly three-fifth of the teachers were living in nuclear families. Average size of the family was 1.98 ± 0.62. Minor variations were noticed in type and size of the family in terms of the type of school, gender and place of posting. Average income of the family was Rs. 30528.2 per month.

Public school teachers held sway over their private school counterparts in terms of family income. Female teachers and those posted in urban schools were in sound financial position than their counterparts. While revealing their ambition in life, three-fifth of the teachers wanted to become school teachers. Female and private school teachers were numerically in preponderant position. Who desired to become school teachers nearly four-fifth of them recalled the first thought to become a school teacher at realistic stage. Two-fifth of the teachers decided themselves to become school teachers and other one-third revealed that their parents took the decision for them. Influence of parents was more on female teachers in the choice of their career.

6.3.2 *Prevalence of Unprofessional Practices*

Before drawing conclusions based on the responses, magnitude of each UPP was analysed. It was found that discrimination against the students, commercial venality, and lack of responsibility were leading UPPs among the teachers. Dereliction of duty, absenteeism, and authoritarianism were next less prevalent UPPs among the teachers. Except commercial venality that was the leading UPP among the private school teachers, public school teachers were front runners in all other five UPPs. The differences were quite significant in terms of dereliction of duty, absenteeism and authoritarianism. Male teachers were quite ahead of their female counterparts in absenteeism and dereliction of duty, whereas female teachers were leading in four other UPPs studied. The differences were quite noticeable in discrimination against the students and authoritarianism. Commercial venality, absenteeism and discrimination against the students were more prevalent UPPs among rural school teachers while dereliction of duty was the leading UPP among urban school teachers.

6.3.3 *Correlates of Unprofessional Practices*

Commercial venality was the most prevalent UPP among the young teachers out of lust for making money. Mostly private school teachers represented the youngest group of teachers indulging in private tutoring due to limited salaries. With the increase in the age of the teachers there was a decrease in the prevalence of various UPPs. Unmarried teachers were generally private school teachers and young computer teachers of public schools, and had inclination towards private tutoring. Desire for lavish living and limited salaries was forcing them to indulge in private tutoring instead of teaching during school hours. Most of them had established private academies that guaranteed passing the board examinations in lieu of money. Many of them, were not dependent on their jobs in the schools, rather they were working there for the advertisement of their academies to get students from the schools. On the other hand, majority of the married teachers were public school teachers and having those UPP among them which were caused by the poor monitoring of the schools.

Absenteeism, dereliction of duty, and lack of responsibility were prominent UPPs among the teachers belonging to General Castes whereas commercial venality, authoritarianism, discrimination against students were the leading UPPs among the teachers belonging to Scheduled Castes and Other Backward Castes. Various UPPs investigated in the study were most prevalent among teachers teaching Middle standard classes followed by masters or mistresses teaching High standard classes and least prevalent among the lecturers teaching the Senior Secondary classes. The prevalence of various types of UPPs was on the average three times more among the teachers that were brought up in the urban environment than their rural brought up counterparts. With the increase in the educational level of the father there was a decrease in the prevalence of various UPPs among the school teachers.

There was a relationship between the lower income of the family at the time of joining teaching profession and higher prevalence of various UPPs among the teachers because on the average more than half of the teachers came from low income families. Commercial venality was associated with lower income of the family whereas absenteeism, lack of responsibility and dereliction of duty were associated with higher income of the family. Getting the status of a teacher by joining teaching profession and later on making good money by indulging in private tutoring attracted the youngsters to become school teachers. Making easy money without taking pains for the duties and responsibilities attracted many youngsters to the profession. Those UPPs that were related with basic value system like commercial venality, authoritarianism, discrimination etc. were more prevalent among the young teachers where as UPPs that were related to professional value system like absenteeism, dereliction of duty, lack of responsibility etc. were more prominent among the experienced teachers.

6.3.4 *Reasons and Remedies for Unprofessional Practices*

Anticipating the poor response in admitting to the prevalence of various unprofessional practices among their fraternity by the school teachers, an attempt was made by asking the teachers to state reasons and remedies for various UPPs in order to judge the grimness of the problem as highlighted by other similar studies. Absenteeism, the first UPP studied among the school teachers, was more prevalent in public schools due to ineffective local and hierarchical monitoring system. The prevailing practice of populism, that principal does not want to spoil relations with subordinates in public schools was another reason for this practice, which was not the case in private schools which, were better governed. The easy going public school teachers are considered the best personnel for doing Census, health surveys and other similar jobs at the cost of teaching. Lack of appreciation for efficient and punctual teachers, disheartened them and others. Strict monitoring by the stakeholders in education like parents, community and awakened students was felt desirable to put things in order.

Most of the public schools in the district do not have fulltime principals due to lack of regular promotion policy. In their absence, senior teachers of the school are given the responsibility to run the school. Without authority he is unable to use strict measures against the staff to contain the UPPs like dereliction of duty. Most of the times, the officiating duties are furthered passed on to junior teachers, when some senior teachers specially female teachers refuse to take the responsibility of officiating principal, thus undermining the worth of the chair.

Due to non-availability and incompetency of the supporting staff, all the non-teaching duties within the school like; maintenance of records, preparing pay-rolls, carrying reports to the district offices etc., rest on the teachers at the cost of teaching. Department of school education has made compulsory for all teachers to attend in-service seminars to reinvent the lost glory of professionalism among them, for the last several years. Some senior fellow teachers are chosen as resource persons in the seminars. Teachers take them lightly and consider them as the wastage of time due to their inability to add to the knowledge and skills of the seminarians due to lack of knowledge of the subject related to pedagogic practices and professional ethics at the cost of their basic duties. Autocratic style of the officiating principal sometimes further polarises the school staff to take part in day-to-day functioning of the school thus further deteriorating the school atmosphere.

Public schools generally cater to the needs of the students coming from lower middle class and poor families. Some of them sometimes happen to be first generation school goers and unaware of their rights and obligations that teachers owe towards them. Further, they have no courage to raise a voice against irresponsible teachers. Here, role of PTA/VEDC members, the ultimate beneficiaries of education system, was advocated in monitoring the school affairs, though that may not be welcomed by the irresponsible teachers. Role of teacher's associations who cater to the welfare of the teachers could also have some significance in this regard. Involvement of responsible teachers in running the day-to-day affairs might convey some message to their irresponsible colleagues. These activities could have a supportive role for the principal in mending the affairs of the school.

Public Schools were also plagued with discrimination against the students on the basis of socio-economic conditions. Who are active, obedient, intelligent and maintain personal hygiene attract teacher's attention while others are not even promoted fearing spoiling teacher's board results. Many are thus devoid of availing life chances due to their miserable conditions. District Roopnagar is easily approachable from Chandigarh, the state Capital of Punjab, and it satellite towns of Panchkula and Mohali. Most of the teachers, specially the female teachers, come from these towns by chartered vehicles, in large groups. They are both kith and kin of the state bureaucracy or political masters and have got posted adjoining to Chandigarh by using their social and cultural capital. They get their postings here, to get coaching of their wards from reputed coaching institutions in Chandigarh for entry into high-tech engineering, medical and other such courses. They are hardly bothered to uplift the students coming from lower socio-economic background and serve as pressure groups if some one dares to question them for that. They are here to preserve their cultural capital with the help of their social capital. School have also become a place for promotion of casteeism . It starts from the head and finds place among student community through teachers. Caste based pressure groups are taking toll on teaching- learning atmosphere of government schools.

The crux of the teaching-learning activity is the teacher-student relationship. If teacher is in the possession of knowledge and desired skill to impart it, his attitude is empathetic, cooperative and supportive, and the student is ready to acquire the knowledge as a virtue then the purpose of the teaching-learning activity is achieved. Primary data support s the prevalence of authoritarian attitude among the school teachers and grein magnitude among government school teachers. This hinders the formation of student-teacher relationship. Indian law does not permit this attitude in school teachers. Neither stakeholder are sensitive about it nor any provision to overcome it.

In-service seminars are only subject oriented, in the absence of resource persons from the fields of Sociology and Psychology. Empathetic attitude was totally missing among the teachers, students were treated as numbers by the teachers, and so many passed or failed, instead of so many personalities made or spoiled. Morality is another virtuous thing that is to be transmitted through the school teacher across generations. It is coerced on the students in stead of nurtured among them by becoming role models. Co-curricular activities are almost non-existent in public schools as they are taken as extra burden on the teacher.

Commercial venality was the only UPP that was heavily prevalent among private school teachers. Private schools that were philanthropic social institutions earlier have now become profit ogranisations. Though principal and members of management committee were governing the schools excellently but there was a large gap what they charged from the students and what they paid to the teachers. Low salary forced private school teachers to indulge in private tutoring, a practice declared unethical by UNESCO. When teachers asked for increment in salary they were told to make way for others willing to work on low salary. This stop-gap-arrangement took the toll on teaching-learning activity. In service seminars, that are thought to motivate the school teachers were restricted only for government school teachers and were not available for private school teachers. The government school teachers indulging in private tutoring were very limited. On the other hand every second private school teacher was found taking tuitions. It seemed that private schools have made education a private commodity or a place to gain teaching experience to other government service.

6.4 Conclusions

The teachers studied were young and majority of them were married. Public school teachers were more experienced than their private school counterparts. The profession was dominated by teachers belonging to both Hindu and Sikh religions. Teachers belonging to Scheduled Caste and Other Backward Castes were in minority and majority of the teachers were Post Graduates. Urban schools had accommodated a major section of female teachers and a vast majority in the sample came from urban background. Higher inter-generational mobility was observed in private school teachers as compared to public school counterparts. A preponderant section of teaching community was living in nuclear family. Female teachers of public schools were financially well off than their counterparts. Female teachers of private schools were more ambitious about the school teaching profession as compared to their colleagues but at the same time a major section of them joined the profession when avenues exhausted for them. For female teachers parents had a role in the choice of the profession.

Among the six UPPs studied among the school teachers, discrimination against the students, commercial venality and lack of responsibility were some prominent UPPs among the school teachers. Besides commercial venality public school teachers were front runners among the other five UPPs. Absenteeism and dereliction of duty were prominent UPPs among male teachers whereas female teachers had inclination towards authoritarianism and discrimination against the students. Rural teachers were leading in commercial venality and absenteeism, while urban teachers were ahead in dereliction of duty.

Reciprocal relationship was found between age and the prevalence of various UPPs among teachers. Married teachers were prominent in UPPs like absenteeism, dereliction of duty and lack of responsibility. A similar observation was noticed among the teachers belonging to General Castes. Commercial venality was the leading UPP among the young unmarried teachers belonging to Scheduled Castes. On the whole UPPs were more prominent among General Castes and least among Other Backward Castes. An inverse relationship was found between UPPs and the classes being taught according to the designation of the teachers. High prevalence of UPPs was found among teachers coming from urban background.

In the absence of regular principal and other monitoring staff, absenteeism was plaguing the public schools. The officiating principals were ineffective in monitoring the public schools and moreover the practice of populism at the part of officiating principals was keeping the teachers away from schools during duty hours. Involvement of public school teachers in non-teaching duties like Census, health surveys etc. at the cost of teaching and was taking the toll of teaching-learning activity. Supportive role of other stakeholders like parents and community was suggested to overcome this practice. This practice is absent in private schools due to effective monitoring system of the local management. Dereliction of duty was also the repercussion of ineffective governance and erosion of professional commitment, among the teaching community. Shortage of non-teaching staff and lack of coordination with the officiating principals in public schools, the involvement of teachers in performing non-teaching duties were keeping them away from classes. Rampant factionalism among teachers due to poor governance in the schools was another reason in spoiling the congenial environment of the public schools.

In-service seminars which were organised only for public school teachers were not found effective to motivate the teachers due to incompetent resource persons. Supportive role teacher associations and other stakeholders were suggested to reinvent the lost professionalism among school teachers. Subjective outlook of teachers and poor socio-economic conditions of the students were the main reasons found for discrimination against students. Caste based polarisation was found among the teaching community in the formation of pressure groups to assert their individual motives. Authoritative attitude was observed among the teaching fraternity and was undermining the formation of student-teacher relationship. Provision of in-service seminars was there for public school teachers to overcome authoritarian attitude but lack of competent resource persons undermined their effectiveness. In spite of legislation, to adopt child centered approach, in the formation of student-teacher relationship but nobody was aware about it. Private schools were better governed than the public schools but they were the breeding grounds for private tutoring. Teachers were underpaid and forced to take tuitions to meet the both ends. Consistent reshuffling of teachers in private schools, due to job insecurity and low pay, was undermining to the teaching-learning activity in private schools. Private schools were virtually left for the commercialisation of education.

6.5 Theoretical Importance and Practical Significance of the Study

In the process of acquisition of formal education the desirable status-roles, contents and context of learning are predefined and determined. Desirable status-role is the action or behaviour expected of the individual holding a particular status in a particular situation of interaction. Sometimes personal belief system, priorities of life, context of activity etc. put such an effect that a particular status-role holder deviates from the desired role. If the deviance is to such an extent that starts affecting the outcome of a particular activity, then the role of the particular status-role holder become undesired. If the status-role holder is a professional then his/her role becomes unprofessional. In case of education, if various status-role holders deviate from the desired roles, then the structure of social relationships change, which ultimately affect the functions of education in society. To study the change in the social structure of education is the concern of sociology. To study the change in the behavioural pattern of a professional (school teacher in this case), is the concern of sociology of professions.

The present study is an endeavour to assess the prevalence of unprofessional practices, reasons behind the prevalence of a particular unprofessional practice and remedial measures in containing that unprofessional practice, among school teachers. Inferences drawn from the study may also help the researchers for doing the comparative studies and setting hypothesis for the future studies. Findings of the study may help the policy makers for the prevention and remedy of the prevalence of unprofessional practices among school teachers in general. Nevertheless, there are certain suggestions for the state and policy makers:

1. In the present system appointments of school teachers are made on the basis of academic and professional qualifications only, and there is no measure to assess the teaching aptitude of the candidates. Some questionnaire to assess the teaching aptitude may help the appointing authorities that right people join the teaching profession.
2. The regular promotion policy may help the public schools to get full fledged principals to strengthen the monitoring system at the institution level as well at the upper level which is the need of hour.
3. The private schools should come in the purview of state auditing agency so that they should not serve as the profit making and teacher exploiting agencies in the name of quality education providers.
4. Public school teachers should be entrusted with teaching duties and should not be engaged in maintaining the school records while in the school and other enumeration duties outside the school.
5. The collective vigilance by the parents and the community, like the case in Himachal Pradesh that played an important role in preserving the accountability of the state run schooling system, should be replicated in the other states.

Appendices

Appendix (i)

Table 1: Frequency of Country Examined in Published Comparative Studies*

Sr. No.	Country	Single Profession (Across Countries)	Multiple Professions (Across Countries)	Total
1	United States	32	67	99
2	United Kingdom	35	50	85
3	Germany	12	20	32
4	France	8	22	30
5	Sweden	13	16	29
6	Canada	17	10	27
7	Netherlands	17	5	22
8	Australia	4	9	13
9	Czechoslovakia/ Czech Republic	3	9	12
10	Italy	3	9	12
11	Finland	8	4	12
12	USSR/Russia	6	5	11
13	India	1	6	7
14	Norway	6	1	7
15	Belgium	2	3	5
16	Greece	2	3	5
17	Israel	1	4	5
18	Japan	3	2	5
19	Denmark	3	1	4
20	Mexico	2	2	4
21	China	2	1	3
22	Egypt	1	2	3
23	New Zealand	2	1	3
24	Poland	1	2	3
25	Spain	2	1	3
26	Nigeria	-	2	2
27	Pakistan	1	1	2
28	Armenia	-	1	1
29	Argentina	-	1	1

Table 1 continue

Table 1 continue

Sr. No.	Country	Single Profession (Across Countries)	Multiple Professions (Across Countries)	Total
30	Bangladesh	1	-	1
31	Bolivia	-	1	1
32	Brazil	-	1	1
33	Colombia	-	1	1
34	Ethiopia	-	1	1
35	Guatemala	1	-	1
36	Hong Kong	1	-	1
37	Indonesia	-	1	1
38	Ireland	-	1	1
39	Lithuania	-	1	1
40	Malaysia	-	1	1
41	Manchuria	-	1	1
42	Philippines	-	1	1
43	Saudi Arabia	1	-	1
44	South Africa	1	-	1
45	Switzerland	-	1	1

* Individual studies may have been coded to more than on category.

Table 2: Frequency of Professions Examined in Published Comparative Studies*

Sr. No.	Country	Single Country (Across Professions)	Multiple Countries (Across Countries)	Total
1	Physicians	30	45	75
2	Lawyers	14	19	33
3	Nurses	14	19	33
4	Midwives	5	22	27
5	Academics/ Professors	8	7	15
6	Teachers	11	2	13
7	Health Workers (allied,etc.)	3	8	11
8	Engineers	6	5	11
9	Pharmacists	6	3	9
10	CAM Professions	4	4	8

Table 2 continue

Table 2 continue

Sr. No.	Country	Single Country (Across Professions)	Multiple Countries (Across Countries)	Total
11	Psychologist/ Mental Health Worker	7	1	8
12	Social Workers	6	2	8
13	Architect	3	3	6
14	Manager	3	3	6
15	Clergy	3	3	6
16	Accountant	2	2	4
17	Dentist	2	2	4
18	Military	1	3	4
19	Scientist	3	1	4
20	Journalist	2	1	3
21	Occupational Therapist	2	1	3
22	Optometrist	3	-	3
23	Veterinarian	2	1	3
24	Banker	-	2	2
25	Business Administrator	2	-	2
26	Chiropodist	1	-	1
27	Library Scientist	1	-	1
28	Masseur	1	-	1
29	Physiotherapist	-	1	1
30	Police Officer	-	1	1
31	Politician	1	-	1
32	Prison Guard	1	-	1
33	Public Relations	1	-	1

* Individual studies may have been coded to more than on category.
CAM: Complementary and alternative medicine

Table 3: Frequency of Themes/Content Areas Addresses in Published Studies*

Level	Highest Order Theme	Theme	Total (Percentage)	Rank Order
Micro	Individual Professional or Local Level Relations	Private Sphere	7.2	15**
		Clients/Patients	12.6	13
		Orientations/DecAision Making	7.2	15**
		Work Conditions	24.6	4
Meso	Intra-professional Level	Education	17.4	9**
		Occupational Distribution	5.8	17
		Professionalisation	16.4	10
	Inter-professional Level	Recruitment	2.9	20
		Inter-professional Relations	13	12
Macro	Inequality and Stratification	Gender/Sexual Stratification	21.7	5
		Race/Ethnicity Stratification	3.4	19
		Social Class Stratification	5.8	17
		Occupational Segregation/Segmentation	8.2	14
		Occupational Stratification	18.4	7
	Profession-state or Profession-political Economy Structural Levelof Relations	Autonomy and Governance Mechanisms	19.8	6
		Relations with State/Regulation	35.3	2
		Work Organisation	41.1	1
		Organisational Change/Restructuring	26.1	3
		Globalisation	6.7	16
	Ideational or Ideological Level	Classifications	2.4	21
		Ethics	3.8	18

Table 3 continue

Table 3 continue

Level	Highest Order Theme	Theme	Total (Percentage)	Rank Order
		Knowledge	15	11
		Professionalism and Professional Socialisation	17.9	8
		Status/Prestige	17.4	9**

*Individual studies may have been coded to more than on category so frequencies will not add up to 100 per cent.

**Indicates a tied position.

Appendix (ii)

Department of Sociology, Guru Nanak Dev University, Amritsar-143005, Punjab.

INTERVIEW SCHEDULE
for

A Sociological Study to Investigate the Prevalence of Unprofessional Practices Among School Teachers in Roopnagar District.

1. Name (in full): Miss/Mrs./Mr.____________________________
2. Age:____
3. Marital Status:

   1. Married 2. Unmarried

   3. Widowed 4. Separated/Divorced

4. Gender

   1. Male 2. Female

5. Religion

   1. Hindu 2. Muslim

   3. Sikh 4. Christian

   5. Jain 6. Buddhist

   7. Any Other (specify)__________________________

6. Caste

   1. SC 2. OBC

   3. General

7. Educational Qualification:
    1. Higher Secondary/Senior Secondary
    2. Graduate
    3. Post Graduate
    4. Doctorate
    5. Others (specify) ______________________________
8. Designation:
    1. Lecturer
    2. Master/Mistress
    3. Teacher (Art&Craft/Phy.Edu./Language)
9. School from which you did your Higher Secondary/Senior Secondary was Located in:
    1. Rural Area (Village)   2. Urban Area (City/Town)
10. Father's highest educational qualification:
    1. Matric/Higher Secondary
    2. Senior Secondary
    3. Graduate
    4. Post Graduate
    5. Others (Specify) _______________________
11. Father's occupation:
    1. Farming
    2. Business and/or industry
    3. Government service (civil and military)
    4. Professions (non-teaching)
    5. Professions (teaching)
    6. Others
    7. No response
12. Approximate income of the family when you joined teaching profession: (Rs)___________________(per month)

    Information about family:-

13. Total number of members in the family (present):

    1. 1-3 2. 4-6
    3. 7-9 4. 10 or More

14. Socio-economic and demographic profile of the family (present):

Relationship with head of the household	Age	Sex	Marital status	Education Occupation	Income per month
1. Self					
2.					
3.					
4.					
5.					
6.					
7.					
8.					
9.					

15. What was your aim in life?

    1. To become a civil/defense servant
    2. To become an engineer/doctor/lawyer
    3. To become a businessman
    4. To go abroad
    5. To become a school teacher
    6. Others (specify)____________________

16. Give the tentative age, when the idea of becoming a teacher came to your mind:______________

17. Who influenced you to become a teacher?

    1. Self 2. Father
    3. Mother 4. Brother
    5. Sister 6. Close relatives
    7. Teachers 8. Two or more

18. When did you join the service as a teacher? ____________(years)

19. Type of the school:

    1. Government 2. Private

20. Whether the school falls in rural or urban area?

    1. Rural (village) 2. Urban (city/town)

21. Classes being taught:
    1. High School
    2. Higher/Senior Secondary School

Overall environment of the school

22. How do you find the overall environment of the school?
    1. Satisfactory
    2. Not satisfactory
23. Do teachers of your school attend school regularly?
    1. Yes
    2. No
24. If no, what are the reasons of their absence?

(You can encircle more than one options)

25. Posted far away from home
26. Doing side business to enhance the earnings
27. Forcibly engaged in non-teaching activities
28. Lack of check on their attendance
29. Having adjustment with the principal
30. Having high bureaucratic and political connections
31. Job security
32. Others are not attending
33. Atmosphere of the school is not good
34. Lack of healthy relations with the colleagues
35. Other (please specify)

(Your opinion is appreciated whether answered in Yes or No)

37. Periodical and surprise check of attendance by higher authorities/school management
38. Greater role of students in persuading teachers to attend the school
39. Involvement of Parent Teachers Association/Village Education Development Committees in checking the attendance of the teachers
40. Increasing casual leave of the teachers
41. Greater role of peer group teachers in persuading to attend the school
42. Becoming the role model at the part of the school principal in the enhancement of the teachers attendance
43. Entry of teachers yearly attendance in their ACRs
44. Rewarding those teachers with highest attendance at school/district/state level functions
45. Abstaining teachers from non teaching duties
46. Posting teachers in the vicinity of their homes
47. Others (please specify)

48. When in school, do teachers of your school attend classes regularly?

1. Yes 2. No

49. If no, what are the reasons that teachers of your school do not attend their classes regularly?

(You can encircle more than one option)

50. Students are not serious in their studies
51. Members of peer group are not attending their classes
52. Intelligence level of students is very low
53. Nobody checks whether you attend the class or not
54. There is no appreciation for those who attend classes regularly
55. Non-teaching work restrain them from attending classes regularly
56. Equation with the principal helps them in not taking classes regularly
57. Officiating principals are not effective in governance
58. Not being paid adequately
59. Non-availability of teaching-learning material
60. Non-conducive teaching-learning atmosphere in the school
61. Others (please specify)

62. Please give your opinion for the improvement in teachers attending their classes regularly.

(Your opinion is appreciated whether answered in Yes or No)

63. Regular and surprise checks of the classroom teaching by the higher officials/members of the management committee of the school
64. Through teacher motivation by encouraging them to attend seminars conducted by psychologists, sociologists, educationists besides subject specialists
65. Through seeking their active participation as a member of the team lead by the principal in running the day to day affairs of the school
66. Giving the teacher an absolute autonomy and making him the master of the class in conducting the teaching-learning process
67. Enhancing close coordination between the members of Parent Teacher Association/Village Education Developmental Committees and the teachers
68. Encouraging the students in motivating the teachers for the importance of their presence in the class for their future prospects
69. Periodical evaluation of the teachers attitude toward work or towards their profession through filling questionnaires by the higher authorities
70. Keeping teachers away from non-teaching activities
71. Others (please specify)

Responsibility towards students

72. Do teachers of your school feel a sense of responsibility towards their students?

    1. Yes 2. No

73. If no, give reasons why teachers do not feel a sense of responsibility towards their students.

(*You can encircle more than one option*)

74. Students are irresponsible and are not serious about their future
75. Transmission of the knowledge of the subject to the student is the only duty of a teacher
76. Teachers are not adequately paid
77. The role of the parents are limited to the fulfillment of physical needs of their wards and are ignorant of the importance of other social needs
78. Members of the peer group are not responsible
79. Members of the peer group indulging in non-teaching activities are appreciated
80. Burdened by personal problems during school hours
81. Preference to other leisure activities at the cost of teaching during school hours
82. Not aware of the importance of regular schooling in molding life of the students
83. Due to job security service is taken for granted
84. Others (please specify)

85. Please give your opinion, how teachers can be made more responsible towards their duties?

(*Your opinion is appreciated whether answered in Yes or No*)

86. Making the students aware about their rights and, the duties teachers are supposed to perform for the welfare of the students
87. Making teachers accountable for their indecent behavior towards the students by the officials in the upper hierarchy/school management
88. Through greater interaction between the members of Parent Teachers Association/Village Education Developmental Committees and the teachers
89. Reminding them the significance of the role of a schoolteacher in shaping the life of a student through motivational seminars and orientation lectures
90. Through greater role of Teachers Associations in inspiring the teachers to become the role models for the students
91. Through decentralisation process at the part of the higher authorities to give the teachers a full autonomy in the classroom affairs

92. By appreciating and encouraging, at the part of the higher authorities/ members of parent-teacher association or village educational developmental committees, those teachers with great sense of responsibility in sharpening the minds, shaping the personalities and molding the characters of the students
93. By posing a full faith and seeking a greater role at the part of the principal from all the members of the teaching community in the school in running day to day affairs of the school
94. Others (please specify)

Relationship with students

95. Do teachers of your school treat all students equally?

    1. Yes   2. No

96. If no, according to your opinion what could be the reasons that all students do not get equal treatment from the teachers? (You can encircle more than one option)

97. All students are not intelligent and are not serious about their studies
98. Students are discriminated according to acceptance to the personal whims of the teachers
99. All students do not belong to the caste the teachers belong to
100. All students do not belong the religion the teachers belong to
101. All students do not have the way of life the teachers believe to live
102. Students are discriminated according to the social class they belong to
103. All students do not belong to the province the teachers belong to
104. Discrimination on the basis of language
105. Discrimination on the basis of cleanliness and personal hygiene
106 .Others (please specify)

107. Please give your opinion, how teachers can be made to treat all students equally?

    (*Your opinion is appreciated whether answered in Yes or No*)

108. By discouraging caste based polarisation among students as well as teachers at part of the principal
109. Giving the campus a secular outlook through mottos, lectures, National song and Anthem etc.
110. Inculcating the habits of cleanliness and personal hygiene among the students through physical education teachers of the school
111. Introduction of the topics based on moral science in the curriculum at the part of the persons responsible for curriculum development
112. Through greater efforts by members of Parent Teachers Association/ Village Education Developmental Committees in inculcating a sense of universalism among the teachers towards the students

113. By addition of columns at the part of official in the upper hierarchy/ school management in assessing the objective outlook of the teachers, in their ACRs , and gradation through the questionnaire filled by the students
114. Through the greater role of the students in persuading teachers to become role models for them in shaping unbiased personalities
115. Through periodical teacher motivational lectures and seminars in understanding the importance of their role in the development of objective personalities in containing the social evils
116. Through self realisation at the part of peer group by the query, "if you had encountered a biased teacher in your student life, would you have become a teacher?"
117. Others (please specify)

118. Do teachers of your school honor the feelings of the students?

1. Yes 2. No

119. If no, please give your opinion why teachers do not honor the feelings of their students? (You can encircle more than one option)

120. Students are not their own children
121. It is the moral duty of the students to obey their teachers
122. Students do not possess the skill and knowledge which the teachers have
123. Students are ignorant of their rights and the duties teachers owe towards their students
124. Teachers are ignorant of the importance of empathetic understanding of the feelings of the students in the development of productive personalities
125. It is good practice for a teacher to have an authoritative image in disciplining the students
126. Teachers got their authoritative outlook from their teachers
127. Principal and members of peer group are authoritative
128. Parents want the teachers of their wards to be authoritative
129. Others (please specify)

130. Please give your opinion how teachers can be made student friendly?

(*Your opinion is appreciated whether answered in Yes or No*)

131. By making students aware of their rights and the obligations teachers owe towards them through declamations, debates, lectures etc. on model teachers
132. Through greater interaction of students with teachers in persuading them the importance of their friendly attitude in the development of constructive personalities
133. A sincere effort on the part of the principal to have non-authoritative outlook and the role of the members of the peer group in maintaining a friendly attitude towards the students in the school

134. Through greater efforts by the members of Parent Teachers Association/ Village Education Developmental Committees in persuading the teachers in the maintenance of student friendly attitude
135. By addition of columns at the part of officials in the upper hierarchy/ school management assessing the non-authoritative attitude of the teachers, in their ACRs , and gradation through the questionnaire filled by the students
136. Through periodical teacher motivational lectures and seminars in understanding the importance of their empathic attitude towards the students in containing the inhibitions and development of balanced personalities
137. Through recommendations from educationists for the use of student oriented teaching methods instead of directional methods
138. At the part of the principals to encourage the teachers for greater participation in co-curricular activities of the students to diffuse their authoritative image
139. Regular therapeutic counselling of teachers with authoritative outlook to overcome it
140. Others (please specify)

Commercialisation of profession

141. Do the services of the teachers of your school are available for private hire and sale?

1. Yes 2. No

142. If yes, please give your opinion why the services of the teachers of your school are available for private hire and sale? (You can encircle more than one option)

143. Salary is not sufficient to fulfill the basic needs of the family
144. The social status of person is determined only by the possession of monetary assets
145. Because the members of peer group are indulging in such practices
146. There is no check from high authorities/school management whether you indulge in such practices or not
147. Lengthy syllabus can not be covered in the school hours
148. The quality of services provided privately is better than those provided during school hours
149. There is no difference in the quality of services provided privately or publicly, but mere for the satisfaction of parents and students
150. The professional ethics like service for the welfare of the community and not for personal gains, has no relevance in the present context
151. Out of the lust for making more money, students are forced to take private tuitions
152 Others (please specify)

153. Please give your opinion, how private hire and sale of the services of the school teachers can be controlled?

(*Your opinion is appreciated whether answered in Yes or No*)

154. Enhancement in the wages to fulfill the basic needs of the family
155. Through greater role of the students in making classroom teaching-learning activity more conducive for timely completion of the curriculum
156. Through greater check on the part of the officials in the upper hierarchy/ school management on the teachers indulging in private tuitions or other side business
157. Through greater efforts by the members of Parent Teachers Association/ Village Education Developmental Committees in persuading the parents not send their wards for private tuitions and on the other hand a constant look on the teaching-learning activity in the school
158. A quick effort on the part of the higher officials/school management to reappoint teachers in case of retirement or transfer and to discourage frequent change of teachers
159. A sincere effort on the part of the national authorities to universalise the content of curriculum and a collective effort by the other agents in the school system to achieve the set standard in education
160. Through periodical in service teacher motivational lectures and seminars by psychologists, sociologists, educationists, social workers and spiritual personalities to remind the teachers the ethics of teaching profession
161. By addition of columns at the part of officials in the upper hierarchy/ school management, in teachers ACRs ,whether they indulge in private hire and sale of their services or not
162. By further decentralisation of evaluation system at the part of the concerned authorities to make it less marks oriented and posing more faith in subject teacher
163. Others (please specify)

164. Rate your opinion about the following items on the five point scale:

5. Strongly Agree 4. Fairly Agree
3. Agree 2. Disagree
1. Strongly Disagree

165.	Teachers are not going to the school when they should be going	5	4	3	2	1
166.	Those who are in school do not teach during their teaching hours	5	4	3	2	1
167.	Not sincere about their duties as teachers	5	4	3	2	1
168.	Treat the students with the distinction of caste, class and creed	5	4	3	2	1

169. Teachers impose themselves as the ultimate authority over the students	5	4	3	2	1
170. The possession of skill and knowledge is meant for private hire and sale, and not for the welfare of the students	5	4	3	2	1

171. Any other remarks

References

Abbott, A., The System of Professions: An Essay on the Division of Expert Labour, Chicago: I.L. University Chicago Press, 1988, cited from *Current Sociology* 57, 475-485, 2009.

————————, "Sociology of Professions", in N. J. Smelser and P. B. Baltes (eds) *International Encyclopedia of the Social and Behavoural Sciences,* Amsterdam: Elsevier Science, 2002, cited from *Current Sociology* 57, 475-485, 2009.

Aikara, Jacob, *Education: Sociological Perspective,* Jaipur: Rawat Publications, 2004.

Aldridge, M. and Evetts, J., "Rethinking the Concept of Professionalism: The Case of Journalism", *The British Journal of Sociology,* 54(4), 547-64, 2003, cited from *Current Sociology* 57, 475-485, 2009.

Altbach, P.G., "The Distorted Guru: The College Teacher in Bombay", in Suma Chitnis and P.G. Altbach (eds), *The Indian Academic Profession,* Delhi: Macmillan, 1979.

ASER (Annual Status of Education Report), 2006, Accessed from www.pratham.org/aser2006.php on August 20, 2008.

Aurora, G.S. and Rao, Radha, "Institutionalisation of Western Science in India " in M.N. Srinivas et al. (eds), *Dimensions of Social Change in India,* New Delhi: Allied Publishers, 506-18, 1977.

Atal, Yogesh, *Indian Sociology from Where to Where,* Jaipur: Rawat Publications, 2003.

Benoit, C. and Heitlinger, A., "Women's Health Care Work in Comparative Perspective: Canada, Sweden, and Czechoslovakia/ Czeh Republic as Case Examples", *Social Science and Medicine* 47(8), 1101-11, cited from *Current Sociology* 57, 475-485, 2009.

Bhoite, V.B., *Sociology of Indian Intellectuals,* Jaipur: Rawat, 1987.

Bledstein, B.J., *The Culture of Professionalism*, New York: Norton, 1976.

Blau, P., et al., "Occupational Choice: A Conceptual Framework", *Industrial and Labour Relations Review,* July, 1956.

Bowles, Samuel, "Unequal Education and the Reproduction of the Social Division of Labour", in *Schooling in a Corporate Society,* (eds),

Martin Carnoy, N.Y.: David Mckay, Inc., 1972, in Parelius, A. P. and Pereluis, R. J., *The Sociology of Education,* New Jersey: Rutgers State University of New Jersey, 1978.

Bowles, S and Gintis, H. T., *Schooling in Capitalist America: Education Reform and the Contradictions of Economic* Life, New York: Basic Books, 1976.

Brint, S., *In an Age of Experts: The Changing Role of Professionals in Politics and Public Life,* Princeton N.Y.: Princeton University Press, 1994, cited from *Current Sociology* 57, 475-485, 2009.

Britto, Rita, *Unequal Schools,* Ph.D. Thesis Submitted to Tata Institute of Social Sciences, Bombay, 1987.

Carr-Saunders, A.M., *Professions: Their Organisation and Place in Society,* London: The Clarendon Press Oxford, 4-6, 1928, in Sheo Kumar Lal, *Readings in Sociology of Professions,* Delhi: Gian Publishing House, 48, 1988.

Carr-Saunders, A. M. and Wilson, P.A., *The Professions,* London: Oxford University Press, 1933, in Sheo Kumar Lal, *Readings in Sociology Of Professions,* Delhi: Gian Publishing House, 62, 1988.

--------, "The Emergence of Professions"; in Sigmund Nosow and William H. Form, (eds), *Men, Work and Society: A Reader in the Sociology of Occupation,* New York: Basic Books, 199-256, 1962.

Chand Vikram K. and Deepak Mishra, "Resuming Punjab's Prosperity", A World Bank Report Released at Institute of Communication and Development, Mohali, 22nd of December, 2004.

Chattergee, B. and Khan, Q., "Basic Education: The Quality Puzzle", *IDPAD News Letter,* 1(1), 2003.

Chandani, Ambika, *The Medical Profession: A Sociological Exploration,* New Delhi: Jainsons Publications, 1985.

Chauhan, Ompal Singh, *A study of Teacher's Professional Responsibility, Teaching Attitude and Organisational Climate between Government and Privately Managed Schools,* Ph.D. Thesis Submitted to Meerut University, 1995.

Census, 2001.

Chitnis, Suma, *The Teachers Role in the College System,* Unpublished Ph.D. Thesis, Bombay: Tata Institute of Social Sciences, 1973.

Chitnis, S. and Altbach, P. G., (eds), *The Academic Profession in India,* New Delhi: MacMillan, 1979.

Chubb, J., and Moe, T., *Politics, Markets and American Schools,* Washington DC: Brookings Institute, 1990, cited from *Current Sociology* 57, 581-605, 2009.

Cogan, Morris L., "Toward a Definition of Profession", *Harvard Educational Review,* 23, 1953, in Chandani, Ambika, *The Medical Profession: A Sociological Exploration,* New Delhi: Jainsons Publications, 7, 1985.

Code of Ethics of the National Education Association of the United States,Adopted by the Representative Assembly, Detroit, Mich., 1952, in William O. Stanley, et al., "Organisation, Functions, and Problemsof the Teaching Profession", in *Social Foundations of Education, University* of Illinois, 1967.

Code of Professional Ethics for Indian School Teachers, NCERT, New Delhi. Accessed from http://www.education.nic.in/cd50years/f/93/HP/93HP0F01.htm on December 19, 2009.

Cohen, L., Wilkinson, A., Arnold, J. and Rachael, F., "'Remember I'm the Bloody Architect!' Architects, Organisations and Discourses of Profession", *Work, Employment and Society* 19(4), 575-96, 2005, cited from *Current Sociology* 57, 475-485, 2009.

Collins, Randall, "Functional and Conflict Theory of Educational Stratification", in J. Karabel, and A.M. Halsey, (eds), *Power and Ideology in Education,* New York: Penguin Books, 1977.

Damle, Y.D., "The Role of a Teacher in Developing Society", in S.P. Ruhela (eds), *Sociology of Teaching Profession,* NCERT, New Delhi, 1970.

Davies, S. and Guppy, N., "Globalisation and Educational Reforms Anglo-American Democracies", *Comparative Education Review* 41, 435-59, 1997, cited from *Current Sociology* 57, 581-605, 2009.

Davies, S. and Quirke, L., "The Impact of Sector on School Organisation: Institutional and Market Logics", *Sociology of Education* 24(1), 60-89, 2007, cited from *Current Sociology* 57, 581-605, 2009.

Derebello, Daphne Margaret, *Formal Schooling and Personal Efficacy,* New Delhi: Sterling, 1979.

De Vries, R., Benoit, C., van Teijlingen, E. and Wrede, S. (eds), Birth by Design: Pregnancy, Maternity Care and Midwifery in North America and Europe, New York: Routledge, 2001, cited from *Current Sociology* 57, 475-485, 2009.

District Information System for Education (DISE), EMIS Wing, Sarva ShikshaAbhiyan Authority, Punjab, 2005

Dubey, S.M., *Social Mobility Among the Professions,* Bombay: Popular Prakashan, 1975.

Durkheim, Emile, *Moral Education: A Study in the Theory and Application of the Sociology of Education,* New York: The Free Press: A Division of Macmillan Publishing Co.,Inc., 1973.

--------, *The Division of Labor in Society*, New York: MacMillan, 1933, in Sheo Kumar Lal (eds), *Readings in Sociology of Professions,* Delhi: Gian Publishing House, 33, 1988.

Dutt, Sunitte, "Towards a True Profession of Teaching", in S.P. Ruhela (eds), *Sociology of the Teaching Profession,* National Seminar on Sociology of Teaching Profession in India, New Delhi: NCERT, 3-11, 1970.

Educating India, "Sarva Shiksha Abhiyan, the Centre's Flagship Scheme to Impove Primary Education, is a Success in Numbers", *An IIM-A Study,* 2006.

"Education in Tarn Taran a Mess", *A Survey Report Published in The Tribune,* July 18, 2008.

Eisenhower, David, "Unproductive Labor and Crisis", in Dale, L. Johnson, *Class and Social Development: A New Theory of Middle Class,* Beverly Hills: Sage Publications, 245-325, 1982.

Esping-Andersen, G., (eds), *Welfare States in Transition: National Adaptations in Global Economics,* London: Sage, 1996, cited from *Current Sociology* 57, 475-485, 2009.

Evetts, J., "Professional Identities: State and International Dynamics in Engineering", in I. Hellberg, M. Sacks, and C. Benoit (eds), *Professional Identities in Transition,* Landskrona: Parajett, 13-25, 1999, cited from *Current Sociology* 57, 475-485, 2009.

------, "The Sociological Analysis of Professionalism: Occupational Change in the Modern Word", International Sociology 18(2), 395-415, 2003, cited from *Current Sociology* 57, 475-485, 2009.

------, "Short Note: The Sociology of Professional Groups: New Directions", cited from *Current Sociology* 54, 133-43, 2006. Foucault, Michel, "Discipline and Punish", in *The Birth of the Prison,* 1975.

Accessed from http://en.wikipedia.org/wiki/Michel_Foucalt on January 1, 2009. Falling 'General' Trend in Public Schools, *A People Forum Survey on Education and Social Reforms,* 2008.

Gallantry, Marc, "The Aborted Restoration of 'Indigenous' Law in India", *Comparative Studies in Society and History,* 14(I), 53-70, 1972.

Gandhi, J.S., *Lawyers and Touts: A Study in Sociology of Legal Profession,* Delhi: Hindustan Publishing Corporation, 1982. Garg, Kanta, *Population Awareness among Secondary Schools in Relation to Qualification, Age and Experience,* Ph.D. Thesis Submitted to Punjabi University, Patiala, 1992.

Gauba, Ved Parkash, *A Study of Educational Aspiration, School Adjustment and Values of +2 Arts and Science Male Students in Relation to School Environment* , Ph.D. Thesis Submitted to Punjabi University, Patiala, 1993.

Gerth, H. H. and Mills, C. W., From *Max Weber,* New York: Oxford University Press, 293, 1948.

Ghuman, R.S., et al., *Rural Students in Universities of Punjab: An Explorative Study,* A Project Report Submitted to Punjabi University, Patiala, 2006.

Ghurye, G.S., *Caste and Class in India,* Bombay: Popular Prakashan, 1950.

– – – –, *Class and Occupations in India,* Bombay: Popular Prakashan, 1961.

Giddens, Anthony, *Globalisation: Runaway World,* BBC Reith Lectures, 1999. Accessed from http://news.bbc.co.uk/hi/english/static/events/reith_99/week1/week1.htm> on August 6, 2008.

– – – –, *The Second Globalisation Debate,* 2000. Accessed from <http://www.edge.org/3rd_culture/giddens/giddens_index.html> on August 3, 2008.

Ginsberg, E., *Occupational Choice An Approach to a General Theory,* New York: Columbia University Press, 1951.

Goode, William J., "Community within Community: The professions", *American Sociological Review,* 22, 194-200, April,1957.

– – – – –, "Encroachment, Charlatanism and the Emerging Professions: Psychology, Sociology and Medicine", *American Sociological Review,* 25, 902-914, 1960.

Gore, M.S. et al., *Field Studies in the Sociology of Education: All India Report,* New Delhi: NCERT, 1970 a.

Gouldner, Alvin W., *For Sociology,* Harmondsworth Middlesex: Penguin Books 1975.

Goyal, Rajinderpal, *Study of Some Personality Correlates of Creativity in Secondary School Teachers Under Training,* Ph.D. Thesis Submitted to Punjabi University, Patiala, 1973.

GreenField Harry, *Accountability in Health Facilities,* New York: Praeger, 1975.

Greenwood, Ernest, "Attributes of a Profession", *Social Work,* 2(3), 44-46, July 1957, in Sheo Kumar Lal (eds), *Readings In Sociology of Professions,* Delhi: Gian Publishing House, 48, 1988.

Gupta, P.L., *Study of Personality Characteristics of Ninth Grade: Over and Under Achieving Boys and Girls at Different Levels of Achievement Motivation,* Ph.D. Thesis Submitted to Punjabi University, Patiala, 1982.

Gupta, Surendra K. and Rani Anita, "Professional Commitment of School Teachers", in Sheo Kumar Lal (eds), *Readings in Sociology of Professions,* Gian Publishing House, Delhi,1988.

Gupta, Ved P., *Personality Characteristics, Adjustment Level, Academic Achievement and Training Attitude of a Successful Teacher,* Ph.D. Thesis Submitted to Punjabi University, Patiala, 1974.

Hall, Oswald, "The Stages of a Medical Career", *The American Journal of Sociology,* 53, 327-336, March 1948, in Chandani, Ambika, *The Medical Profession: A Sociological Exploration,* New Delhi: Jainsons Publications, 3, 1985.

Halsey, A. H., "Towards Meritocracy? A Case of Britain", in Karabel, J. and Halsey, A. H. (eds), *Power and Ideology in Education,* New York: Oxford University Press, 1977a.

Hanlon, G., "Professionalism as Enterprise: Service Class Politics and the Redefinition of Professionalism", *Sociology* 32(1), 43-63, cited from *Current Sociology* 57, 475-485, 2009.

Harinder, *T.V. Viewing Behavior of Urban Primary School Students of Punjab,* Ph.D. Thesis Submitted to Punjabi University, Patiala, 2002.

Haug, M.R., "Deprofessionalisation: An Alternative Hypothesis for the Future", in P. Halmos (eds), *Professionalisation and Change,* University of Keel, 195-212, 1973.

Hellberg, I., Saks, M. and Benoit, C., *Professional Identities in Transition: Cross Cultural Dimensions,* Goteborg, Department of Sociology, Goteborg University, 1999, cited from *Current Sociology* 57, 475-485, 2009.

Heredia, R.C., "The College Teacher in a Metropolitan University", in Suma Chitnis and P.G. Altbach, (eds), *The Indian Academic Profession,* Delhi: Macmillan, 1979.

Huges, Everett C., *Men and their Work,* New York: The Free Press, 46-55, 1958.

– – – – – –, "Professions", *Daedalus,* Vol.92, Fall, 657, 1963. Jayaram, N. and Sivaramakrishnan G., "Teachers and Unionism: The Organisation of Academic Profession", in Suma Chitnis and P.G Altbach (eds), *The Indian Academic Profession,* New Delhi: Macmillan, 1979.

John, W.N., *A Study of Teachers Professional Values andProfessional Growth in Relation to Principal's Decision Making Style,* Ph. D. Thesis Submitted to Gorakhpur University, 1994.

Johnson, Dale L. and Chistine, O' Donnell, "Accumulation Crisis and Service Professionals", Economics Education Project (eds), *Crisis in the Public Sector,* 45, 1981.

Johnson, T., Larkin, G., and Saks, M. (eds), *Health Professions and the State in Europe,* London: Routledge, 1995, cited from *current Sociology* 57, 475-485, 2009.

Kahl, J. A., Educational and Occupational Aspirations of 'Common Man' Boys, *Harward Educational Review, 23,* Summer, 1953.

Kapoor, Khem Chand, *Environmental Awareness and Attitude Towards Environmental Education in Relation to Socio-economic Status of Students and Teachers of 10+2 School of Arunachal Pradesh,* Research Project Sponsored by ICSSR, 63, 2000.

Kaur, Sarbjit, *Value Dimension of Post Graduate Students in Relation to Levels of Aspiration and Intelligence,* Ph.D. Thesis Submitted to Punjabi University, Patiala, 1994.

Khana, Kirti, *Academic Role Structure and Modernization,* Unpublished Ph.D. Thesis Submitted to University of Jodhpur, Jodhpur, 1979. Lane, Jeremy F., *Pierre Bourdeu: A Critical Introduction,* 2008. Accessed from <http://en.wikipedia.org/wiki/Pierre_Bourdieu> on August 16, 2008.

Larson, M.S., *The Rise of Professionalism,* London: University of California Press, 1977. Laski, H. J., "The Decline of the Professions", *Harper's Monthly*

Magazine, 565-857, November 1935, in Sheo Kumar Lal (eds), *Readings in Sociology of Professions,* Delhi: Gian Publishing House, 1988.

Leach, Edward, "The Family: A Runaway Word", in Haralambos, M., *Sociology: Themes and Perpectives,* New Delhi: Oxford University Press, 2007.

Lortie, Dan C., *School Teacher: A Sociological Study,* Chicago: The University of Chicago Press, 1975. Madan, T.N., "Doctors in a North Indian City: Recruitment, Role Perception and Role Performance", in Saberwal, Satish (eds), *Beyond the Village,* Shimla: Indian Institute of Advanced Study, 80, 1972,

---------, *Doctors and Society: The Asian Case Studies,* New Delhi: Vikas, 1980. Malavika, C., *Career Orientation and Commitment of School Teachers: Study in the Sociology of Professions among Women Teachers in Six Delhi Schools,* Unpublished Ph.D. Thesis Submitted to Delhi: Delhi University, 1970.

Malaviya, A., "Commitment and Rural Bias of Teachers for Rural Orientation of Home Science Education", *Journal of Higher Education,* Monsoon-Autumn, 77-83, 1984.

Mandal Commission Report, 1980, Accessed from http://en.wikipedia.org/wiki/Indian_Caste_System on 25 April, 2009.

Marshall, T.H., "The Recent History of Professionalism in Relation to Social Structure and Social Polity", *Canadian Journal of Economic and Political Science,* 5, 325-340, August 1939, in Sheo Kumar Lal (eds), *Readings in Sociology of Professions,* Delhi: Gian Publishing House, 69, 1988.

Marshall, T.N., "Professionalism and Social Policy", in William, H. Form, *Men Work and Society: A Reader in the Sociology of Occupations,* New York: Basic Books, 225-235, 1962.

Marx, K., *Capital,* Vol. 1, New York: International Publishers, 508, 1967.

Miller, D. C. and Form, W. H., *Industrial Sociology,* New York: Harper and Bros., 1951. Millerson, Geoffery, *The Qualifying Association,* London: Routledge and Kegan Paul, 4-5, 1964.

Mishra, B.B., *India's Middle Class: Their Growth in Modern Times,* London: Oxford University Press, 1961.

Morrison, C., "Kinship in Professional Relations: A Study of North Indian District Lawyers", *Comparative Studies in Society and History,* January 1972.

Mukherji, D.P., *Diversities*, New Delhi: People's Publishing House, 1958. Nahar, Umed Raj, "Teaching in University System: Needed Area of Research", *in* Sheo Kumar Lal (eds), *Readings in Sociology of Professions,* New Delhi: Gian Publishing House, 1988.

National Sample Survey, 2000, Accessed from http://en.wikipedia.org/wiki/Indian_Caste_System on 25 April, 2009. NUEPA (National University of Educational Planning and Administration), *An Analytical Report of Education Indicators,* New Delhi, 2005-06. Oommen, T.K., *Doctors and Nurses,* Delhi: Vikas, 1978.

Oppenheimer, Martin, et al., "Professionsand Middle Class, Professionalisation/ Deprofessionalisation", in Dale L. Johnson, *Class and Social Development: A New Theory of the Middle Class,* Baverly Hills: Sage Publications, 245-325, 1982.

Panday, Rajendra, "Whither Professionalism?", in Sheo Kumar Lal (eds), *Readings in Sociology of Professions,* New Delhi: Gian Publishing House, 1988.

Parelius, Ann Parker and Parelius, Robert J., *The Sociology of Education,* New Jersy: Prentice-Hall Inc., 1978.

Parsons, T., "The Professional Social Structure", *Social Force,* 17, 455-467, May 1939, in Lal, Sheo Kumar, *Reading in Sociology of Professions,* New Delhi: Gian Publishing House, 633, 1988.

———————, "The Professions", *International Encyclopedia of Social Sciences,* Vol. 12, 545, 1968.

———————, "The Family: Basic and Irreducable", in Haralambos, M., *Sociology: Themes and Perpectives,* New Delhi: Oxford University Press, New Delhi, 2007.

Public Interest Litigation (PIL), Punjab and Haryana High Court, Chandigarh, 2007.

Punjab Education Development (amendment) Bill, 2007.

Raju, P. Mohan, *A Study of Factors Contributing to Commitment to the Teaching Profession,* Ph. D. Thesis Submitted to University of Delhi, 1992.

Ramana, P.V.L., *Modernist Orientations and Role Performance of Lady Teachers of Vishakhapatnam Municipal Schools,* Unpublished Doctoral Thesis, Waltair, Andhra University, 1986.

Rao, C.P. and Venkataramana V., *A Functional Analysis of Unionism Among College Teachers,* Sheo Kumar lal (eds), *Readings in Sociology Of Professions,* New Delhi: Gian Publishing House, 1988.

Rao, S.N., *Work Adjustment and Job Satisfaction of Teachers,* Delhi: Mittal, 1986.

Reiff, R., "The Danger of the Techini-pro: Democratising the Human Services Professions", *Social Policy,* Vol.2, 63, May-June 1971.

Riska, E. and Wegar, K. (eds), *Gender, Work, and Medicine: Women And Medical Division of Labour,* London: Sage, 1993, cited from *Current Sociology* 57, 475-485, 2009.

Rosenberg, M., *Occupations and Values,* Glencoe: Ill. Free Press, 1957.

Rousseau, Jeen-Jacques, *The Social Contact and Discourses,* New York: E.P. Dutton and Co., 1950, in Sheo Kumar Lal (eds), *Reading in Sociology of Professions*, New Delhi: Gian Publishing House, 74, 1988.

Ruhela, S.P., (eds), *Sociology of Teaching Profession: National Seminar on Sociology of Teaching Profession in India*, New Delhi: NCERT, 1970c.

Saroha, Kaushalya, *A Study of Self Concept, Socio-economic Status and Social Adjustment of School Teachers of Haryana State,* Ph.D Thesis Submitted to Jamia Millia Islamia University, 1995.

Schultz, Theodor, "Investment in Human Capital", American Economic Review, Presidential Address to the American Economic Association, March 1961, in "Human Capital", *Encyclopedia of Social Sciences,* Vol.2, New York, 1968.

Sciulli, D., "Continental Sociology of Professions Today: Conceptual Cotributions", *Current Sociology* 53(6), 915-942, 2005.

Sen, Amartya, "The Idea of Justice: Underdogs Remain Underdogs", *First Hiren Mukherje Memorial Lecture,* New Delhi: Parliament Hall, August 11, 2008.

Seventh All India Educational Survey, Chandigarh: SCERT Punjab, 2002.

Shaffer, Dale Eugene, *Maturity of Librarianship as a Profession,* Metuchen, New Jersy, Scavecrow Press, 1968, in Chandani, Ambika, *The Medical Profession: A Sociological Exploration,* New Delhi: Jainsons Publications, 3, 1985.

Shah, B.V., *The Role of the Secondary Teacher: A Sociology Survey,* New Delhi: NCERT, 1970.

Sharma, Menakshi, *Study of Satisfaction and Dissatisfaction with in School Among Adolescet Boys in Relation to Their responsibility, Characteristics, Intelligence, Scholastic Performance and Socio-economic status,* Ph.D. Thesis Submitted to Punjabi University, Patiala, 1980.

Sharma, S.L., *Modernizing Effect of University Education,* New Delhi: Allied, 1979.

Singh, Hardeep, *A Study of Socio-personal Background, Achievements, Adjustment and Job Satisfaction of Physical Education College Teachers,* Ph.D. Thesis Submitted to Punjabi University, Patiala, 2001.

Singh, R.P., *The Indian Teacher,* Delhi: National Publishing House, 1969. Singh, Yogendra, "Academic Role Structure and Modernisation: A Study of Rajisthan University Teachers" in Suma Chitnis and P.G.

Altbach (eds), *The Indian Academic Profession: Crisis and Change in the Teaching Community,* Delhi: Macmillan, 1979.

Singhal, R.P., *Indian Schools: A Study of Teacher-Pupil Ratio,* New Delhi: Vikas, 1988.

Sinha, B.N., *University Teachers and Their Problems,* New Delhi: Puja, 1982.

Skospol, T., *States and Social Revolutions: A Comparative Analysis of France, Russia and China,* Cambridge: Cambridge University Press, 1979, cited from *Current Sociology* 57, 475-485, 2009.

Srivastava, R.N., *Sociology of Professions: An Overview with Analytical note on University Teaching as a Profession,* in Lal, Sheo Kumar, *Reading in Sociology of Professions,* Delhi: Gian Publishing House, 1988.

Swank, D., *Global Capital, Political Institutions, and Policy Change in Developed Welfare States,* Cambridge: Cambridge University Press, 2002, cited from *Current Sociology* 57, 475-485, 2009.

Swanson, G., *Framework for Comparative Research: Structural Athropology and Theory of Action: Essay in Trend and Applications,* Berkeley: University of California, 1971, cited from *Current Sociology* 57, 475-485, 2009.

Tapodhan, Harish Chandra, N., *A Study of Professional Attitudes of Secondary School Teachers of Gujrat State,* Ph.D Thesis Submitted to Gujrat University, 1991.

Tawney, R.H., *The Acquisitive Society,* New York: Harcout Brace, 1920, in Chandani, A., *A Sociological Study of the Doctors of Jodhpur City,* Unpublished Ph.D. Thesis, Jodhpur: University of Jodhpur, 1977.

The constitution (Seventy-third Amendment) Act, 1992.

The constitution (Seventy-fourth Amendment) Act, 1992.

Tilly, C., *The Formation of National States in Western Europe,* Princeton N.J.: Princeton University Press, 1975, cited from *Current Sociology* 57, 475-485, 2009.

Torstendahl, R., "The Need for a definition of 'Profession'", *Current Sociology* 53, 947-51, 2005.

Torstendahl, R. and Burrage, M., (eds), *Professions in Theory and History: Rethinking the Study of the Professions,* London: Sage, 1990, cited from *Current Sociology* 57, 475-485, 2009.

UNESCO, *International Institute of Educational Planning Study on Corruption in Education*, New Delhi, 2007.

Wadhawan, C.L., *School Teachers in Delhi: Relationship Between their Social Background and Professionalisation*, Ph.D. Thesis Submitted in Education at Jamia Millia Islamia University, New Delhi, 1980.

Webb, Sidney and Beatrice, Webb, "Special Supplement on Professional Association", *New Statesman*, 9(211), Saturday, April 21, 1917, in Chandani, A., *A Sociological Study of the Doctors of Jodhpur City*, Unpublished Ph.D. Thesis, Jodhpur: University of Jodhpur, 1977.

Weber, Max, *The Study of Social and Economic Organisation*, Glencoe Ill.: The Free Press, 1947, in Lal, Sheo Kumar, *Reading in Sociology of Professions*, New Delhi: Gian Publishing House, 1988.

Webster's Seventh New Collegiate Dictionary, Calcutta: Scientific Book Agency, 680, 1969, in Chandani, Ambika, *The Medical Profession: A Sociological Exploration*, New Delhi: Jainsons Publications, 2, 1985.

Wallerstein, I. M., *The Politics of Word Economy*, Cambridge: Cambridge University Press, 1984, cited from *Current Sociology* 57, 475-485, 2009.

Waller, Willard, *The Sociology of Teaching*, N.Y.: Russel and Russel, 1961, in Parelius, A. P. and Pereluis, R. J., *The Sociology of Education*, Rutgers the State University of New Jersey, 1978.

Wilensky, Harold H., " The Professionalisation of Everyone?", *American Journal of Sociology*, Vol.70, 1964.

Wilson Bryan, R., " The Teacher's Role: A Sociological Analysis", *The British Journal of Sociology*, 15-32, in Lal, Sheo Kumar, *Reading in Sociology of Professions*, New Delhi: Gian Publishing House, 1988.

Index

A

Abbott, 10
A body of abstract knowledge, 6
Absenteeism, 25
Accumulative, 3
A code of ethics among American school teachers, 79
A code of ethics among Indian school teachers, 83
Age, 36
Age and unprofessional practices, 94
Age at which first thought of becoming a school teacher came in mind, 68
Age at which first thought of becoming a school teacher came in mind and UPPs, 108
Aikara J., 1, 18, 77
Aim in life and UPPs, 107
Aims and objectives of study, 25
Altbach, 10, 12
Altruistic, 6
Amendment (73rd and 74th) Act 1992, 29
Anomic, 3
Authority, 4
Aurora and Rao, 10
Atal, 10, 18
Attributional analysis of professions, 6

B

Benoit and Heitlinger, 10
Bhoite, 10, 14
Blau, 71
Bledstein, 8
Bordieu P., 24
Boules and Gintis, 35,51
Bowles, 5
Brint, 10
Britto, 10, 13
Bureaucrats, 4
Burrage and Torstendahl, 10

C

Calling, 8
Capitalism, 5
Capitalist, 4
Capitalist economies, 5
Capitalists, 4
Career decision makers, 71
Career decision makers and UPPs, 108
Carr-Saunders, 4, 6
Caste, 43
Caste and UPPs, 96
Census 2001, 27, 41, 43, 44
Chand and Mishra, 19, 86, 90, 117, 126
Chandani, 9
Change, 5
Change in status quo, 3
Chatteregee and Khan, 2
Chauhan, 10, 15, 17, 86, 88, 91, 117
Chitnis, 10, 11
Chitnis and Altbach, 10
Chubb and Moe, 10
Class, 5
Client, 7
Coercion, 5
Coercive institution, 5
Cogan, 4
Cognitively encompassing, 3
Cohen et al., 8
Cohesion, 3
Colleague-colleague relations, 8
Collective identity, 4

Community sanction, 4, 7
Commercial venality, 26
Conclusions, 75, 90, 114, 176, 188
Conflict approach, 5
Conflict, 5
Control and regulation of behaviour, 4
Corrective measures to contain absenteeism, 122
Corrective measures to contain authoritarianism, 159
Corrective measures to contain commercial venality, 168
Corrective measures to contain dereliction of duty, 131
Corrective measures to contain discrimination against students, 150
Corrective measures to contain lack of responsibility, 141
Cosmopolitanism, 8
Culture, 4
Customer, 7

D

Damale, 10
Davis and Guppy, 10
Davis and Quirke, 10
Deference to authority, 5
Derebello, 10, 11, 16
Dereliction of duty, 25
Designation and UPPs, 98
De Vries et al., 10
Discipline, 5
Discrimination, 26
DISE, 43, 44
Disenchanted, 3
Disinterestedness, 8
Division of labour, 1, 3
Dubey, 10
Durkheim E., 3, 24
Dutt, 10, 11, 16, 86, 90
Derebello, 10, 11, 16

E

Economy, 1
Educational attainment in previous generation, 51
Educational attainment of teachers, 46
Educational level of father and UPPs, 101
Efficient, 3
Emotional neutrality, 8
Esping-Anderson, 10
Ethical codes, 4
Evetts, 9, 10
Examination, 23
Exchange relations, 9

F

Family, 1
Faucault M., 23
Formation of social personality, 1
Functional specificity, 7

G

Galanter, 10
Gandhi, 10
Garg, 10
Gauba, 10
Ghuman, 22
Ghurye, 9
Giddens, 23
Ginsberg, 68
Girth and Mills, 3
God, 2
Good work, 8
Goode, 4, 6
Good society, 23
Gore et al., 10, 11
Goyal, 10
Greenwood, 4
Gupta, 10
Gupta and Rani, 10, 14, 17, 38, 49, 67, 68, 89, 91, 94, 114
Guru, 22
Gurukul, 22

H

Hall, 2
Hanlon, 10
Harinder, 10, 16, 18
Hasley, 51
Hellberg et al., 10
Heredia, 10, 13
Hierarchical observation, 23

I

Ideal-type, 3
IIM-A study, 19, 117, 132, 177
Income of family while joining teaching profession and UPPs, 102
Individual functions of education, 1
Intellectualised, 3

J

Jayaram and Sriramakrishna, 10, 12
John, 10, 15
Johnson et al., 9

K

Kapoor, 10, 16, 18, 107, 115
Kaur, 10
Khanna, 10, 11

L

Lack of responsibility, 26
Lais-sez-faire, 23
Larson, 9
Leach, 59
Learned professions, 2
Length of service, 73
Length of service and UPPs, 109
Logical, 3
Lortie, 56, 65, 71

M

Malavika, 10
Malaviya, 10 , 14
Mandal commission, 43
Marital status, 39
Marital status and UPPs, 94
Marx K., 5
Major findings of study, 182
Madan, 9
Matrix, 2
Marshall, 4
Method of research, 26
Miller and Form, 71
Millerson, 4
Mishra, 10
Moral code of ethics, 4
Morrison, 10
Mukergee, 9

N

Nahar, 10
National sample survey, 43
Nehru J., 9
Non-professional occupation, 7
Normalising judgment, 23
NUEPA, 10, 127

O

Occupational change, 9
Occupational preference, 65
Occupation of father and UPPs, 101
Oppenheimer, 9
Oppenheimer and Dale, 5, 9
Oommen, 9
Orzack, 10

P

Parelious and Parelious, 35
Parsons T., 4, 6, 7, 8, 59
Peasant proprietors, 4
PED (amendment) Bill, 21
People Forum, 21, 142
PIL, 22
Place of origin and rearing, 49
Polity, 1

Power/knowledge, 23
PRATHAM ASER (rural), 22, 118
Present income of the family, 63
Present income of the family and UPPs, 102
Prevalence of unprofessional practices, 86
Priest, 2
Profess, 2
Profession, 5
Profession as defined, 2
Professional associations and code of conduct, 8
Professional authority, 7
Professional body, 4
Professional-client relationship, 7
Professional complex, 4
Professional culture, 8
Professional ethics, 8
Professional fraternity, 4
Professional occupation, 7
Professionalisation, 6, 8
Professionalism, 8
Professions by criteria, 6
Profitable, 3
Prolonged socialisation, 4
Protected or institutional market, 5
PTA, 28
Punctuality, 5

Q

Qualitative educational system, 2

R

Raju, 10, 15, 17, 108, 115, 117
Ramana, 13, 17, 107, 115
Rao, 10, 13
Rao and Venkataramana, 10
Rational, 3
Rationality, 6
Religion, 1, 41
Religious community, 2
Reasons for absenteeism, 118
Reasons for authoritarianism, 156
Reasons for commercial venality, 164
Reasons for dereliction of duty, 126
Reasons for discrimination against students, 147
Reasons for lack of responsibility, 138
Religion and UPPs, 96
Review of literature, 9
Rika and Wegar, 9
Role-performer, 2
Roopnagar, 26, 44
Rosenberg, 71
Rousseau, 8
Ruhela, 10, 11, 16

S

SAIES, 27
Sample, 31
Saroha, 10, 16, 17, 107, 115
Schooling in childhood and UPPs, 99
Sciulli, 4, 10
Self good, 22
Sen, 21, 86, 91, 117, 122, 142, 169, 177
Service orientation, 6
Shaffer, 2
Shah, 10, 11, 16, 86, 90, 162, 178
Sharma, 10, 18
Singh, 10, 12, 16
Singhal, 10, 14, 17
Sinha, 10, 13
Skocpol, 10
Social change, 1
Social control, 9
Social force, 4
Social good, 22
Socialist, 4
Social institutions, 1
Societal functions, 1
Social mobility, 1
Social order, 2, 3
Social position, 1
Social stability, 1
Sociological orientation of profession, 3
Sociology of professions, 2
Srivastava, 10, 14

State, 4
Status-role, 2
Stratification, 1
Structural-functional approach, 3
Sub-culture, 2
Survey report, 22, 126, 177
Swank, 10
Swanson, 10
Systematic, 3, 4

T

Tapodhan, 10, 14, 17, 86, 88, 89, 91, 96, 98, 114
Tawney, 4
Teaching profession, 10
Tilly, 10
Torstendahl, 4, 10
Type and size of family, 59

U

UNESCO IIEP, 20, 86, 90, 117, 178
Universalism, 8
Unprofessional practices defined, 85
Unrestricted economic interest, 4
Urban proprietary groups, 4
Use value, 9

V

VEDC, 29

W

Wadhawan, 10, 13, 17, 32, 49, 58, 88, 91, 107, 115, 117, 132
Waller, 5
Wallerstein, 10
Webb and Beatrice, 4
Weber, 3, 6
Webster, 2
Welfare state, 23
Wilinsky, 7
Wilson, 6
Workers, 4